IZAAK WALTON

THE LIVES OF DR. JOHN DONNE, SIR HENRY WOTTON, MR. RICHARD HOOKER, MR. GEORGE HERBERT

1670

A Scolar Press Facsimile

THE SCOLAR PRESS LIMITED
MENSTON, ENGLAND
1969

THE SCOLAR PRESS LIMITED
20 Main Street, Menston, Yorkshire, England

Printed in Great Britain by
The Scolar Press Limited
Menston, Yorkshire, England

0854171657

NOTE

Reproduced (original size) by permission of the Curators of the Bodleian Library. Shelf-mark: Wood. 229(2).

Before their first collective publication with the life of Herbert in 1670 Izaak Walton's biographies of Donne, Wotton and Hooker had all appeared separately. When a life was in print Walton continued to revise the text so that each new edition varies with its predecessor.

The life of John Donne was first published as part of the edition of Donne's *LXXX Sermons*. Walton had been assisting Henry Wotton in the preparation of the edition and when Wotton died in 1639 Walton completed the life for publication the following year.

Walton's life of Wotton was first published with Wotton's *Reliquiæ Wottonianæ* in 1651 — a second edition of which appeared in 1654. Walton then revised and enlarged the life of Donne and published the second edition in 1658.

At the request of the Archbishop of Canterbury, Gilbert Sheldon, Walton completed the work he had already begun on the life of Hooker. The archbishop's interest in Hooker had been aroused by Dr. John Gauden's life published in 1662. As Walton explains:

... *about that time*, Doct. Ga. (*then Lo. B. of* Exeter) *publisht* the Life of Mr. Ric. Hooker, (*so he called it*) *with* ... *many dangerous mistakes, both of him and his* Books:

The archbishop therefore asked Walton to:

... *rectifie the Bishops mistakes, by giving the World a truer account of* Mr. Hooker *and his* Books:

(To the Reader, A5 verso)

The Life of Mr. Rich. Hooker was published in 1665 and reprinted the following year as part of an edition of Hooker's works.

The collected *Lives*, 1670, was next to appear containing the first edition of the life of Herbert. Later in the year some of the misprints were corrected and *The Life of Mr. George Herbert* was reprinted separately.

There was a third edition of *Reliquiæ Wottonianæ* in 1672, and in 1674 the life of Herbert was included in the third edition of *The Temple*. The *Lives* were reprinted in 1675 and this text is undoubtedly the second edition although called the 'Fourth Edition'.

Modern editions of the *Lives* include those by A. W. Pollard, 1901, and G. Keynes, in *The Compleat Walton*, 1929. See also J. E. Butt, "A Bibliography of Walton's *Lives*" in *Proceedings of the Oxford Bibliographical Society*, Vol. II, pt. 4, 1930, pp. 327-49.

Reference: Wing. W671.

Viri ſeraphici Joannis Donne Qua =
dragenarij Effigies vera, Qui poſt
eam ætatem Sacris initiatus Ec =
cleſiæ Sti Pauli Decanus obijt.
Anõ { Dõm 1631°
{ Ætatis ſuæ 59°

Lombart ſculp Alendre

THE
LIVES

Of
- Dr. *John Donne*,
- Sir *Henry Wotton*,
- Mr. *Richard Hooker*,
- Mr. *George Herbert*.

Written by IZAAK WALTON.

To which are added some Letters written by
Mr. *George Herbert*, at his being in *Cambridge :* with others to his Mother, the
Lady *Magdalen Herbert*, written by *John Donne*, afterwards Dean of St. *Pauls.*

Eccles. 44. 7.
These were honourable men in their Generations.

LONDON,
Printed by *Tho. Newcomb* for *Richard Marriott.*
Sold by most Booksellers. 1670.

To the Right Honorable
And
Reverend Father in GOD

GEORGE

Lord Bishop of Winchester, and Prelate of the most noble Order of the Garter.

My Lord,

 *Did some years past, present you with a plain relation of the life of Mr* Richard Hooker, *that humble man, to whose memory,* Princes *and the most* learned of this **Nation** *have*

A 3   *paid*

The Epiſtle

paid a reverence at the mention of his name ---- And, now with Mr. Hookers I preſent you alſo, the life of that pattern of primitive piety, Mr. George Herbert; and, with his, the life of Doctor Donne, and your friend Sir Henry Wotton, all reprinted.-- The two firſt were written under your roof: for which reaſon, if they were worth it, you might juſt-ly challenge a Dedication. And indeed, ſo you might of Doctor Donnes, and Sir Henry Wottons: becauſe, if I had been fit for this Undertaking, it would not have been by acquir'd Learning or Study, but by the ad-vantage of forty years friendſhip,

and

Dedicatory.

and thereby the hearing of and discoursing with your Lordship, which hath inabled me to make the relation of these Lives passable in an eloquent and captious age.

And indeed, my Lord, though, these relations he well-meant Sacrifices to the Memory of these Worthy men: yet, I have so little Confidence in my performance, that I beg pardon for superscribing your name to them; And, desire all that know your Lordship, to apprehend this not as a Dedication, (at least, by which you receive any addition of honour;) but rather, as an humble, and a more publick

ac-

The Epiſtle, &c.
acknowledgment of your long continued : and, your now daily Favours of to

My Lord

Your moſt affectionate

and

moſt humble Servant

Izaak Walton.

To the Reader.

THough, the several Introductions to these several Lives, have partly declared the reasons how, and why I undertook them: yet, since they are come to be review'd, and, augmented, and reprinted : and, the four are become one Book ; I desire leave to inform you that shall become my Reader, that when I look back upon my mean abilities, 'tis not without some little wonder at my self, that I am come to be publickly in print. And, though I have in those Introductions declar'd some of the accidental reasons : yet, let me add this to what is there said : that, by my undertaking to collect some notes for Sir Henry Wottons writing the life of Doctor Donne, and Sir Henry's dying before he perform'd it, I became like those that enter
easily

eafily into a Law-fute, *or a* quarrel, *and having begun, cannot make a fair retreat and be quiet, when they defire it.* And really, *after fuch a manner, I became in-gag'd, into a neceffity of writing* the life *of* Doctor Donne: Contrary, *to my firft Intentions. And th t begot a like ne-ceffity of writing the life of his and my honoured friend,* Sir Henry Wotton.

And, *having writ thefe two lives;* I *lay quiet twenty years, without a thought of either troubling my felf or others, by any new ingagement in this kind.* But, *about that time,* Doct. Ga. (*then* Lo. B. *of* Exeter) *publifht* the Life of Mr. Ric. Hooker, (*fo he called it*) *with fo many dangerous miftakes, both of him and* his Books : *that difcourfing of them with his* Grace, Gilbert *that now* is Lord Arch bifhop *of* Canterbury, *he injoyned me to examine fome Circumftan-ces, and then rectifie the Bifhops mif-takes, by giving the World a truer ac-count of* Mr. Hooker *and his* Books ;
and

and I *know* I *have done so. And, indeed, till* his Grace *had laid this injunction upon me,* I *could not admit a thought of any fitness in me to undertake it: but when he had twice injoyn'd me to it,* I *then trusted his judgment, and submitted to his Commands; considering that if* I *did not,* I *could not forbear accusing my self of disobedience: And, indeed of* Ingratitude *for his many favours.* Thus I became ingaged into the third Life.

For the life of Mr. George Herbert, I *profess it to be a* Free-will-offering, *and writ, chiefly to please my self: but not without some respect to posterity, for though he was not a man that the next age can forget, yet many of his particular acts and vertues might have been neglected, or lost, if* I *had not collected and presented them to the* Imitation *of those that shall succeed us: for* I *conceive writing to be both a safer and truer preserver of mens Vertuous actions,*

nice one!   *then*

then tradition. I am *to tell the Reader,
that though this life of* Mr. *Herbert
was not by me writ in haſte , yet,* I
intended it a Review, *before it ſhould be
made publick: but, that was not allowed
me, by reaſon of my abſence from* London *when 'twas printing ; ſo that the
Reader may finde in it, ſome double expreſſions , and ſome not very proper, and
ſome that might have been contracted,
and ſome faults that are not juſtly chargable upon me but the Printer : and yet
I hope none ſo great, as may not by this
Confeſſion purchaſe pardon, from a good
natur'd Reader.*

And now, I *wiſh that as* Joſephus
(that learned Jew *) and others, ſo theſe
men had alſo writ their own lives :
and ſince 'tis not the faſhion of theſe times;
that their friends would do it for them,
before delayes make it too difficult. And
I deſire this the more : becauſe 'tis an honour due to the dead, and a debt due
to thoſe that ſhall live, and ſucceed us.*
    For

To the Reader.

For when the next age shall (as this do's) *admire the Learning and clear Reason which* Doctor Sanderson (the late Bishop of Lincoln) *hath demonstrated in his Sermons and other writings*, *who*, *if they love vertue*, *would not rejoyce to know that this good man was as remarkable for the* meekness and innocence of his life, *as for his great learning*; *and as remarkable for his* Fortitude, *in his long and* patient *suffering* (*under them*, *that then call'd themselves the Godly Party*) *for that* Doctrine, *which he had* preach'd and printed, *in the happy daies of the Nations and the Churches peace? And*, *who would not be content to have the like account of* Doctor Field, *and others of noted learning? And though I cannot hope*, *that my example or reason can perswade to this*: *yet*, *I please my self*, *that I shall conclude my Preface*, with wishing that it were so.

J. W.

ERRATA.

If these mistakes (which spoil the sence) be first corrected by the Reader, he will do me some, and himself a greater Courtesy.

Doct. Donne.
Pag. 29. lin. 15. r. *perform*
30. l. 24. r. *do it*
32. l. 2. r. *fortune*
63. l. 21. r. *Dort*

In Sir H. Wotton.
29. l. 10. r. *famed*
35. l. 9. *as well*
37. l. 22. dele Mr. *Bedell*
38. l. 17. dele *mis-*
41. l. 8. r. *delivery*
45. l. 5. r. *mont*
47. l. 19. r. *Sysiphus*
53. l. 7. r. *against*
56 l. 24. r. *Elegy*
75. l. 19. r. *those.*

In Mr. Hoooker.
25. l... r. *assiduous : still*
42. l. 7. r. *God and so* ⎫ These must be thus
42. l. 11. r. *and in wicked* ⎬ corrected, or that Para-
42. l. 15. dele *(it)* ⎭ graph will not be sence,
56. l. 20. r. *answers.*

In George Herbert,
14. l. 4. r. *his*
24. dele *of*
32. l. 22. r. *Parish Church*
33. l. 26. r. *she*
34. l. 4. dele *at*
49. l. 10. r. *wants it*
63. l. 24. dele *too*
65. l. 24. r. *spirits and*
72. l. 3. r. *for the*
80. l. 1. r. *to their.*

The Copy of a Letter writ to Mr. Isaac Walton, by Doctor King Lord Bishop of Chichester.

Honest Isaac,

Though a Familiarity of more then Forty years continuance, and the constant experience of your Love even in the worst times, be sufficient to indear our Friendship; yet, I must confess my Affection much improved, not onely by Evidences of private Respect to many that know and love you, but by your new Demonstration of a publick Spirit, testified in a diligent, true, and useful Collection of so many Material Passages as you have now afforded me in the Life of Venerable Mr. *Hooker,* of which, since desired by such a Friend as your self, I shall not deny to give the Testimony of what I know concerning him and his learned Books : but shall first here take a fair occasion to tell you, that you have been happy in choosing to write the Lives of three such Persons, as Posterity hath just cause to honour; which they will do the more for the true Relation of them

B   by

by your happy Pen ; of all which I shall give you my unfeigned Censure.

I shall begin with my most dear and incomparable Friend Dr. *Donne*, late Dean of St. *Pauls* Church, who not onely trusted me as his Executor, but three days before his death delivered into my hands those excellent Sermons of his now made publick: professing before Dr. *Winniff*, Dr. *Monford*, and, I think, your self then present at his bed side, that it was by my restless importunity, that he had prepared them for the Press ; together with which (as his best Legacy) he gave me all his Sermon-Notes, and his other Papers, containing an Extract of near Fifteen hundred Authours. How these were got out of my hands, you, who were the Messenger for them, and how lost both to me and your self, is not now seasonable to complain: but, since they did miscarry, I am glad that the general Demonstration of his Worth was so fairly preserved, and represented to the World by your Pen in the History of his Life ; indeed so well, that beside others, the best Critick of our later time (Mr. *John Hales* of *Eaton* Colledge) affirm'd to me, *He had not seen a Life written with more advantage to the Subject, or more reputation to the Writer, then that of Dr.* Donnes.

After the performance of this task for Dr. *Donne*, you undertook the like office for our Friend Sir *Henry Wotton*: betwixt which two
there

there was a Friendſhip begun in *Oxford*, continued in their various Travels, and more confirmed in the religious Friendſhip of Age: and
doubtleſs this excellent Perſon had writ the
Life of Dr. *Donne*, if Death had not prevented him; by which means his and your Pre-
collections for that Work fell to the happy Menage of your Pen: a Work which you would
have declined, if imperious Perſuaſions had not
been ſtronger then your modeſt Reſolutions a-
gainſt it. And I am thus far glad, that the firſt
Life was ſo impoſed upon you, becauſe it gave
an unavoidable Cauſe of Writing the ſecond;
if not? 'tis too probable, we had wanted both,
which had been a prejudice to all Lovers of Honour and ingenious Learning. And let me not
leave my Friend Sir *Henry* without this Teſtimony added to yours; That he was a Man of
as Florid a Wit and as Elegant a Pen, as any
former (or ours which in that kind is a moſt excellent) Age hath ever produced.

And now having made this voluntary Obſer-
vation of our two deceaſed Friends, I proceed
to ſatisfie your deſire concerning what I know
and believe of the ever-memorable Mr. *Hooker*,
who was *Schiſmaticorum Malleus*, ſo great a
Champion for the Church of *Englands* Rights
againſt the Factious Torrent of Separatiſts, that
then ran high againſt Church-Diſcipline: and
in his unanſwerable Books continues to be ſo
againſt the unquiet Diſciples of their Schiſm,

which

which now under other Names ftill carry on
their Defign; and, who (as the proper Heirs of
Irrational Zeal) would aga n rake into the fcarce
clofed Wounds of a newly bleeding State and
Church.

And firft, though I dare not fay that I knew
Mr. *Hooker*; yet, as our Ecclefiaftical Hiftory
reports to the honour of S *Ignatius*, that he
lived in the time of St. *John*, and had feen him
in his Childhood; fo, I alfo joy that in my Minority I have often feen Mr. *Hooker* with my Father, who was then Bifhop of *London*, from
whom, and others, at that time, I have heard
moft of the material paffages which you relate
in the Hiftory of his Life, and from my Father
received fuch a Charaɛter of his *Learning, Humility*, and other Virtues, that like Jewels of
unvaluable price, they ft ll caft fuch a luftre as
Envy or the Ruft of Time fhall never darken.

From my Father I have alfo heard all the
Circumftances of the Plot to defame him; and
how Sir *Edwin Sandys* outwitted his Accufers,
and gained their Confeffion; and I could give
an account of each particular of that Plot, but
that I judge it fitter to be forgotten, and rot in
the fame grave with the malicious Authors.

I may not omit to declare, that my Fathers
Knowledge of Mr. *Hooker* was occafioned by
the Learned Dr. *John Spencer*, who after the
Death of Mr. *Hooker* was fo careful to preferve
his unvaluable Sixth, Seventh, and Eighth
Books

Books of *ECCLESIASTICAL POLITY*, and his other Writings, that he procu ed *Henry Jackson*, then of *Corpus Christi* Colledge, to transcribe for him all Mr. *Hookers* remain ng written Papers, many of which were impe fe&, for his Study had been rifled, or worse used, by Mr *Chark*, and another, of Principles too like his: but, these Papers were endeavored to be compleated by his dear friend Dr. *Spencer*, who bequeathed them as a precious Legacy to my Father, after whose Death they rested in my hand, till Dr. *Abbot*, then Archbishop of *Canterbury*, commanded them out of my custody by authorizing Dr. *John Barkeham* to require, and bring them to him to his Palace in *Lambeth*; at which time, I have heard, they were put into the Bishops Library, and that they remained there till the Martyrdom of Archbishop *Laud*; and, were then by the Brethren of that Faction given with all the Library to *Hugh Peters*, as a Reward for his remarkable Service in those sad times of the Churches Confusion; and though they could hardly fall into a fouler hand; yet there wanted not other Endeavours to corrupt and make them speak that Language for which the Faction then fought, which, indeed was *To subject the Soveraign Power to the People*.

But I need not strive to vindicate Mr. *Hooker* in this particular, his known Loyalty to his Prince whilest he lived, the Sorrow expressed

by

by King *James* at his Death, the Value our
late Soveraign (of ever-bleſſed Memory) put
upon his Works, and now, the ſingular Character of his Worth by you given in the paſſages of his Life, eſpecially in your *Appendix* to
it, do ſufficiently clear him from that Imputa-
tion: and I am glad you mention how much
value *Thomas Stapleton*, Pope *Clement* the VIII.
and other Eminent men of the Romiſh Perſwaſion, have put upon his Books: having been told
the ſame in my Youth by Perſons of worth that
have travelled *Italy*.

Laſtly, I muſt again congratulate this Undertaking of yours, as now more proper to you
then any other perſon, by reaſon of your long
Knowledge and Alliance to the worthy Family of the *Cranmers*, (my old Friends alſo) who
have been men of noted Wiſdom, eſpecially
Mr. *George Cranmer*, whoſe Prudence added to
that of Sir *Edwin Sandys*, proved very uſeful in
the Completing of Mr. *Hookers* matchleſs
Books; one of their Letters I herewith ſend
you, to make uſe of, if you think fit. And
let me ſay further; you merit much from many of Mr. *Hookers* beſt Friends then living,
namely, from the ever renowned Archbiſhop
Whitgift, of whoſe incomparable Worth, with
the Character of the Times, you have given
us a more ſhort and ſignificant Account then I
have received from any other Pen. You have
done much for Sir *Henry Savile*, his Contemporary

porary and familiar Friend; amongft the furviving Monuments of whofe Learning (give
me leave to tell you fo) two are omitted, his
Edition of _Euclid_, but efpecially his Tranflati-
of _King James his Apology for the Oath of Alle-
geance_ into elegant Latine; which flying in that
drefs as far as _Rome_, was by the Pope and Con-
clave fent to _Salamanca_ unto _Francifcus Sua-
rez_, (then refiding there as Prefident of that
Colledge) with a Command to anfwer it.
When he had perfeded the Work, which he
calls _Defenfio Fidei Catholica_, it was tranfmit-
ted to _Rome_ for a view of the Inquifitors; who
according to their cuftom blotted out what
they pleafed, and (as Mr. _Hooker_ hath been
ufed fince his Death) added whatfoever might
advance the Popes Supremacy, or carry on their
own Intereft, commonly coupling _Deponere &
Occidere_, the Depofing and Killing of Princes; which cruel and unchriftian Language
Mr. _John Saltkel_, his _Amanuenfis_, when he
wrote at _Salamanca_, (but fince a Convert,
living long in my Fathers houfe) often pro-
feffed, the good Old man (whofe Piety and
Charity Mr. _Saltkel_ magnified much) not
onely difavowed, but detefted. Not to
trouble you further; your Reader (if according to your defire, my Approbation of
your Work carries any weight) will here
find many juft Reafons to thank you for it;

B 4   and

and for this Circumſtance here mentioned
(not known to many) may happily apprehend one to thank him, who heartily wiſhes
your happineſs, and is unfainedly ,

Chicheſter,
Novem. 17.
1664.

Sir,

Your ever-faithful and

affectionate old Friend

Henry Chicheſter.

THE
LIFE
OF
Dr JOHN DONNE,
late Dean of St *Paul's Church*,
L O N D O N.

The Introduction.

IF *that great Master of Language and Art,
Sir* Henry Wotton, *the late Provost of*
Eaton Colledge, *had liv'd to see the Publication of these Sermons, he had presented the
World with the* Authors Life *exactly written;
And, 'twas pity he did not; for it was a work worthy his undertaking, and he fit to undertake it:
betwixt whom, and the Author, there was so mutual a knowledge, and such a friendship contracted
in their Youth, as nothing but death could force
a separation. And though their bodies were divided, their affections were not: for, that learned
Knight's love followed his Friends fame beyond*

death

death and the forgetful grave ; which he testified by intreating me, whom he acquainted with his designe, to inquire of some particulars that concern'd it ; not doubting but my knowledge of the Author, and love to his memory, might make my diligence useful : I did most gladly undertake the employment, and continued it with great content 'till I had made my Collection ready to be augmented and compleated by his curious Pen : but then, Death prevented his intentions.

When I heard that sad news, and heard also that these Sermons *were to be printed, and want the* Authors Life*, which I thought to be very remarkable : Indignation or grief (indeed I know not which) transported me so far, that I reviewed my forsaken Collections, and resolv'd the World should see the best plain Picture of the* Authors Life *that my artless Pensil, guided by the hand of truth, could present to it.*

And, if I shall now be demanded as once Pompey's *poor bondman was,* " (The grateful " wretch had been left alone on the Sea-shore, " with the forsaken dead body of his once glorious " lord and master : and, was then gathering the " scatter'd pieces of an old broken boat to make a " funeral pile to burn it (which was the custom " of the Romans;) *who art thou that alone hast the honour to bury the body of* Pompey *the great ? so, who I am that do thus officiously set the Authors memorie on fire ? I hope the question will prove to have in it more of wonder then dis-*
dain ;

dain ; But wonder indeed the Reader may, that I who profeß my self artleß should presume with my faint light to shew forth his Life whose very name makes it illustrious! but be this to the dis-advantage of the person represented: Certain I am, it is to the advantage of the beholder, who shall here see the Authors Picture in a natural dreß, which ought to beget faith in what is spoken: for, he that wants skill to deceive may safely be trusted.

And if the Authors glorious spirit, which now is in Heaven, can have the leasure to look down and see me, the poorest, the meanest of all his friends, in the midst of this officious dutie, con-fident I am that he will not disdain this well-meant sacrifice to his memory: for, whilst his Conversation made me and many others happy below, I know his Humility and Gentleneß was then eminent ; and, I have heard Divines say, those Vertues that were but sparks upon Earth, become great and glorious flames in Heaven.

Before I proceed further, I am to in-treat the Reader to take notice, that when *Doctor Donn's* Sermons were first printed, this was then my excuse for daring to write his life ; and, I dare not now appear without it.

The Life.

After *John Donne* was born in *London*, of good and vertuous Parents : and, though his own Learning and other multiplyed merits may juftly appear fufficient to dignifie both Himfelf and his Pofteritie : yet, the Reader may be pleafed to know, that his Father was mafculinely and lineally defcended from a very antient Family in *Wales*, where many of his name now live, that deferve and have great reputation in that Countrey.

By his Mother he was defcended of the Family of the famous and learned Sir *Tho. Moor*, fometime Lord *Chancellour* of *England*: as alfo, from that worthy and laborious *Judge Raftall*, who left Pofterity the vaft Statutes of the Law of this Nation moft exactly abridged.

He had his firft breeding in his Fathers houfe, where a private Tutor had the care of him, until the ninth year of his age ; and, in his tenth year was fent to the Univerfity of *Oxford*, having at that time a good command both of the French and Latine Tongue. This and fome other of his remarkable Abilities,
made

made one give this censure of him, *That this age had brought forth another Picus Mirandula*; of whom Story sayes, *That he was rather born than made wise by study*.

There he remained in *Hart-Hall*, having for the advancement of his studies Tutors of several Sciences to attend and instruct him, till time made him capable, and his learning expressed in publick exercises declared him worthy to receive his first degree in the Schools, which he forbore by advice from his friends, who being for their Religion of the Romish perswasion, were *conscionably* averse to some parts of the Oath that is always tendered at those times; and, not to be refused by those that expect the titulary honour of their studies.

About the fourteenth year of his age he was transplanted from *Oxford* to *Cambridge*; where, that he might receive nourishment from both Soils, he staid till his seventeenth year; all which time he was a most laborious Student, often changing his studies, but endeavouring to take no degree, for the reasons formerly mentioned.

About the seventeenth year of his age, he was removed to *London*, and then admitted into *Lincolns-Inne*, with an intent to study the *Law*; where he gave great testimonies of his Wit, his Learning, and of his Improvement in that profession: which never served him for

other

other ufe than an Ornament and Self-fatif-faction.

His Father died before his admiffion into this Society; and being a Merchant left him his portion in money (it was 3000 l.) His Mother and thofe to whofe care he was committed, were watchful to improve his knowledge, and to that end appointed him Tutors in the *Mathematicks,* and all the *Liberal Sciences,* to attend him. But with thefe Arts they were advifed to inftil particular Principles of the *Romish Church,* of which thofe Tutors profeft (though fecretly) themfelves to be members.

They had almoft obliged him to their faith; having for their advantage (befides many opportunities) the example of his dear and pious Parents, which was a moft powerful perfwafion, and did work much upon him, as he profeffeth in his Preface to his *Pfeudo-Martyr;* a Book of which the Reader fhall have fome account in what follows.

He was now entered into the eighteenth year of his age, and at that time had betrothed himfelf to no Religion that might give him any other denomination than a Chriftian. And Reafon and Piety had both perfwaded him that there could be no fuch fin as Schifme, if an adherence to fome vifible Church were not neceffary.

He did therefore at his entrance into the nineteenth year of his age (though his youth and

and ftrength then promifed him a long life) yet being unrefolved in his Religion, he thought it neceffary to rectifie all fcruples that concerned that: and therefore waving the Law, and betrothing himfelf to no Art or Profeffion, that might juftly denominate him; he begun to furvey the Body of Divinity, as it was then controverted betwixt the *Reformed* and the *Roman Church*. And as *Gods bleffed Spirit did then awaken him to the fearch, and in that induftry did never forfake him,* (they be his own words *) *fo he calls the fame holy Spirit to witnefs this Proteftation; that, in that difquifition and fearch, he proceeded with humility and diffidence in himfelf; and, by that which he took to be the fafeft way; namely, frequent Prayers, and an indifferent affection to both parties;* and indeed truth had too much light about her to be hid from fo fharp an Inquirer, and he had too much ingenuity not to acknowledge he had found her.

* in his Preface to *Pfeudo-Martyr.*

Being to undertake this fearch, he believed the *Cardinal Bellarmine* to be the beft defender of the *Roman caufe,* and therefore betook himfelf to the examination of his Reafons. The Caufe was weighty, and wilful delays had been inexcufable both towards God and his own Confcience; he therefore proceeded in this fearch with all moderate hafte, and before the twentieth year of his age, did fhew the then *Dean* of *Gloucefter* (whofe name

my

my memory hath now loft) all the Cardinals works marked with many weighty obfervations under his own hand ; which works were bequeathed by him at his death as a Legacy to a moft dear Friend.

The year following he refolved to travel; and the Earl of *Effex* going firft the *Cales*, and after the *Ifland voyages*, he took the advantage of thofe opportunities, waited upon his Lordfhip, and was an eye-witnefs of thofe happy and unhappy employments.

But he returned not back into *England*, till he had ftaid fome years firft in *Italy*, and then in *Spain*, where he made many ufeful obfervations of thofe Countreys, their Laws and manner of Government, and returned perfect in their Languages.

The time that he fpent in *Spain* was at his firft going into *Italy* defigned for travelling the *Holy Land*, and for viewing *Jerufalem* and the Sepulchre of our Saviour. But at his being in the furtheft parts of *Italy*, the difappointment of Company, or of a fafe Convoy, or the uncertainty of returns for Money into thofe remote parts, denied him that happinefs which he did often occafionally mention with a deploration.

Not long after his return into *England*, that exemplary Pattern of Gravity and Wifdom, the Lord *Elfemore*, then Keeper of the Great Seal, and *Lord Chancellour* of *England*, taking notice

notice of his Learning, Languages, and other Abilities, and much affecting his Perfon and Condition, took him to be his chief Secretary; fuppofing and intending it to be an Introduction to fome more weighty Employment in the State; for which, his Lordfhip did often proteft, he thought him very fit.

Nor did his Lordfhip in this time of Mafter *Donne's* attendance upon him, account him to be fo much his Servant, as to forget he was his Friend; and to teftifie it, did always ufe him with much courtefie, appointing him a place at his own Table, to which he efteemed his Company and Difcourfe a great Ornament.

He continued that employment for the fpace of five years, being daily ufeful, and not mercenary to his Friends. During which time he (I dare not fay unhappily) fell into fuch a liking, as (with her approbation) increafed into a love with a young Gentlewoman that lived in that Family, who was Niece to the Lady *Elfemore*, and daughter to Sir *George Moor*, then Chancellor of the Garter and Lieutenant of the Tower.

Sir *George* had fome intimation of it, and knowing prevention to be a great part of wifdom, did therefore remove her with much hafte from that to his own houfe at *Lothefley*, in the County of *Surry*; but too late, by reafon of fome faithful promifes which were fo
inter-

interchangeably paſſed, as never to be violated by either party.

Theſe promiſes were onely known to them-ſeves, and the friends of both parties uſed much diligence, and many arguments to kill or cool their affections to each other: but in vain, for, love is a flattering miſchief, that hath de-nyed aged and wiſe men a foreſight of thoſe evils that too often prove to be the children of that blind father; a paſſion that carries us to commit *Errors* with as much eaſe as whirl-winds remove feathers, and begets in us an unwearied induſtry to the attainment of what we deſire. And ſuch an Induſtry did, notwith-ſtanding much watchfulneſs againſt it, bring them ſecretly together (I forbear to tell how) and to a marriage too without the allowance of thoſe friends, whoſe approbation always was and ever will be neceſſary to make even a vertuous love become lawful.

And that the knowledge of their marriage might not fall, like an unexpected tempeſt, on thoſe that were unwilling to have it ſo; but that preapprehenſions might make it the leſs enormous, it was purpoſely whiſpered into the ears of many that it was ſo, yet by none that could atteſt it. But to put a period to the jealouſies of Sir *George*, (Doubt often beget-ting more reſtleſs thoughts then the certain knowledge of what we fear) the news was in favour to Mr. *Donne*, and with his allowance,

made

made known to Sir *George* by his honorable
friend and neighbour *Henry* Earl of *Northum-*
berland: but it was to Sir *George* fo immeafu-
rably unwelcome, and fo tranfported him,
that as though his paffion of anger and incon-
fideration might exceed theirs of love and errour, he prefently engaged his Sifter the Lady *Elfemore*, to joyn with him to procure her
Lord to difcharge Mr. *Donne* of the place he
held under his Lordfhip.   This requeft was
followed with violence; and though Sir
George were remembred, that Errors might be
overpunifhed, and defired therefore to forbear
till fecond confiderations might clear fome
fcruples, yet he became reftlefs until his fuit
was granted, and the punifhment executed.
And though the *Lord Chancellor* did not at
Mr. *Donnes* difmifsion, give him fuch a Commendation as the great Emperour *Charles* the
fifth, did of his Secretary *Erafo*, when he prefented him to his Son and Succeffor *Philip* the
Second; faying, *That in his* Erafo, *he gave to*
him a greater gift then all his Eftate, and all the
Kingdomes which he then refigned to him: yet
he faid, *He parted with a Friend, and fuch a*
Secretary as was fitter to ferve a King then a
fubject.

And yet this Phyfick of Mr. *Donnes* difmif-
fion was not ftrong enough to purge out all
Sir *George* 's choler, for he was not fatisfied
till Mr. *Donne* and his fometime Compupil

in *Cambridge* that married him, namely, *Samuel Brook* (who was af er Doctor in Divinity, and Master of Trinity Colledge) and his brother Mr. *Christopher Brook*, sometime Mr. *Donnes* Chamber-fellow in *Lincolns Inn*, who gave Mr. *Donne* his Wife, and witnessed the marriage, were all committed, and to three several prisons.

Mr. *Donne* was first enlarged, who neither gave rest to his body or brain, nor to any friend in whom he might hope to have an interest, untill he had procured an enlargement for his two imprisoned friends.

He was now at liberty, but his dayes were still cloudy: and being past these troubles, others did still multiply upon him; for his wife was (to her extreme sorrow) detained from him; and though with *Jacob* he endured not an hard service for her, yet he lost a good one, and was forced to make good his title to her, and to get possession of her by a long and restless suit in Law; which proved troublesom and chargeable to him, whose youth, and travel, and needless bounty, had brought his estate into a narrow compass.

It is observed, and most truly, that silence and submission are charming qualities, and work most upon passionate men; and it proved so with Sir *George*; for these and a general report of Mr. *Donnes* merits, together with his winning behaviour, (which when it would intice,

intice, had a strange kind of elegant irresistible art) these and time had so dispassionated Sir *George*, that as the world had approved his Daughters choice, so he also could not but see a more then ordinary merit in his new son: and this at last melted him into so much remorse (for Love and Anger are so like Agues, as to have hot and cold fits; and love in Parents, though it may be quenched, yet is easily rekindled, and expires not, till death denies mankind a natural heat) that he labored his Sons restauration to his place; using to that end both his own and his Sisters power to her Lord; but with no success; for his Answer was, *That though he was unfeignedly sorry for what he had done, yet it was inconsistent with his place and credit, to discharge and readmit servants at the request of passionate petitioners.*

Sir *Georges* endeavour for Mr. *Donnes* readmission, was by all means to be kept secret (for men do more naturally reluct for errours, then submit to put on those blemishes that attend their visible acknowledgment.) But however it was not long before Sir *George* appeared to be so far reconciled, as to wish their happiness, and not to deny them his paternal blessing, but yet refused to contribute any means that might conduce to their livelihood.

Mr *Donnes* estate was the greatest part spent

in many and chargeable Travels, Books and dear-bought Experience: he out of all employment that might yield a support for himself and wife, , who had been curiously and plentifully educated; both their natures generous, and accuftomed to conferr, and not to receive Courtefies; these and other confiderations, but chiefly that his wife was to bear a part in his fufferings furrounded him with many fad thoughts, and fome apparent apprehenfions of want.

But his forrows were leffened and his wants prevented by the feafonable courtefie of their noble kinfman Sir *Francis Wolly* of *Pirford* in *Surrie,* who intreated them to a cohabitation with him ; where they remained with much freedom to themfelves, and equal content to him for many years; and, as their charge encreafed (fhe had yearly a child) fo did his love and bounty.

It hath been obferved by wife and confidering men, that Wealth hath feldom been the Portion, and never the Mark to difcover good People; but, that Almighty God, who difpofeth all things wifely, hath of his abundant goodnefs denied it (he onely knows why) to many, whofe minds he hath enriched with the greater Bleffings of *Knowledge* and *Vertue,* as the fairer Teftimonies of his love to Mankind; and this was the prefent condition of this man of fo excellent Erudition and Endowments ;
whofe

whofe neceffary and daily expences were hardly reconcileable with his uncertain and narrow
eftate. Which I mention, for that at this time
there was a moft generous offer made him for
the moderating of his worldly cares; the de-
claration of which fhall be the next employment of my Pen.

God hath been fo good to his Church, as to
afford it in every age fome fuch men to ferve
at his Altar as have been pioufly ambitious of
doing good to mankind; a difpofition that
is fo like to God himfelf, that it owes it felf
only to him who takes a pleafure to behold it
in his Creatures. Thefe times he did blefs with
many fuch; fome of which ftill live to be Patterns of Apoftolical Charity, and of more
than Humane Patience. I have faid this, becaufe I have occafion to mention one of them
in my following difcourfe; namely, Dr. *Morton*, the moft laborious and learned Bifhop of
Durham, one that God hath bleffed with perfect intellectuals, and a cheerful heart at the
age of 94 years (and is yet living:) one that
in his days of plenty had fo large a heart as to
ufe his large Revenue to the encouragement of
Learning and *Vertue*; and is now (be it fpoken
with forrow) reduced to a narrow eftate, which
he embraces without repining; and ftill fhews
the beauty of his mind by fo liberal a hand, as
if this were an age in which *to morrow were to
care for it felf.* I have taken a pleafure in gi-

ving

ving the Reader a short, but true character of
this good man, from whom I received this following relation. He sent to Mr. *Donne*, and
intreated to borrow an hour of his time for a
Conference the next day. After their meeting
there was not many minutes passed before he
spake to Mr. *Donne* to this purpose; ' Mr. *Donne*,
" The occasion of sending for you is to propose
" to you what I have often revolv'd in my own
" thought since I last saw you: which, never-
" theless, I will not do but upon this condition,
" that you shall not return me a present answer,
" but forbear three days, and bestow some part
" of that time in Fasting and Prayer; and after
" a serious consideration of what I shall pro-
" pose, then return to me with your answer.
" Deny me not, Mr. *Donne*, for it is the effect
" of a true love, which I would gladly pay as a
" debt due for yours to me.

This request being granted, the
Doctor exprest himself thus :

' Mr. *Donne*, I know your Education and
' Abilities; I know your expectation of a State-
' employment; and I know your fitness for it;
' and I know too the many delays and contin-
' gencies that attend Court-promises; and let
' me tell you, my love begot by our long friend-
' ship, our familiarity and your merits hath
' prompted me to such an inquisition of your
' present

' prefent temporal eftate, as makes me no
' ftranger to your neceffities, which are fuch as
'your generous fpirit could not bear, if it were
' not fupported with a pious Patience : you
'know I have formerly perfwaded you to wave
' your Court-hopes, and enter into ho'y Or-
' ders; which I now again perfwade you to
' embrace, with this reafon added to my for-
' mer requeft: The King hath yefterday made
' me Dean of *Gloucefter*, and I am poffeffed of a
' Benefice, the profits of which are equal to
' thofe of my Deany; I will think my Dean-
' ry enough for my maintenance (who am and
' refolve to die a fingle man) and will quit my
' Benefice, and eftate you in it, (which the
' Patron is willing I fhall do) if God fhall in-
' cline your heart to embrace this motion.
(' *Remember*, Mr. *Donne*, no mans Education or
' Parts make him too good for this employ-
' ment, *which is to be an Ambaffadour for the*
' *God of glorie, who by a vile death opened the*
' *gates of life to mankind.* Make me no prefent
' anfwer; but remember your promife, and re-
' turn to me the third day with your Refolu-
' tion.

At the hearing of this, Mr. *Donne's* faint
breath and perplext countenance gave a vifible
teftimony of an inward conflict; but he performed his promife and departed without re-
turning an anfwer till the third day, and then
it was to this effect;

" My

" My moſt worthy and moſt dear friend,
" ſince I ſaw you I have been faithful to my
" promiſe, and have alſo meditated much of
" your great kindneſs, which hath been ſuch as
" would exceed even my gratitude; but that
" it cannot do; and more I cannot return you;
" and I do that with an heart full of Humility
" and Thanks, though I may not accept of
" your offer; but, Sir, my refuſal is not for
" that I think my ſelf too good for that calling,
" for which Kings, if they think ſo, are not
" good enough: nor for that my Education
" and Learning, though not eminent, may not,
" being aſſiſted with God's Grace and Humili-
" ty, render me in ſome meaſure fit for it: but,
" I dare make ſo dear a friend as you are my
" Confeſſor; ſome irregularities of my life
" have been ſo viſible to ſome men, that
" though I have, I thank God, made my peace
" with him by penitential reſolutions againſt
" them, and by the aſſiſtance of his Grace ba-
" niſh'd them my affections; yet this, which
" God knows to be ſo, is not ſo viſible to man,
" as to free me from their cenſures, and it may
" be that ſacred calling from a diſhonour. And
" beſides, whereas it is determined by the beſt
" of *Caſuiſts*, that *God's Glory ſhould be the firſt*
" *end, and a maintenance the ſecond motive to*
" *embrace that calling*; and though each man
" may propoſe to himſelf both together; yet
" the firſt may not be put laſt without a violation

"tion of Conscience, which he that searches
"the heart will judge. And truly my present
"condition is such, that if I ask my own Con-
"science, whether it be reconcileable to that
"rule, it is at this time so perplexed about it,
"that I can neither give my self nor you an an-
"swer. You know, Sir, who sayes, *Happy is*
"*that man whose Conscience doth not accuse him*
"*for that thing which he does.* To these I might
"adde other reasons that disswade me; but I
"crave your favour that I may forbear to ex-
"press them, and thankfully decline your
"offer.

This was his present resolution, but the heart
of man is not in his own keeping; and he was
destined to this sacred service by an higher
hand; a hand so powerful, as at last forced him
to a compliance: of which I shall give the
Reader an account before I shall give a rest to
my Pen.

Mr. *Donnne* and his wife continued with Sir
Francis Wolly till his death: a little before
which time, Sir *Francis* was so happy as to
make a perfect reconciliation betwixt Sir
George and his forsaken son and daughter; Sir
George conditioning by bond, to pay to Mr.
Donne 800 l. at a certain day, as a portion
with his wife, or 20 l. quarterly for their
maintenance: as the interest for it, till the
said portion was paid.

Most of those years that he lived with Sir
Francis,

Francis, he ſtudied the *Civil* and *Cannon Laws*; in which he acquired ſuch a perfection, as was judged to hold proportion with many who had made that ſtudy the employment of their whole life.

Sir *Francis* being dead, and that happy family diſſolved, Mr. *Donne* took for himſelf an houſe in *Micham* (near to *Croydon* in *Surrey*) a place noted for good air and choice company: there his wife and children remained: and for himſelf he took lodgings in *London*, near to White-Hall, whither his friends and occaſions drew him very often, and where he was as often viſited by many of the Nobility and others of this Nation, who uſed him in their Counſels of greateſt conſideration.

Nor did our own Nobility onely value and favour him, but his acquaintance and friendſhip was ſought for by moſt Ambaſſadours of forraign Nations, and by many other ſtrangers, whoſe learning or buſineſs occaſioned their ſtay in this Nation.

He was much importuned by many friends to make his conſtant reſidence in *London*, but he ſtill denyed it, having ſetled his dear wife and children at *Micham*, and near ſome friends that were bountiful to them and him: for they, God knows, needed it : and that you may the better now judge of the then preſent Condition of his minde and fortune, I ſhall preſent
you

you with an extract collected out of some few
of his many Letters.

　　――――*And the reason why I did not send an
answer to your last weeks letter, was, because it
found me under too great a sadness; and at present
'tis thus with me: There is not one person, but
my self, well of my family: I have already lost
half a Child, and with that mischance of hers,
my wife is fallen into such a discompofure, as
would afflict her too extremely, but that the sickness of all her children stupifies her: of one of
which, in good faith, I have not much hope:
and these meet with a fortune so ill provided for
Phyfick, and such relief, that if God should ease
us with burials, I know not how to performe even
that: but I flatter my self with this hope, that I
am dying too: for, I cannot waste faster then by
such griefs. As for,　――――*

　　　　　　　　　　From my hospital
*Aug.*10.　　　　　　　at *Micham,*

　　　　　　　JOHN DONNE.

Thus he did bemoan himself:　And thus in
　　other letters.

　　　――――*For, we hardly discover a sin, when it
is but an omiſſion of some good, and no accusing
act; with this or the former, I have often sus-
pected my self to be overtaken; which is, with an*
　　　　　　　　　　　　　　　　　over

*over earnest desire of the next life: and though
I know it is not mearly a weariness of this, because
I had the same desire when I went with the tide,
and injoyed fairer hopes then I now doe: yet I
doubt worldly troubles have increased it: 'tis
now Spring, and all the pleasures of it displease
me; every other tree blossoms, and I wither: I
grow older and not better; my strength deminisheth and my lode grows heavier; and yet, I
would fain be or do something; but that I cannot
tell what, is no wonder in this time of my sadness,
for, to chuse is to do, but to be no part of my body,
is as to be nothing, and so I am, and shall so judge
my self, unless I could be so incorporated into a
part of the world, as by business to contribute
some sustentation to the whole. This I made account, I began early when I understood the study
of our Laws: but was diverted by leaving that
and imbracing the worst voluptuousness,* an hydroptique immoderate desire of humane learning and languages: *Beautiful ornaments indeed
to men of great fortunes; but mine was grown
so low as to need an occupation: which I thought I
entred well into it, when I subjected my self to
such a service as I thought might exercise my poor
abilities: and there I stumbled, and fell too: and
now I am become so little, or such a nothing, that I
am not a subject good enough for one of my own
letters,* ———*I fear my present discontent does
not proceed from a good root, that I am so well
content to be nothing, that is, dead. But, Sir,*
though

though my fortune hath made me such, as that I
am rather a Sickness or a Disease of the world,
than any part of it, and therefore neither love it
nor life; yet I would gladly live to become some
such thing as you should not repent loving me:
Sir, your own Soul cannot be more zealous of your
good then I am, and, God who loves that zeal in
me, will not suffer you to doubt it: you would
pity me now, if you saw me write, for my pain
hath drawn my head so much awry, and holds it
so, that my eye cannot follow my pen. I therefore receive you into my Prayers with mine own
weary soul, and, Commend my self to yours. I
doubt not but next week will bring you good news,
for I have either mending or dying on my side:
but, If I do continue longer thus, I shall have
Comfort in this, That my blessed Saviour in ex-
ercising his Justice upon my two worldly parts,
my Fortune and my Body, reserves all his
Mercy for that which most needs it, my Soul?
that is, I doubt, too like a Porter, which is very
often near the gate, and yet goes not out. Sir, I
profess to you truly, that my lothness to give over
writing now, seems to my self a sign that I shall
write no more ——

Sept. 7.

Your poor friend, and
Gods poor patient

JOHN DONNE.

By

By this you have feen a part of the picture of his narrow fortune, and the perplexities of his generous minde, and thus it continued with him for about two years; all which time his family remained conftantly at *Micham*, and to which place he often retir'd himfelf, and deftined fome dayes to a conftant ftudy of fome points of Controverfy betwixt the *Englifh* and *Roman Church*; and efpecially thofe of *Supremacy* and *Allegiance*: and, to that place and fuch ftudies he could willingly have wedded himfelf during his life: but the earneft perfwafion of friends became at laft to be fo powerful as to caufe the removal of himfelf and family to *London*, where Sir *Robert Drewry*, a Gentleman of very noble eftate, and a more liberal mind, affigned him a very choice and ufeful houfe rent-free, next to his own in *Drewry-lane*; and was alfo a cherifher of his ftudies, and fuch a friend as fympathized with him and his in all their joy and forrows.

Many of the Nobility were watchful and folicitous to the King for fome fecular preferment for him: His Majefty had formerly both known and put a value upon his company, and had alfo given him fome hopes of a State-employment, being alwayes much pleafed when Mr. *Donne* attended him, efpecially at his meals, where there were ufually many deep difcourfes of general learning, and very often friendly debates or difputes of Religion betwixt

twixt his Majesty and those Divines, whose places required their attendance on him at those times: particularly the Dean of the Chappel; who then was Bishop *Montague*) the publisher of the learned and eloquent Works of his Majesty) and the most reverend Doctor *Andrews*, the late learned Bishop of *Winchester*, who then was the Kings Almoner.

About this time there grew many disputes that concerned the *Oath of Supremacy* and *Allegiance*, in which the King had appeared and engaged himself by his publick writings now extant: and his Majesty discoursing with Mr. *Donne* concerning many of the reasons which are usually urged against the taking of those Oaths, apprehended such a validity and clearness in his stating the Questions, and his Answers to them, that his Majesty commanded him to bestow some time in drawing the Arguments into a method, and then write his Answers to them: and having done that, not to send, but be his own messenger and bring them to him.   To this he presently applyed himself, and within six weeks brought them to him under his own hand-writing, as they be now printed, the Book bearing the name of *Pseudo-martyr.*

When the King had read and considered that Book, he perswaded Mr. *Donne* to enter into the Ministry; to which at that time he was, and appeared very unwilling, apprehending

D   it

it (such was his miſtaking modeſty) to be too weighty for his Abilities; and though his Majeſty had promiſed him a favour, and many perſons of worth mediated with his Majeſty for ſome ſecular employment for him, to which his Education had apted him, and particularly the Earl of *Somerſet,* when in his height of favour; who being then at *Theobalds* with the King, where one of the Clerks of the Council died that night, and the Earl having ſent for Mr. *Donne* to come to him immediately, ſaid, Mr. *Donne, To teſtifie the reality of my Affection, and my purpoſe to preferre you, Stay in this Garden till I go up to the King and bring you word that you are Clark of the Council: doubt not my doing this, for I know the King loves you, and will not deny me.* But the King gave a poſitive denyal to all requeſts; and having a diſcerning ſpirit, replyed, *I know Mr.* Donne *is a learned man, has the abilities of a learned Divine; and will prove a powerful Preacher, and my deſire is to prefer him that way.* After that

* In his Book of Devoti- ..s. time, as he profeſſeth, * *The King deſcended to a perſwaſion, almoſt to a ſolicitation of him to enter into ſacred Orders :* which though he then denyed not, yet he deferred it for almoſt three years. All which time he applyed himſelf to an inceſſant ſtudy of Textual Divinity, and to the attainment of a greater perfection in the learned Languages. *Greek* and *Hebrew.*

In the firſt and moſt bleſſed times of Chriſtia-

ftianity, when the Clergy were look'd upon
with reverence, and deferved it, when they
overcame their oppofers by high examples of
Vertue, by a bleffed Patience and long Suffering: thofe onely were then judged worthy
the Miniftry, whofe quiet and meek fpirits did
make them look upon that facred calling with
an humble adoration and fear to undertake it ;
which indeed requires fuch great degrees of *humility*, and *labour* and *care*, that none but fuch
were then thought worthy of that celeftial
dignity. And fuch onely were then fought out,
and folicited to undertake it.   This I have
mentioned becaufe forwardnefs and inconfide-
ation, could not in Mr. *Donne*, as in many
others, be an argument of infufficiency or un-
fitnefs for he had confidered long, and had
many ftrifes within himfelf concerning the
ftrictnefs of life and competency of learning required in fuch as enter into facred Orders ; and
doubtlefs, confidering his own demerits, did
humbly ask God with St. *Paul, Lord, who is
fufficient for thefe things ?* and, with meek
Mofes, Lord, who am I ?   And fure, if he had
confulted with flefh and blood, he had not put
his hand to that holy plough.   But, God who
is able to prevail, wreftled with him, as the *Angel* did with *Jacob, and marked him;* mark'd
him for his own ; mark'd him with a bleffing ;
a bleffing of obedience to the motions of his
bleffed Spirit. And then, as he had formerly

D 2   asked

asked God with *Moses, Who am I ?* So now being infpired with an apprehenfion of Gods particular mercy to him, in the Kings and others folicitations of him, he came to ask *King Davids* thankful queftion, *Lord, who am I, that thou art fo mindful of me ?* So mindful of me, as to lead me for more then forty years through this wildernefs of the many temptations, and various turnings of a dangerous life : fo merciful to me, as to move the learned'ft of Kings, to defcend to move me to ferve at thy Altar : fo merciful to me, as at laft, to move my heart to imbrace this holy motion: thy motions I will and do imbrace : And, I now fay with the bleffed Virgin, *Be it with thy fervant as feemeth beft in thy fight*: and fo, *bleffed Jefus,* I do take the cup of Salvation, and will call upon thy Name, and will preach thy Gofpel.

Such ftrifes as thefe St. *Auftine* had, when St. *Ambrofe* indeavoured his converfion to Chriftianity, with which he confeffeth, he acquainted his friend *Alipius.* Our learned Author, (a man fit to write after no mean Copy) did the like. And declaring his intentions to his dear friend Dr. *King* then *Bifhop* of *London,* a man famous in his generation, and no ftranger to Mr. *Donnes* abilities. (For he had been Chaplain to the Lord Chancellor, at the time of Mr. *Donnes* being his Lordfhips Secretary) That Reverend man did receive the news with much gladnefs ; and, after fome expreffions of

joy,

joy, and a perſwaſion to be conſtant in his pious purpoſe, he proceeded with all convenient ſpeed to ordain him both *Deacon* and *Prieſt.*

Now the *Engliſh Church* had gain'd a ſecond St. *Auſtine*, for, I think, none was ſo like him before his Converſion: none ſo like St. *Ambroſe* after it: and if his youth had the infirmities of the one, his age had the excellencies of the other, the learning and holineſs of both.

And now all his ſtudies which had been occaſionally diffuſed, were all concentred in Divinity. Now he had a new calling, new thoughts, and a new imployment for his wit and eloquence. Now all his earthly affections were changed into divine love; and all the faculties of his own ſoul were ingaged in the Converſion of others: In preaching the glad tidings of Remiſſion to repenting Sinners; and peace to each troubled ſoul. To theſe he app'yed himſelf with all care and diligence; and now, ſuch a change was wrought in him, that he could ſay with David, *Oh how amiable are thy Tabernacles, O Lord God of Hoſts!* Now he declared openly, *that when he required a temporal, God gave him a ſpiritual bleſſing.* And that, *he was now gladder to be a door-keeper in the houſe of God, then he could be to injoy the nobleſt of all temporal imployments.*

Preſently after he entred into his holy profeſſion, the King ſent for him, and made him

him his Chaplain in ordinary; and promised to take a particular care for his preferment.

And though his long familiari·y with Scholars, and persons of greareſt quality, was ſuch as might have given ſome men boldneſs enough to have preached to any eminent Auditory, yet his modeſty in this imployment was ſuch, that he could not be perſwaded to it, but went uſually accompanied with ſome one friend, to preach privately in ſome village, not far from *London:* his firſt Sermon being preached at *Paddington.* This he did, till His Majeſty ſent and appointed him a day to preach to him at *White-hall,* and, though much were expected from him, both by His Majeſty and others, yet he was ſo happy (which few are) as to ſatisfie and exceed their expectations: preaching the Word ſo, as ſhewed his own heart was poſſeſt with thoſe very thoughts and joyes that he labored to diſtill into others: A Preacher in earneſt, weeping ſometimes for his Auditory, ſometimes with them: alwayes preaching to himſelf, like an Angel from a cloud, but in none; carrying ſome, as St. *Paul* was, to Heaven in holy raptures, and inticing others by a ſacred Art and Courtſhip to amend their lives; here picturing a vice ſo as to make it ugly to thoſe that practiſed it; and a vertue ſo, as to make it be beloved even by thoſe that luv'd it not; and, all this with a moſt particuticular grace and an unexpreſſible addition of comelineſs.

There may be ſome that may incline to think (ſuch indeed as have not heard him) that my affection to my Friend, hath tranſported me to an immoderate Commendation of his Preaching. If this meets with any ſuch, Let me intreat, though I will omit many, yet that they will receive a double witneſs for what I ſay, it being atteſted by a Gentleman of worth, (Mr. *Chidley,* a frequent hearer of his Sermons) being part of a funeral Elogie writ by him on Doctor *Donne,* and a known truth, though it be in Verſe.

—— Each Altar had his fire ——
He kept his love, but not his object : wit,
He did not baniſh, but tranſplanted it ;
Taught it both time & place, and brought it home
To Piety, *which it doth beſt become.*
For ſay, had ever pleaſure ſuch a dreß ?
Have you ſeen crimes ſo ſhip't, or lovelineß
Such as his lips did clothe Religion in ?
Had not reproof a beauty, paſſing ſin ?
Corrupted nature ſorrowed that ſhe ſtood
So neer the danger of becoming good.
And, when he preach't ſhe wiſh't her ears exempt
From Piety, *that had ſuch pow'r to tempt.*
How did his ſacred flattery beguile
Men to amend ? ——

More

More of this, and more witneffes might be brought, but I forbear and return.

That Summer, in the very fame moneth in which he entred into facred Orders, and was made the *Kings Chaplain*, His Majefty then going his Progrefs , was intreated to receive an entertainment in the Univerfity of *Cambridge*. And Mr. *Donne* attending his Majefty, at that time, his Majefty was pleafed to recommend him to the Univerfity, to be made *Doctor* in *Divinity* ; *Doctor Harfnet* (after Archbifhop of *York*) was then *Vice-Chancellour*, who knowing him to be the Author of that learned Book the *Pfeudo-Martyr*, required no other proof of his Abilities, but propofed it to the *Univerfity*, who prefently affented, and expreft a gladnefs, that they had fuch an occafion to intitle him to be theirs.

His Abilities and Induftry in his Profeffion were fo eminent, and he fo known and fo beloved by Perfons of Quality, that within the firft year of his entring into facred Orders, he had fourteen Advowfons of feveral Benefices prefented to him: But they were in the Countrey, and he could not leave his beloved *London*, to which place he had a natural inclination, having received both his Birth and Education in it, and, there contracted a friendfhip with many, whofe converfation multiplyed the joyes of his life: But, an imployment that might affixe him to that place would be welcome, for he needed it.   Im-

Immediately after his return from *Cam-bridge,* his wife died, leaving him a man of an unfetled eftate, and (having buried five) the careful father of feven children then living, to whom he gave a voluntary affurance never to bring them under the fubjection of a ftep-mother; which promife he kept moft faith-fully, burying with his tears all his earthly joyes in his moft dear and deferving wives grave; be-taking himfelf to a moft retired and folitary life.

In this retirednefs which was often from the fight of his deareft friends, he became *cruci-fied to the world* , and all thofe vanities, thofe imaginary pleafures that are dayly acted on that reftlefs ftage; and, they crucified to him. Nor is it hard to think (being pafsions may be both changed and heightned by accidents) but that that abundant affection which once was betwixt him and her, who had long been the delight of his eyes, the Companion of his youth; her, with whom he had divided fo many pleafant forrows and contented fears, as Common-people are not capable of; She, being now removed by death, a commeafura-ble grief took as full a poffefsion of him as joy had done; and fo indeed it did: for, now his very foul was elemented of nothing but fad-nefs; now grief took fo full a poffefsion of his heart, as to leave no place for joy: If it did, It was a joy to be alone, where like a *Pelican in*

the

the wildernefs, he might bemoan himfelf without witnefs or reftraint, and pour forth his paffions like *Job* in the days of his affliction, *Oh that I might have the defire of my heart ! Oh that God would grant the thing that I long for !* For then, *as the grave is become her houfe,* fo I would haften to make it mine alfo; *that we two might there make our beds together in the dark.* Thus as the *Ifraelites* fate mourning by the rivers of *Babylon*, when they remembred *Sion*; fo he gave fome eafe to his oppreffed heart by thus venting his forrows : Thus he began the day, and ended the night ; ended the reftlefs night and began the weary day in *Lamentations*. And, thus he continued till a confideration of his new ingagements to God, and St. *Pauls Wo is me, if I preach not the Gofpel :* difper'ft thofe fad clouds that had now benighted his hopes, and forc'd him to behold the light.

His firft motion from his houfe was to preach, where his beloved wife lay buried (in St *Clements* Church, near Temple-Bar *London*) and his Text was a part of the Prophet *Jeremy*'s Lamentation : *Lo, I am the man that have feen affliction.*

And indeed, his very words and looks teftified him to be truly fuch a man ; and they, with the addition of his fighs and tears, expreft in his Sermon, did fo work upon the affections of his hearers, as melted and moulded them into a companionable fadnefs ; and fo they left the
Con-

Congregation; but then their houses presented them with objects of diversion, and his presented him with no diversions, but with fresh objects of sorrow, in beholding many helpless children, a narrow fortune, and, a consideration of the many cares and casualties that attend their education.

In this time of sadness he was importuned by the grave Benchers of *Lincolns Inne*, once the friends of his youth, to accept of their Lecture, which by reason of Dr. *Gatakers* removal from thence was then void: of which he accepted; being most glad to renew his intermitted friendship with those whom he so much loved, and where he had been a *Saul*, though not to persecute Christianity, or to deride it, yet in his irregular youth to neglect the visible practise of it: there to become a *Paul*, and preach salvation to his beloved brethren.

And now his life was as a *Shining light* among his old friends: now he gave an ocular testimony of the strictness and regularity of it; now he might say as St *Paul* adviseth his *Corinthians*, *Be ye followers of me*, *as I follow Christ*, *and walk as yee have me for an example*; not the example of a busie-body; but, of a contemplative, a harmless, an humble and an holy life and conversation.

The love of that noble society was expressed to him many wayes: for, besides fair lodgings that were set apart and newly furnished for him, with

with all neceſſaries, other courteeſies were
daily added; indeed ſo many and ſo freely, as
if they meant their gratitude ſhould exceed his
merits; and, in this love-ſtrife of deſert and liberality, they continued for the ſpace of two
years, he preaching faithfully and conſtantly to
them, and they liberally requiting him. About
which time the Emperour of *Germany* died,
and the Palſgrave, who had lately married the
Lady *Elizabeth* the Kings onely daugher, was
elected and crowned King of *Bohemia*, the unhappy beginning of many miſeries in that Nation.

    King *James*, whoſe Motto (*Beati pacifici*)
did truly ſpeak the very thoughts of his heart,
endeavoured firſt to prevent, and after to com-
poſe the diſcords of that diſcompoſed State;
and amongſt other his endeavours did then ſend
the Lord *Hay* Earl of *Doncaſter* his Ambaſſadour to thoſe unſetled Princes; and by a ſpe-
cial command from his Majeſty Dr *Donne* was
appointed to aſſiſt and attend that employment
to the Princes of the Union: for which the
Earl was moſt glad, who had alwayes put a
great value on him, and taken a great pleaſure
in his converſation and diſcourſe: and his friends
of *Lincolns Inne* were as glad, for, they feared
that his immoderate ſtudy and ſadneſs for his
wives death, would, as *Jacob* ſaid, *make his
daies few*, and reſpecting his bodily health, *evil*
too: and of this there were ſome viſible ſigns.
At

At his going he left his friends of *Lincolns-Inne*, and they him with many reluctations: for, though he could not say as *S. Paul* to his *Ephesians, Behold you to whom I have preached the Kingdom of God, shall from henceforth see my face no more*; yet, he believing himself to be in a Consumption, questioned, and they feared it: (all concluding that his troubled mind, with the help of his unintermitted studies, hastened the decays of his weak body:) And God turned it to the best; for this employment (to say nothing of the event of it) did not onely divert him from those too serious studies and sad thoughts, but seemed to give him a new life by a true occasion of joy, to be an eye-witness of the health of his most dear and most honoured Mistress the Qu. of *Bohemia*, in a forraign Nation; and, to be a witness of that gladness which she expressed to see him: Who, having formerly known him a Courtier, was much joyed to see him in a Canonical habit, and more glad to be an ear-witness of his excellent and powerful Preaching.

About fourteen moneths after his departure out of *England*, he returned to his friends of *Lincolns-Inne* with his sorrows moderated, and his health improved; and there betook himself to his constant course of Preaching.

About a year after his return out of *Germany*, Dr. *Cary* was made Bishop of *Exeter*, and by his removal the Deanry of St. *Pauls* being va-
cant

cant, the King sent to Dr. *Donne*, and appointed him to attend him at Dinner the next day. When his Majesty was sate down, before he had eat any meat, he said after his pleasant manner, *Dr. Donne, I have invited you to Dinner; and, though you sit not down with me, yet I will carve to you of a dish that I know you love well; for knowing you love* London, *I do; therefore make you Dean of* Pauls; *and when I have dined, then do you take your beloved dish home to your study; say grace there to your self, and much good may it do you.*

Immediately after he came to his Deanry, he employed work-men to repair and beautifie the Chappel; suffering, as holy *David* once vowed, *his eyes and temples to take no rest, till he had first beautified the house of God.*

The next quarter following, when his Father-in-law Sir *George Moor*, (whom Time had made a lover and admirer of him,) came to pay to him the conditioned summe of twenty pounds; he refused to receive it, and said (as good *Jacob* did, when he heard his beloved son *Joseph* was alive, *It is enough,*) You have been kind to me and mine: I know your present condition is such as not to abound: and I hope mine is or will be such as not to need it: I will therefore receive no more from you upon that contract; and in testimony of it freely gave him up his bond.

Immediately after his admission into his
Deanry

Deanry, the Vicarage of St. *Dunstan* in the West, *London*, fell to him by the death of Dr. *White*, the Advowson of it having been given to him long before by his honourable friend, *Richard* Earl of *Dorset*, then the Patron, and confirmed by his brother the late deceased *Edward*, both of them men of much honour.

By these and another Ecclesiastical endowment which fell to him about the same time, given to him formerly by the Earl of *Kent*, he was enabled to become charitable to the poor, and kind to his friends, and to make such provision for his children, that they were not left scandalous, as relating to their or his Profession and Quality.

The next *Parliament*, which was within that present year, he was chosen *Prolocutor* to the *Convocation*; and about that time was appointed by his Majesty, his most gracious Master, to preach very many occasional Sermons, as at St. *Paul*'s Cross, and other places. All which employments he performed to the admiration of the Representative Body of the whole Clergy of this Nation.

He was once, and but once, clouded with the Kings displeasure ; and , it was about this time; which was occasioned by some malicious whisperer, who had told his Majesty that Dr. *Donne* had put on the general humour of the Pulpits, and was become busie in insinuating
a fear

a fear of the Kings inclining to *Popery*, and a dif-like of his Government: and particularly, for his then turning the Evening Lectures into *Ca-techifing*, and expounding the *Prayer* of our *Lord*, and of the *Belief*, and *Commandments*. His Majefty was the more inclineable to be-lieve this, for that a Perfon of Nobility and great note, betwixt whom and Dr. *Donne*, there had been a great friendfhip, was at this very time difcarded the Court (I fhall forbear his name, unlefs I had a fairer occafion) and juftly committed to prifon; which begot many ru-mours in the common people, who in this Na-tion think they are not wife, unlefs they be bufie about what they underftand not: and efpeci-ally about Religion.

The King received this news with fo much difcontent and reftlefnefs, that he would not fuffer the Sun to fet and leave him under this doubt; but fent for Dr. *Donne*, and required his anfwer to the Accufation; which was fo clear and fatisfactory, that the King faid *he was right glad he refted no longer under the fufpicion.* When the King had faid this, Doctor *Donne* kneeled down and thanked his Majefty, and protefted his anfwer was faithful and free from all collufion, and therefore *defired that he might not rife, till, as in like cafes he always had from God, fo he might have from his Majefty, fome af-furance that he ftood clear and fair in his opinion.* Then the King raifed him from his knees with
his

his own *hands*, and *protested he believ'd him: and that he knew he was an honest man, and doubted not but that he loved him truly.* And, having thus difmiffed him, he called fome Lords of his Council into his Chamber, and faid with much earneftnefs, *My Doctor is an honest man: and my Lords, I was never better fatisfied with an anfwer then he hath now made me: and I always rejoyce when I think that by my means he became a Divine.*

He was made Dean the fiftieth year of his age; and in his fifty fourth year a dangerous ficknefs feized him, which inclined him to a Confumption. But God, as *Job* thankfu'ly acknowledged, *preferved his fpirit*, and ke, t his intellectuals as clear and perfect, as when that ficknefs firft feized his body: but it continued long and threatned him with death; which he dreaded not.

In this diftemper of body, his dear friend Doctor *Henry King* (then chief Refidenciary of that Church, and late Bifhop of *Chichefter*) a man generally known by the Clergy of this Nation, and as generally noted for his o liging nature, vifited him daily; and obferving that his ficknefs rendred his recovery doubtful, he chofe a feafonable time to fpeak to him, to this purpofe.

'Mr. *Dean*, I am by your favour no ftranger
'to your temporal eftate, and you are no
'ftranger to the Offer lately made us, for

E   'the

'the renewing a Leafe of the beft Prebends
'Corps belonging to our Church; and you
'know, 'twas denied, for that our Tenant be-
'ing very rich, offered to fine at fo low a rate
'as held not proportion with his advantages:
'but I will either raife him to an higher fumme,
'or procure that the other Refidenciaries fhall
'joyn to accept of what was offered: one of
'thefe I can and will by your favour do without
'delay, and without any trouble either to your
'body or mind; I befeech you to accept of my
'offer, for I know it will be a confiderable addi-
'tion to your prefent eftate, which I know
'needs it.

To this, after a fhort paufe, and raifing himfelf upon his bed, he made this reply.

'My moft dear friend, I moft humbly thank
'you for your many favours, and this in particu-
'lar: But, in my prefent condition, I fhall not
'accept of your propofal; for doubtlefs there
'is fuch a Sin as *Sacriledge*; if there were not,
'it could not have a name in Scripture: And
'the Primitive Clergy were watchful againft
'all appearances of that evil; and indeed then
'all Chriftians lookt upon it with horrour and
'deteftation: Judging it to be even an *open de-*
'*fiance of the Power and Providence of Almighty*
'*God, and a fad prefage of a declining Religion.*
'But in ftead of fuch Chriftians, who had fe-
'lected times fet apart to faft and pray to God,
'for a pious Clergy which they then did obey;
'Our

'Our times abound with men that are busie
'and litigious about trifles and Church-Cere-
'monies; and yet so far from scrupling *Sacri-*
'*ledge*, that they make not so much as a *quare*
'what it is: But, I thank God I have; and,
'dare not now upon my sick-bed, when Al-
'mighty God hath made me useless to the ser-
'vice of the Church, make any advantages out
'of it. But, if he shall again restore me to such
'a degree of health, as again to serve at his
'*Altar*, I shall then gladly take the reward
'which the bountiful Benefactours of this
'Church have designed me; for God knows
'my Children and Relations will need it. In
'which number my Mother (whose Credulity
'and Charity has contracted a very plentiful to
'a very narrow estate) must not be forgotten:
'But Doctor *King*, if I recover not, that little
'worldly estate that I shall leave behind me,
'(that very little, when divided into eight parts,)
'must, if you deny me not so Charitable a fa-
'vour, fall into your hands as my most *faith-*
'*ful friend* and Executor; of whose Care and
'Justice, I make no more doubt then of Gods
'blessing on that which I have conscientiously
'collected for them; but it shall not be aug-
'mented on my sick-bed; and, this I declare
'to be my unalterable resolution.

The reply to this was only a promise to observe his request.

Within a few days his distempers abated;
and

and as his ſtrength increaſed, ſo did his thank-
fulneſs to Almighty God, teſtified in his moſt
excellent Book of *Devotions*, which he publi-
ſhed at his Recovery. In which the Reader
may ſee, the moſt ſecret thoughts that then
poſſeſt his Soul, Paraphraſed and made publick: a book that may not unfitly be called a
a *Sacred picture of Spiritual Extaſies*, occaſioned
and applyable to the emergencies of that ſickneſs; which book being a compoſition of *Meditations, Diſquiſitions* and *Prayers*, he writ on his
ſick-bed; herein imitating the Holy Patriarchs,
who were wont to build their Altars in that
place, where they had received their bleſsings.

This ſickneſs brought him ſo near to the
gates of death, and he ſaw the grave ſo ready
to devour him, that he w uld often ſay his
recovery was ſupernatural: But that God that
then reſtored his health continued it to him, till
the fifty-ninth year of his life. And then in
Auguſt 1630. being with his eldeſt Daughter
Mrs. *Harvy* at Abury hatch in *Eſſex*, he there
fell into a fever, which with the help of his
conſtant infirmity (vapors from the ſpleen) haſte-
ned him into ſo viſible a Conſumption, that his
beholders might ſay, as St *Paul* of himſelf, *He
dies dayly;* and he might ſay with *Job, My
welfare paſſeth away as a cloud, the dayes of my
affliction have taken hold of me, and weary nights
are appointed for me.*

R a-

Reader, This ſickneſs continued long, not onely weakning but wearying him ſo much, that my deſire is, he may now take ſome reſt: and that before I ſpeak of his death, thou wilt not think it an impertinent digreſsion to look back with me, upon ſome obſervations of his life, which, whilſt a gentle ſlumber gives reſt to his ſpirits, may, I hope, not unfitly exerciſe thy conſideration.

His marriage was the remarkable errour of his life; an errour which though he had a wit able and very apt to maintain Paradoxes, yet, he was very far from, juſtifying it: and though his wives Competent years, and other reaſons might be juſtly urged to moderate ſevere Cenſures; yet he would occaſionally condemn himſelf for it: and doubtleſs it had been attended with an heavy Repentance, if God had not bleſt them with ſo mutual and cordial affections, as in the midſt of their ſufferings made their bread of ſorrow taſte more pleaſantly then the banquets of dull and low-ſpirited people.

The Recreations of his youth were *Poetry*, in which he was ſo happy, as if nature and all her varieties had been made onely to exerciſe his ſharp wit, and high faćy; and in thoſe pieces which were facetiouſly Compoſed and careleſly ſcattered (ⁱmoſt of them being written before the twentieth year of his age) it may appear by

E 3   his

his choice Metaphors, that both *Nature* and all the *Arts* joyned to assist him with their utmost skill.

It is a truth, that in his penitential years, viewing some of those pieces too loosely scattered in his youth, he wish't they had been abortive, or so short liv'd that his own eyes had witnessed their funera's: But, though he was no friend to them, he was not so fallen out with heavenly Poetry as to forsake that: no nor in his declining age; witnessed then by many Divine Sonnets, and other high, holy, and harmonious Composures. Yea, even on his former sick-bed he wrote this heavenly *Hymne*, expressing the great joy that then possest his soul in the Assurance of Gods favour to him.

An Hymne to God the Father.

Wilt thou forgive that sin where I begun,
Which was my sin, though it were done before?
Wilt thou forgive that sin through which I run,
And do run still though still I do deplore?
When thou hast done, thou hast not done?
     For I have more.

Wilt thou forgive that sin, which I have wonne
Others to sin and made my sin their door?
Wilt thou forgive that sin which I did shun
A year or two, but wallowed in a score?
                When

When thou haft done, thou haft not done,
For I have more.

I have a fin of fear, that when I've fpun
My laft thread, I fhall perifh on the fhore :
But fwear by thy felf that at my death thy Son
Shall fhine as he fhines now, and heretofore ;
And having done that thou haft done,
I fear no more.

I have the rather mentioned this *Hymne,* for
that he caus'd it to be fet to a moft grave and
folemn Tune, and to be often fung to the *Organ*
by the *Chorifters* of St. *Pauls* Church, in his
own hearing, efpecially at the Evening Service ; and at his return from his Cuftomary Devotions in that place, did occafionally fay to
a friend, *The words of this* Hymne *have reftored
to me the fame thoughts of joy that poffeft my Soul
in my ficknefs when I compofed it. And, O the
power of Church-mufick ! that Harmony added to
it has raifed the Affections of my heart, and quic-
ned my graces of zeal and gratitude ;* and I obferve, *that I alwayes return from paying this
publick duty of* Prayer *and* Praife *to* God, *with
an unexprefsible tranquillity of mind ,* and a wil-
lingnefs *to leave the world.*

After this manner did the Difciples of our
Saviour, and the beft of Chriftians in thofe A-
ges of the Church neareft to his time, offer
their praifes to Almighty God. And the reader

of St. *Augustines* life may there find, that towards his diffolution he wept abundantly, that the enemies of Chriftianity had broke in upon them, and prophaned and ruin'd their *Sanctuaries*, and becaufe their *Publick Hymns* and Lauds were loft out of their Churches. And after this manner have many devout Souls lifted up their hands and offered acceptable Sacrifices unto Almighty God where Dr. *Donne* offered his.

But now, oh Lord ⸺ 1656.

Before I proceed further, I think fit to inform the reader, that not long before his death he caufed to be drawn a figure of the Body of Chrift extended upon an Anchor, like thofe which Painters draw when they would prefent us with the picture of Chrift crucified on the Crofs: his, varying no otherwife then to affix him to an Anchor (the Emblem of hope) this he caufed to be drawn in little, and then many of thofe figures thus drawn to be ingraven very fmall in *Helitropian* Stones, and fet in gold, and of thefe he fent to many of his deareft friends to be ufed as *Seales*, or *Rings*, and kept as memorials of him, and of his affection to them.

His dear friends and benefactors, Sir *Henry Goolier*, and Sir *Robert Drewry*, could not be of that number; Nor could the Lady *Magdalen Herbert*, the mother of *George Herbert*, for they had put off mortality, and taken poffeffion of
the

the grave before him: But Sir *Henry Wootton*, and Dr. *Hall* the then late deceafed Bifhop of *Norwitch* were; and, fo were Dr. *Duppa* Bifhop of *Salisbury,* and Dr. *Henry King* Bifhop of *Chiche-fter,* (lately deceafed) men in whom there was fuch a Commixture of general *Learning,* of natural *eloquence,* and Chriftian *humility,* that they deferve a Commemoration by a pen equal to their own , which none hath exceeded.

And in this enumeration of his friends, though many muft be omitted, yet that man of primitive piety Mr. *George Herbert* may not; I mean that *George Herbert,* who was the Author of the *Temple* or *Sacred Poems and Ejaculations.* (A Book, in which by declaring his own fpiritual Conflicts he hath Comforted and raifed many a dejected and difcompofed Soul, and charmed them into fweet and quiet thoughts: A Book, by the frequent reading whereof, and the affiftance of that Spirit that feemed to infpire the Author, the Reader may attain habits of *Peace* and *Piety* , and all the gifts of the *Holy Ghoft* and *Heaven:* and may by ftill reading, ftill keep thofe facred fires burning upon the Altar of fo pure an heart, as fhall free it from the anxieties of this world, and keep it fixt upon things that are above;) betwixt him and Dr. *Donne* there was a long and dear friendfhip, made up by fuch a Sympathy of inclinations , that they coveted and

joy-

joyed to be in each others Company ; and this happy friendſhip was ſtill maintained by many ſacred indearments ; of which, that which followeth may be ſome Teſtimony.

　To Mr. *George Herbert*, ſent him with one of my Seales of the *Anchor* and *Chriſt*. (A ſheaf of Snakes uſed heretofore to be my Seal, which is the Creſt of our poor Family.)

Qui prius aſſuetus ſerpeatum falce tabellas
　　Signare, hæc noſtræ Symbola parva domus
Adſcitus domui domini. ——

Adopted in Gods family, and ſo
　My old Coat loſt into new Arms I go.
The Croſs *my ſeal in Baptiſm, ſpread below,*
　Does by that form into an Anchor grow.
Croſſes grow Anchors, bear as thou ſhould'ſt do
　Thy Croſs, and that Croſs grows an Anchor too.
But he that makes our Croſſes Anchors thus
　Is Chriſt ; *who there is crucified for us.*
Yet with this I may my firſt Serpents hold :
　(God gives new bleſſings, & yet leaves the old)
The Serpent may as wiſe my pattern be ;
　My poyſon, as he feeds on duſt, that's me.
And, as he rounds the earth to murder, ſure
　He is my death ; but on the Croſs *my cure :*
Crucifie nature then ; and then implore
　All grace from him, crucify'd there before.
When all is Croſs, *and that* Croſs *Anchor grown,*
　This ſcales a Catechiſm, not a ſeal alone.

Under

Under that little seal great gifts I send,
  Both works & prayers, pawns & fruits of a friend,
Oh may that saint that rides on our great Seal,
  To you that bear his name large bounty deal.

J. Donne.

In Sacram Anchoram Piscatoris *Geo. Herbert.*

Quod Crux nequibat fixa clavique additi,
Tenere Christum scilicet ne ascenderet
Tuive Christum ――――

Although the Cross could not Christ here detain,
When nail'd unto't, but he ascends again:
Nor yet thy eloquence here keep him still,
But only whilest thou speak'st; this Anchor will:
Nor canst thou be content, unless thou to
This certain Anchor add a seal, and so
The water and the earth, both unto thee
Do owe the Symbole of their certainty.
Let the world reel, we and all ours stand sure,
This Holy Cable's from all storms secure.

G. Herbert.

I return to tell the Reader, that besides
these verses to his dear Mr. *Herbert,* and that
Hymne that I mentioned to be sung in the
Quire of St *Pauls Church*; he did also shorten
and

and beguile many sad hours by composing other sacred Ditties ; and he writ an Hymn on his death-bed, which bears this title.

An Hymn to God, my God, in my sickness, March 23. 1630.

Since I am coming to that holy room,
Where, with thy quire of Saints for ever more
I shall be made thy musique, as I come
I tune my Instrument here at the dore,
And, what I must do then, think here before.

Since my Physitians by their loves are grown
Cosmographers ! and I their map, who lye
Flat on this bed ————

So, in his purple wrapt, receive me, Lord !
By these, his thorns, give me his other Crown :
And, as to other souls I preach'd thy Word,
Be this my text : my Sermon to mine own.
That, he may raise; therefore, the lord throws down.

If these fall under the censure of a soul, whose too much mixture with earth makes it unfit to judge of these high raptures and illumi-
nations

nations; let him know that many holy and devout men have thought the Soul of *Prudentius* to be moſt refined, when not many dayes before his death *he charged it to preſent his God each morning and evening with a new and ſpiritual ſong*; juſtified by the example of King *David* and the good King *Hezekias*, who upon the renovation of his years paid his thankful vowes to Almighty God in a *royal Hymn*, which he concludes in theſe words, *The Lord was ready to ſave, therefore I will ſing my ſongs to the ſtringed inſtruments all the dayes of my life in the temple of my God.*

The latter part of his life may be ſaid to be a continued ſtudy; for as he uſually preached once a week, if not oftner, ſo after his Sermon he never gave his eyes reſt, till he had choſen out a new Text, and that night caſt his Sermon into a form, and his Text into diviſions; and the next day betook himſelf to conſult the Fathers, and ſo commit his meditations to his memory, which was excellent. But upon Saturday he uſually gave himſelf and his mind a reſt from the weary burthen of his weeks meditations, and uſually ſpent that day in viſitation of friends, or ſome other diverſions of his thoughts; and would ſay, that *he gave both his body and mind that refreſhment, that he might be enabled to do the work of the day following, not faintly, but with courage and chearfulneſs.*

Nor was his age onely ſo induſtrious, but in the

the moſt unſetled dayes of his youth, his bed
was not able to detain him beyond the hour of
four in a morning : and it was no common buſineſs that drew him out of his chamber till paſt
ten. All which time was employed in ſtudy ;
though he took great liberty after it: and if this
ſeem ſtrange, it may gain a belief by the viſible
fruits of his labours : ſome of which remain as
teſtimonies of what is here writen : for he left
the reſultance of 1400. Authors, moſt of them
abridged and analyſed with his own hand ; he
left alſo ſixſcore of his Sermons,all written with
his own hand ; alſo an exact and laborious Treatiſe concerning *ſelf-murther*, called *Biathana-*
tos ; wherein all the Laws violated by that Act
are diligently ſurveyed and judiciouſly cenſured:
a Treatiſe written in his younger dayes, which
alone might declare him then not onely perfect
in the *Civil* and *Canon Law*, but in many other
ſuch ſtudies and arguments , as enter not into
the conſideration of many that labour to be
thought great Clerks, and pretend to know all
things.

　　Nor were theſe onely found in his ſtudy ; but
all buſineſſes that paſt of any publick conſequence, either in this, or any of our neighbour
nations, he abbreviated either in Latine, or in
the Language of that Nation, and kept them
by him for uſeful memorials. So he did the copies of divers Letters and caſes of Conſcience
that had concerned his friends, with his obſer-
　　　　　　　　　　　　　　　　　vations

vations and folutions of them; and, divers other bufineffes of importance; all particularly and methodically digefted by himfelf.

He did prepare to leave the world before life left him, making his will when no faculty of his foul was damp'd or made defective by pain or ficknefs, or he furprized by a fudden apprehenfion of death: but it was made with mature deliberation, expreffing himfelf an impartial father by making his childrens portions equal; and a lover of his friends, whom he remembred with Legacies fitly and difcreetly chofen and bequeathed. I cannot forbear a nomination of fome of them; for, methinks they be perfons that feem to challenge a recordation in this place; as namely, to his Brother-in-law Sir *Th. Grimes*, he gave that ftriking Clock which he had long worn in his pocket—to his dear friend and Executor Dr. *King* (late Bifhop of *Chicefter*) that model of gold of the Synod of *Dort*, with which the States prefented him at his laft being at the *Hague*——and the two Pictures of *Padre Paulo* and *Fulgentio*, men of his acquaintance when he travelled *Italy*, and of great note in that Nation for their remarkable learning.——To his ancient friend Dr. *Brook*, (that married him) Mafter of *Trinity Colledge* in *Cambridge*, he gave the Picture of the bleffed Virgin and *Jofeph*. To Dr. *Winniff* (who fucceeded him in the Deanry) he gave a Picture called the *Sceleton*.——To the fucceeding Dean,

Dean, who was not then known, he gave many
neceſſaries of worth, and uſeful for his houſe;
and alſo ſeveral Pictures and Ornaments for the
Chappel, with a deſire that they might be regi-
ſtred, and remain as a Legacy to his Succeſſors.
——— To the Earls of *Dorſet* and of *Carlile*,
he gave ſeveral Pictures, and ſo he did to many
other friends; Legacies, given rather to expreſs
his affection, than to make any addition to their
Eſtates : but unto the Poor he was full of Charity, and unto many others, who by his conſtant
and long continued bounty might intitle themſelves to be his Alms-people; for all theſe he
made proviſion, and ſo largely, as having then ſix
children living, might to ſome appear more than
proportionable to his Eſtate. I forbear to mention any more, leſt the Reader may think I tre-
ſpaſs upon his patience: but I will beg his favour to preſent him with the beginning and end
of his Will.

In the Name of the bleſſed and glorious Tri-
nity, Amen. *I* John Donne, *by the mercy of*
Chriſt Jeſus, *and by the calling of the Church*
of England Prieſt, *being at this time in good*
health and perfect underſtanding (praiſed be
God therefore) do hereby make my laſt Will and
Teſtament in manner and form following:

Firſt, I give my gracious God an intire ſacri-
fice of body and ſoul, with my moſt humble thanks
for that aſſurance which his bleſſed Spirit im-
prints

prints in me now of the salvation of the one,
and the Resurrection of the other ; and for that
constant and chearful resolution which the same
Spirit hath establisht in me to live and dye in
the Religion now professed in the Church of
England. *In expectation of that Resurrection,*
I desire my body may be buried (in the most
private manner that may be) in that place of
*St.*Pauls *Church* London, *that the now Residen-*
tiaries have at my request designed for that pur-
pose, &c. *And this my last Will and Testament,*
made in the fear of God (whose mercy I hum-
bly beg, and constantly relie upon in Jesus Christ)
and in perfect love and charity with all the
world (whose pardon I ask, from the lowest of
my servants, to the highest of my Superiors)
written all with my own hand, and my name sub-
scribed to every page, of which there are five in
number.

Sealed Decem. 13. 1630.

Nor was this blessed sacrifice of Charity expressed onely at his death, but in his life also,
by a cheerful and frequent visitation of any
friend whose mind was dejected , or his fortune
necessitous ; he was inquisitive after the wants
of Prisoners , and redeemed many from thence
that lay for their Fees or small Debts ; he was
a continual Giver to poor Scholars, both of this
and foreign Nations. Besides what he gave
with his own hand, he usually sent a Servant, or

a difcreet and trufty Friend , to diftribute his Charity to all the Prifons in *London* at all the Feftival times of the year, efpecially at the *Birth* and *Refurrection* of our Saviour. He gave an hundred pounds at one time to an old Friend, whom he had known live plentifully , and by a too liberal heart and carelefnefs became decayed in his Eftate: and, when the receiving of it was denied, by the Gentlemans faying, *He wanted not* ; for as there be fome fpirits fo generous as to labour to conceal and endure a fad poverty , rather than thofe blufhes that attend the confeffion of it ; fo there be others to whom Nature and Grace have afforded fuch fweet and compaffionate fouls , as to pity and prevent the Diftreffes of Mankind ; which I have mentioned becaufe of Dr. *Donne*'s Reply , whofe Anfwer was , *I know you want not what will fuftain nature , for a little will do that; but my defire is, that you who in the dayes of your plenty have cheered and raifed the hearts of fo many of your dejected friends , would now receive this from me, and ufe it as a cordial for the cheering of your own :* and fo it was received. He was an happy reconciler of many differences in the Families of his Friends and Kindred , (which he never undertook faintly; for fuch undertakings have ufually faint effects;) and they had fuch a faith in his judgement and impartiality, that he never advifed them to any thing in vain. He was even to her death a
moft

moſt dutiful Son to his Mother, careful to provide for her ſupportation, of which ſhe had
been deſtitute, but that God raiſed him up to
prevent her neceſſities; who having ſucked in
the Religion of the *Roman Church* with her
Mothers Milk, ſpent her Eſtate in foreign
Countreys, to enjoy a liberty in it, and died in
his houſe but three Moneths before him.

And to the end it may appear how juſt a
Steward he was of his Lord and Maſters Revenue, I have thought fit to let the Reader
know, that after his entrance into his Deane-
ry, as he numbred his years, he (at the foot
of a private account (to which God and his
Angels were only witneſſes with him) compu-
ted firſt his Revenue, then what was given to
the Poor, and other Pious Uſes: and laſtly,
what reſted for him and his; he then bleſt each
years poor remainder with a thankful Prayer;
which, for that they diſcover a more than common Devotion, the Reader ſhall partake
ſome of them in his own words:

So all is that remains ⎫
   this year   ⎬
                      ⎭

Deo Opt. Max. benigno
Largitori, à me & ab iis
Quibus hæc à me reſervantur,
Gloria & gratia in æternum.
          Amen.

F 2   So,

So, that this year, God hath ⎱
blessed me and mine with ⎰

Multiplicatæ sunt super
Nos misericordiæ tuæ
Domine. —— ——

Da Domine, ut quæ ex immensâ
Bonitate tuâ nobis elargiri
Dignatus sis, in quorumcunque
Manus devenerint, in tuam
Semper cedant gloriam.
                    Amen.

In fine horum sex Annorum manet ——

Quid habeo quod non accepi à Domino?
Largitur etiam ut quæ largitus est
Sua iterum fiant, bono eorum usu ; ut
Quemadmodum nec officiis hujus mundi,
Nec loci in quo me posuit; dignitati, nec
Servis, nec egenis, in toto hujus anni
Curriculo mihi conscius sum me defuisse;
Ita & liberi, quibus quæ supersunt,
Supersunt, grato animo ea accipiant,
Et beneficum authorem recognoscant.
                    Amen.

But I return from my long Digression.
We left the Author sick in *Essex*, where he
was forced to spend much of that Winter, by
                    reason

reason of his disability to remove from that
place: And having never for almost twenty
years omitted his personal attendance on His
Majesty in that month in which he was to attend and preach to him ; nor, having ever been
left out of the Roll and number of Lent-Prea-
chers; and there being then (in *January* 1630.)
a report brought to *London*, or raised there, that
Dr. *Donne* was dead: That report, gave him
occasion to write this following Letter to a dear
friend.

Sir,
    " This advantage you and my other friends
" have by my frequent fevers, that I am so much
" the oftner at the gates of Heaven; and this
" advantage by the solitude and close imprison-
" ment that they reduce me to after, that I am
" so much the oftner at my prayers, in which I
" shall never leave out your happiness ; and I
" doubt not among his other blessings, God
" will add some one to you for my prayers. A
" man would almost be content to dye (if there
" were no other benefit in death) to hear of so
" much sorrow, and so mnch good testimony
" from good men as I (God be blessed for it)
" did upon the report of my death ; yet I per-
" ceive it went not through all, for one writ to
" me that some (and he said of my friends)
" conceived I was not so ill as I pretended, but
" withdrew my self to live at ease, discharged
           " of

"of preaching. It is an unfriendly, and God
"knows an ill-grounded interpretation; for I
"have alwayes been forrier when I could not
"preach, than any could be they could not hear
"me. It hath been my defire, and God may be
"pleafed to grant it, that I might dye in the
"Pulpit; if not that, yet, that I might take
"my death in the Pulpit, that is, dye the foon-
"er by occafion of thofe labours. Sir, I hope
"to fee you prefently after *Candlemas*, about
"which time will fall my *Lent-Sermon at Court*,
"except my *Lord Chamberlain* believe me to be
"dead, and fo leave me out of the Roll; but as
"long as I live, and am not fpeechlefs, I would
"not willingly decline that fervice. I have bet-
"ter leifure to write, than you to read; yet I
"would not willingly opprefs you with too
"much Letter. God blefs you and your Son as
"I wifh,

Your poor friend and fervant
in Chrift Jefus,
J. Donne.

Before that month ended, he was appointed
to preach upon his old conftant day, the firft
Friday in *Lent*; he had notice of it, and had in
his ficknefs fo prepared for that imployment,
that as he had long thirfted for it: fo, he refolved his weaknefs fhould not hinder his journey;
he came therefore to *London*, fome few dayes
before his appointed day of preaching. At his
coming

coming thither, many of his friends (who with sorrow saw his sickness had left him onely so much flesh as did onely cover his bones)doubted his strength to perform that task,and, did therefore dissiwade him from undertaking it, assuring him however,it was like to shorten his life; but, he passionately denied their requests; saying, *he would not doubt that that God who in so many weaknesses had assisted him with an unexpected strength, would now withdraw it in his last employment ; professing an holy ambition to perform that sacred work.* And, when to the amazement of some beholders he appeared in the Pulpit,many of them thought he presented himself not to preach mortification by a living voice: but, mortality by a decayed body and dying face. And doubtless, many did secretly ask that question in *Ezekiel*; *Do these bones live? or,can that soul organize that tongue, to speak so long time as the sand in that glass will move towards its centre, and measure out an hour of this dying mans unspent life?* Doubtless it cannot; and yet, after some faint pauses in his zealous prayer,his strong desires enabled his weak body to discharge his memory of his preconceived meditations,which were of dying, the Text being, *To God the Lord belong the issues from death.* Many that then saw his tears, and heard his faint and hollow voice, professing they thought the Text prophetically chosen, and that *Dr.* Donne *had preach't his own funeral Sermon.*

Ezek.
37. 3.

F 4   Being

Being full of joy that God had enabled him to perform this defired duty, he haftened to his houfe, out of which he never moved, till like St. *Stephen, he was carried by devout men to his Grave.*

The next day after his Sermon, his ftrength being much wafted, and his fpirits fo fpent, as indifpofed him to bufinefs, or to talk : A friend that had often been a witnefs of his free and facetious difcourfe, asked him, *Why are you fad?* To whom he replied with a countenance fo full of cheerful gravity, as gave teftimony of an inward tranquillity of mind, and of a foul willing to take a farewell of this world. And faid,

'I am not fad, but moft of the night paft I
'have entertained my felf with many thoughts
'of feveral friends that have left me here, *and*
'*are gone to that place from which they fhall not*
'*return:* And, that within a few dayes *I alfo*
'*fhall go hence, and be no more feen.* And, my
'preparation for this change is become my
'nightly meditation upon my bed, which my
'infirmities have now made reftlefs to me. But,
'at this prefent time I was in a ferious contem-
'plation of the providence and goodnefs of
'God to me, who am lefs than the leaft of his
'mercies; and looking back upon my life paft,
'I now plainly fee it was his hand that prevented
'me from all temporal employment; and, it
'was his Will that I fhould never fettle nor
'thrive

' thrive till I entred into the Miniftry ; in which,
' I have now liv'd almoft twenty years (I hope
' to his glory) and by which I moft humbly
' thank him , I have been enabled to require
' moft of thofe friends which fhewed me kind-
' nefs when my fortune was very low , as God
' knows it was : and (as it hath occafioned the
' expreffion of my gratitude) I thank God
' moft of them have ftood in need of my requi-
' tal. I have liv'd to be ufeful and comfortable
' to my good Father-in-law Sir *George Moore,*
' whofe patience God hath been pleafed to ex-
' ercife with many temporal Croffes ; I have
' maintained my own Mother , whom it hath
' pleafed God after a plentiful fortune in her
' younger dayes, to bring to a great decay in her
' very old age. I have quieted the Confcien-
' ces of many that have groaned under the bur-
' then of a wounded fpirit , whofe prayers I
' hope are available for me. I cannot plead inno-
' cency of life, efpecially of my youth : But , I
' am to be judged by a merciful God, *who is not*
' *willing to fee what I have done amifs.* And ,
' though of my felf I have nothing to prefent to
' him but fins and mifery ; yet, I know he looks
' not upon me now as I am of my felf, but as I
' am in my Saviour, and hath given me even at
' this time fome teftimonies by his Holy Spirit,
' that I am of the number of his Elect : *I*
' *am therefore full of joy , and fhall dye in*
' *peace.*

I

I must here look so far back , as to tell the Reader, that at his first return out of *Essex* to preach his last Sermon, his old Friend and Physitian, Dr. *Fox*, a man of great worth, came to him to consult his health ; and that after a sight of him, and some queries concerning his distempers, he told him, *That by Cordials, and drinking milk twenty dayes together, there was a probability of his restauration to health*; but he passionately denied to drink it. Nevertheless, Dr. *Fox*, who loved him most intirely, wearied him with sollicitations, till he yielded to take it for ten dayes; at the end of which time, he told Dr. *Fox*, *he had drunk it more to satisfie him, than to recover his health; and that he would not drink it ten dayes longer upon the best moral assurance of having twenty years added to his life, for he loved it not; and that he was so far from fearing death, which is the King of terrors, that he longed for the day of his dissolution.*

It is observed, that a desire of glory or commendation is rooted in the very nature of man ; and, that those of the severest and most mortified lives, though they may become so humble as to banish self-flattery, and such weeds as naturally grow there; yet, they have not been able to kill this desire of glory, but that like our radical heat it will both live and dye with us; and, many think it should do so ; and, we want not sacred examples to justifie the desire of having our memory to out-live our lives : which I mention,

mention, becaufe Dr. *Donne*, by the perfuafion of Dr. *Fox*, eafily yielded at this very time to have a Monument made for him; but Dr. *Fox* undertook not to perfuade how or what it fhould be; that was left to Dr. *Donne* himfelf.

This being refolved upon, Dr. *Donne* fent for a Carver to make for him in wood the figure of an *Urn*, giving him directions for the compafs and height of it; and, to bring with it a board of the height of his body. Thefe being got, then without delay a choice Painter was to be in a readinefs to draw his picture, which was taken as followeth. —— Several Charcole-fires being firft made in his large Study, he brought with him into that place his winding-fheet in his hand; and, having put off all his cloaths, had this fheet put on him, and fo tyed with knots at his head and feet, and his hands fo placed, as dead bodies are ufually fitted to be fhrowded and put into the grave. Upon this *Urn* he thus ftood with his eyes fhut, and with fo much of the fheet turned afide as might fhew his lean, pale, and death-like face; which was purpofely turned toward the Eaft, from whence he expected the fecond coming of his and our Saviour. Thus he was drawn at his juft height; and when the picture was fully finifhed, he caufed it to be fet by his bed-fide, where it continued, and became his hourly object till his death: and, was then given to his deareft friend and Executor Dr.

King,

King, who caused him to be thus carved in one entire piece of white Marble, as it now stands in the Cathedral Church of St. *Pauls* ; and by Dr. *Donne*'s own appointmen', these words were to be affixed to it as his Epitaph :

JOHANNES DONNE
Sac. Theol. Professor

Post varia Studia quibus ab annis tenerrimis fideliter, nec infeliciter incubuit ;
Instinctu & impulsu Sp. Sancti, Monitu & Hortatu
REGIS JACOBI, *Ordines Sacros amplexus Anno sui Jesu,* 1614. *& sue ætatis* 42.
Decanatu hujus Ecclesiæ indutus 27. *Novembris* 1621.

Exutus morte ultimo Die Martii 1631.

Hic licet in Occiduo Cinere Aspicit Eum Cujus nomen est Oriens.

Upon *Monday* following , he took his last leave of his beloved Study ; and, being sensible of his hourly decay, retired himself to his bed-chamber : and, that week sent at several times for

for many of his moſt conſiderable friends, with whom he took a ſolemn and deliberate farewell; commending to their conſiderations ſome ſentences uſeful for the regulation of their lives, and then diſmiſt them, as good *Jacob* did his ſons, with a ſpiritual benediction. The *Sunday* following he appointed his ſervants, that if there were any buſineſs undone that concerned him or themſelves, it ſhould be prepared againſt *Saturday* next; for, after that day he would not mix his thoughts with any thing that concerned this world; nor ever did: But, as *Job*, ſo he *waited for the appointed time of his diſſolution.*

And now he had nothing to do but to dye; to do which, he ſtood in need of no longer time, for he had ſtudied long, and to ſo happy a perfection, that in a former ſickneſs he called God to witneſs * *he was that minute ready to deliver his ſoul into his hands, if that minute God would determine his diſſolution.* In that ſickneſs he beg'd of God the conſtancy to be preſerved in that eſtate for ever; and his patient expectation to have his immortal ſoul diſrob'd from her garment of mortality, makes me confident he now had a modeſt aſſurance that his Prayers were then heard, and his Petition granted. He lay fifteen dayes earneſtly expecting his hourly change; and, in the laſt hour of his laſt day, as his body melted away and vapoured into ſpirit, his ſoul having, I verily believe, ſome Revelation of

In his Book of Devotions.

of the Beatifical Vision, he said, *I were miserable if I might not dye*; and after those words closed many periods of his faint breath, by saying often, *Thy Kingdom come, Thy Will be done*. His speech, which had long been his ready and faithful servant, left him not till the last minute of his life, and then forsook him; not to serve another Master, but dyed before him; for that it was become uselefs to him that now conversed with God on earth, as Angels are said to do in heaven, *onely by thoughts and looks*. Being speechlefs, he did as St. *Stephen, look stedfastly towards heaven, till he saw the Son of God standing at the right hand of his Father:* and being satisfied with this blefled fight, as his soul afcended, and his laft breath departed from him, he closed his own eyes; and then, difpofed his hands and body into such a pofture as required not the leaft alteration by thofe that came to shroud him.

Thus *variable*, thus *vertuous* was the Life; thus *excellent*, thus *exemplary* was the Death of this memorable man.

He was buried in that place of St. *Pauls* Church which he had appointed for that ufe fome years before his death; and, by which he paffed daily to pay his publick devotions to Almighty God (who was then ferved twice a day by a publick form of Prayer and Praifes in that place) but, he was not buried privately, though he defired it; for, befide an unnumbred number
ber

ber of others, many perfons of Nobility, and of eminency for Learning, who did love and honour him in his life, did fhew it at his death, by a voluntary and fad attendance of his body to the grave, where nothing was fo remarkable as a publick forrow.

To which place of his Burial fome mournful Friend repaired, and, as *Alexander the Great* did to the grave of the famous *Achilles*, fo they ftrewed his with an abundance of curious and coftly Flowers; which courfe they (who were never yet known) continued morning and evening for many dayes; not ceafing till the ftones that were taken up in that Church to give his body admiffion into the cold earth (now his bed of reft) were again by the Mafons art fo levelled and firmed, as they had been formerly; and, his place of Burial undiftinguifhable to common view.

Nor was this all the Honour done to his reverend Afhes; for, as there be fome perfons that will not receive a reward for that for which God accounts himfelf a Debtor: perfons, that dare truft God with their Charity, and without a witnefs; fo there was by fome grateful unknown Friend, that thought Dr. *Donne's* memory ought to be perpetuated, an hundred Marks fent to his two faithful Friends * and Dr. *King* Executors, towards the making of his Monu- and Dr. ment. It was not for many years known by *Monfort.* whom; but, after the death of Dr. *Fox*, it was

known

known that it was he that fent it; and he lived
to fee as lively a reprefentation of his dead
Friend, as Marble can exprefs; a Statue indeed
fo like Dr. *Donne*, that (as his Friend Sir *Henry Wotton* hath exprefled himfelf) *it feems to
breath faintly; and, Pofterity fhall look upon it as
a kind of artificial Miracle.*

*He was of Stature moderately tall, of a ftrait
and equally-proportioned body, to which all his
words and actions gave an unexpreffible addition
of Comelinefs.*

*The melancholy and pleafant humor were in him
fo contempered, that each gave advantage to the
other, and made his Company one of the delights
of Mankind.*

*His fancy was unimitably high, equalled onely
by his great wit, both being made ufeful by a commanding judgement.*

*His afpect was chearful, and fuch as gave a
filent teftimony of a clear knowing foul, and of a
Confcience at peace with it felf.*

*His melting eye fhewed that he had a foft heart,
full of noble compaffion; of too brave a foul to offer injuries, and too much a Chriftian not to pardon
them in others.*

*He did much contemplate (efpecially after he
entred into his Sacred Calling) the mercies of
Almighty God, the immortality of the Soul, and
the joyes of Heaven; and would often fay, Bleffed be God that he is God divinely like himfelf,*

He

He was by nature highly passionate, but more apt to reluct at the excesses of it. A great lover of the offices of humanity, and of so merciful a spirit, that he never beheld the miseries of Mankind without pity and relief.

He was earnest and unwearied in the search of knowledge; with which his vigorous soul is now satisfied, and employed in a continual praise of that God that first breathed it into his active body; that body which once was a Temple of the Holy Ghost, *and is now become a small quantity of* Christian dust:

But I shall see it reanimated.

J. W.

G   A N

An EPITAPH written by Dr.
Corbet, late Bishop of *Oxford*,
on his Friend Dr. *Donne*.

HE *that wou'd write an Epitaph for thee,*
And write it well, must first begin to be
Such as thou wert; for, none can truly know
Thy life and worth, but he that hath liv'd so.
He must have wit to spare, and to hurle down,
Enough to keep the Gallants of the Town.
He must have learning plenty, both the Laws,
Civil *and* Common, *to judge any* Cause.
Divinity great store above the rest,
Not of the last Edition, but the best.
He must have language, travel, all the Arts,
Judgement to use, or else he wants thy parts.
He must have friends the highest, able to do,
Such as Mecœnas, *and* Augustus *too.*
He must have such a sickness, such a death,
Or else his vain descriptions come beneath.
    He that would write an Epitaph *for thee,*
    Should first be dead; let it alone for me.

TO

To the Memory of my ever desired Dr. *Donne*. An *Elegy* by *H. King*, late Bishop of *Chicester*.

TO have liv'd eminent in a degree
    Beyond our loftiest thoughts, that is like thee;
Or t'have had too much merit, is not safe,
For such excesses find no Epitaph.
    At common graves we have poetick eyes,
Can melt themselves in easie Elegies;
Each quill can drop his tributary verse,
And pin it like the hatchments to the herse:
But at thine, Poem or Inscription
(Rich soul of wit and language) we have none.
Indeed a silence does that Tomb befit,
Where is no Herauld left to blazon it.
Widow'd invention justly doth forbear
To come abroad, knowing thou art not there:
Late her great Patron, whose prerogative
Maintain'd and cloath'd her so, as none alive
Must now presume to keep her at thy rate,
Though he the Indies for her dower estate.
Or else that awful fire which once did burn
In thy clear brain, now fallen into thy Urn,

G 2   *Lives*

Lives there to fright rude Empericks from thence,
Which might profane thee by their Ignorance.
Whoever writes of thee, and in a stile
Unworthy such a theme, does but revile
Thy precious dust, and wakes a learned spirit,
Which may revenge his rapes upon thy merit :
For all a low-pitch't fancy can devise
Will prove at best but hallowed injuries.

Thou like the dying Swan did'st lately sing
Thy mournful dirge in audience of the King ;
When pale looks and faint accents of thy breath
Presented so to life that piece of death,
That it was fear'd and prophesi'd by all
Thou thither cam'st to preach thy Funerall.
Oh hadst thou in an Elegiack knell
Rung out unto the World thine own farewell,
And in thy high victorious numbers beat
The solemn measures of thy griev'd retreat,
Thou might'st the Poets service now have mist,
As well as then thou didst prevent the Priest :
And nev'r to the World beholden be,
So much as for an Epitaph for thee.

I do not like the office ; nor is't fit
Thou who didst lend our age such sums of wit,
Should'st now re-borrow from her bankrupt mine
That oare to bury thee which first was thine :
Rather still leave us in thy debt, and know,
Exalted Soul, more glory 'tis to owe
Thy memory what we can never pay,
Than with embas'd Coyn those Rites defray.

Commit

Commit we then thee to thy self, nor blame
Our drooping loves that thus to thine own fame
Leave thee Executor, since but thine own
No pen could do thee Justice, nor bayes Crown
Thy vast deserts ; save that, we nothing can
Depute to be thy ashes guardian :
So, Jewellers no Art or Metal trust
To form the Diamond, but the Diamonds dust.

H. K.

An E L E G Y on Dr.
D O N N E.

OUr Donne *is dead : and, we may sighing say,*
We had that man where language chose to stay
And shew her utmost power. I wou'd not praise
That, and his great Wit, which in our vain dayes
Makes others proud ; but, as these serv'd to unlock
That Cabinet his mind, where such a stock
Of knowledge was repos'd, that I lament
Our just and general cause of discontent.

And, I rejoyce I am not so severe,
But as I write a Line, to weep a tear
For his decease : such sad Extremities
Can make such men as I write Elegies.

G 3   *And*

And wonder not ; for, when so great a loss
Falls on a Nation, and they slight the Cross,
God hath rais'd Prophets to awaken them
From their dull Lethargy: witness my Pen,
Not us'd to upbraid the World: though now it must
Freely, and boldly, for, the Cause is just.

Dull age! oh, I wou'd spare thee, but thou'rt worse:
Thou art not only dull, but, hast a Curse
Of black Ingratitude: if not, Could'st thou
Part with this matchless man, and make no vow
For thee and thine successively to pay,
Some sad remembrance to his dying day ?

Did his Youth scatter Poetry, wherein
Lay Loves Philosophy? Was every sin
Pictur'd in his sharp Satyrs, made so foul
That some have fear'd sins shapes, & kept their soul
Safer by reading Verse? Did he give dayes,
Past marble Monuments to those whose praise
He wou'd perpetuate? Did he (I fear
Envy will doubt) these at his twentieth year?

But more matur'd: did his rich soul conceive,
And, in harmonious holy numbers weave
* La Co-*A Crown of Sacred * Sonnets, fit to adorn*
rona.   *A dying Martyrs brow : or, to be worn*
On that blest head of Mary Magdalen,
After she wip'd Christs feet ; but not, till then.
Did he (fit for such Penitents as she
And he to use) leave us a Letanie,

                     Which

Which all devout men love : and, doubtleſs ſhall
As times grow better, grow more Claſſicall.
Did he write Hymns, *for Piety and Wit,*
Eqnal to thoſe great grave Prudentius *writ ?*
Spake he all Languages ? Knew he all Laws ?
The grounds and uſe of Phyſick : but, becauſe
'Twas mercenary, wav'd it : went to ſee
That happy place of Chriſts Nativity.
Did he return and preach him ? preach him ſo
As ſince St. Paul *none ever did ! they know :*
Thoſe happy ſouls that hear'd him know this truth.
Did he confirm thy ag'd ? convert thy youthe
Did he theſe wonders ! and, is his dear loſs
Mourn'd by ſo few ? few for ſo great a Croſs.

But ſure, the ſilent are ambitious all
To be cloſe Mourners at his Funerall.
If not, in common pity, they forbear
By Repetitions to renew our care :
Or knowing grief conceiv'd, and hid , conſumes
Mans life inſenſibly, as poyſon fumes
Corrupt the brain, take ſilence for the way
To'inlarge the ſoul from theſe walls, mud, and clay,
Materials of this body : to remain
With him in Heaven, where no promiſcuous pain
Leſſens thoſe joyes we have : for, with him all
Are ſatisfied, with joyes eſſentiall.

Dwell on theſe joyes my thoughts : oh, do not call
Grief back, by thinking on his Funerall :

Forget he lov'd me : waste not my swift years
Which haste to Davids seventy, fill'd with fears
And sorrows for his death. Forget his parts,
They find a living grave in good mens hearts.
And, for my first is daily paid for sin :
Forget to pay my second sigh for him.
Forget his powerful preaching : and, forget
I am his Convert. Oh my frailty ! let
My flesh be no more heard - it will obtrude
This Lethargy : so shou'd my gratitude,
My vows of gratitude shou'd so be broke ;
Which, can no more be, than his vertues spoke
By any but himself : for which cause, I
Write no Incomiums, but this Elegy.
Which, as a Free-will offering, I here give
Fame and the World : and, parting with it, grieve,
I want abilities, fit to set forth,
A Monument, great, as Donne's matchless worth.

April 7. 1631.   Iz: Wâ.

F I N I S.

PHILOSOPHVS

CLAVEM CVLCORD
ET

W. Dolle F

THE
LIFE
OF
Sr HENRY WOTTON,
SOMETIME
Provost of *Eaton Colledge.*

There are them that have left a name behinde them; so that their praise shall be spoken of : *Ecclus.* 44. 8.

LONDON,
Printed by *Thomas Newcomb,* for *Richard Marriot,* and sold by most Booksellers. 1 6 7 0.

THE
LIFE
OF
Sir HENRY WOTTON.

IR *Henry Wotton*, (whose Life, I now intend to write) was born in the year of our Redemption, 1 5 6 8. in *Bocton-hall*, (commonly called, *Bocton*, or *Bougton* place) in the Parish of *Bocton Malherb*, in the fruitful Country of *Kent*: *Becton-hall* being an *ancient* and *goodly structure*, beautifying, and being beautified by the Parish Church of *Bocton Malherb* adjoyning unto it : and, both seated within a fair Park of the *Wottons*, on the Brow of such a *Hill*, as gives the advantage of a large Prospect, and of equal *pleasure* to all Beholders.

But this House and Church, are not remarkable for any thing so much, as for that the memorable Family of the *Wottons* have so long inhabited the one, and now lie buried in the

B 2   other,

other, as appears by their many *Monuments* in that Church; the *Wottons* being a Family, that hath brought forth divers Persons eminent for Wisdom and Valour, whose Heroick Acts, and Noble Imployments, both in *England* and in forraign parts, have adorn'd themselves, and this Nation: which they have served abroad faithfully, in the discharge of their great trust, and prudently in their Negotiations with several Princes; and also serv'd it at home with much Honour and Justice, in their wise managing a great part of the publick affairs thereof, in the various times both of War and Peace.

But, lest I should be thought by any, that may incline, either to deny or doubt this Truth, not to have observed *Moderation* in the commendation of this Family; And also, for that I believe the *Merits* and *Memory* of such persons, ought to be thankfully recorded; I shall offer to the consideration of every Reader, out of the testimony of their *Pedegree*, and our *Chronicles*, a part (and but a part) of that just Commendation which might be from thence enlarged, and shall then leave the indifferent Reader to judge, whether my errour be an *excess* or *defect* of Commendations.

Sir *Robert Wotton* of *Bocton Malherb* Knight, was born in the year of Christ 1463. He living in the Reign of King *Edward* the fourth, was by him trusted to be Lieutenant of *Guisnes*, to be Knight Porter, and Comptroller of *Callais* ;

lais; where he dyed, and lies honourably buried.

Sir *Edward Wotton* of *Bocton Malherb* Knight, (Son and Heir of the said Sir *Robert*) was born in the year of Chrift, 1489. in the Reign of King *Henry* the Seventh. He was made Treasurer of *Callais,* and of Privie-Councel to King *Henry* the Eight, who offered him to be Lord Chancellour of *England,* but (faith * *Hollinfhed)* out of a virtuous modefty he refufed it.

* In his Chronicle

Thomas Wotton of *Bocton Malherb* Efquire, Son and Heir of the faid Sir *Edward,* (and the Father of our Sir *Henry,* that occafions this relation) was born in the year of Chrift 1521. He was a Gentleman excellently educated, and ftudious in all the *Liberal Arts;* in the knowledg whereof, he attained unto a great perfection, who though he had (befides thofe abilities, a very Noble, and plentiful eftate, and the ancient Intereft of his *Predeceffors)* many invitations from Queen *Elizabeth* to change his Country Recreations and Retirement for a Court-Life, offering him a Knight-hood (fhe was then with him at his *Bocton-hall*) and that to be but as an earneft of fome more honorable and more profitable imployment under Her, yet, he humbly refufed both; being a man of great modefty, of a moft plain and fingle heart, of an antient freedom, and integrity of mind. A commendation which Sir *Henry Wotton* took occafion often to remember with great gladnefs

A 3   nefs

ness, and thankfully to boast himself the Son of such a Father: From whom indeed he derived that noble ingenuity that was alwayes practised by himself, and which he ever both commended and cherish'd in others. This *Thomas* was also remarkable for Hospitality, a great Lover, and much beloved of his Country; to which may justly be added, that he was a Cherisher of *Learning*, as appears by that excellent Antiquary M. *William Lambert*, in his perambulation of *Kent*.

This *Thomas* had four sons, Sir *Edward*, Sir *James*, Sir *John*, and Sir *Henry*.

Sir *Edward* was Knighted by Queen *Elizabeth*, and made Comptroller of Her Majesties Houshould. He was (saith *Cambden*) a man remarkable for many and great Imployments in the State, during her Reign, and sent several times *Ambassadour* into Forraign Nations. After her death, he was by King *James* made Comptroller of his Houshold, and called to be of his Privy-Councel, and by him advanced to be *Lord Wotton*, *Baron* of *Merley* in *Kent*, and made Lord Lieutenant of that County.

Sir *James* (the second son) may be numbred among the Martial men of his age, who was in the 38 of Queen *Elizabeths* Reign (with *Robert Earl of Sussex*, *Count Lodowick of Nassaw*, *Don Christophero*, son of *Antonio* King of *Portugal*, and divers other Gentlemen of Noblenesss and Valour) Knighted in the Field near *Cadiz* in
Spain,

Spain, after they had gotten great Honour and Riches, besides a notable retaliation of Injuries by taking that Town.

Sir *John*, being a Gentleman excellently accomplished, both by Learning and Travel, was Knighted by Queen *Elizabeth*, and by her look'd upon with more then ordinary favour, and intentions of preferment ; but Death, in his younger years, put a period to his growing hopes.

Of Sir *Henry*, my following difcourfe shall give an account.

The defcent of thefe fore-named *Wottons*, were all in a direct Line ; and moft of them and their actions, in the memory of thofe with whom we have converfed : But, if I had look'd fo far back, as to Sir *Nicolas Wotton*, (who lived in the Reign of King *Richard* the fecond ;) or before him, upon divers others of great note in their feveral Ages, I might by fome be thought tedious ; and yet others may more juftly think me negligent, if I omit to mention *Nicholas Wotton*, the fourth Son of Sir *Robert*, whom I firft named.

This *Nicholas Wotton was Doctor of Law*, and fometime *Dean of Canterbury:* a man whom God did not onely blefs with a long life, but with great abilities of mind, and an inclination to imploy them in the fervice of his Country, as is teftified by his feveral Imployments ; * having been fent nine times *Ambaffadour* unto forraign

raign Princes; and being a Privy-*Councellor* to King *Henry* the eighth, to *Edward* the sixth, to Queen *Mary* and Queen *Elizabeth*; who alfo, after he had (during the Wars between *England, Scotland* and *France*) been three feveral times (and not unfuccefsfully) imployed in Committies for fetling of peace betwixt this and thofe Kingdomes, dyed (faith learned *Cambden*) full of Commendations for Wifdom and Piety. He was alfo by the Will of King *Henry* the eighth, made one of his Executors, and chief *Secretary* of State to his Son, that pious Prince *Edward* the fixth. Concerning which *Nicholas Wotton*, I fhall fay but this little more; That he refufed (being offered it by * Holin- Queen *Elizabeth*) to be * *Arch-bifhop* of *Canter-*
fhed. *bury*, and that he dyed not rich, though he lived in that time of the diffolution of *Abbeys*.

More might be added: but by this it may appear, that Sir *Henry Wotton*, was a Branch of fuch a kindred as left a Stock of Reputation to their Pofterity; fuch Reputation, as might kindle a generous emulation in ftrangers, and preferve a noble ambition in thofe of his name and Family to perform Actions worthy of their Anceftors.

And, that Sir Henry Wotton *did fo, might appear more perfectly then my Pen can exprefs it, if of his many furviving friends, fome one of higher parts and imployment, had been pleafed to have commended his to Pofterity; But, fince fome*
years

years are now past, and they have all (I know not why) forborn to do it; my gratitude to the memory of my dead friend, and the renewed request of some * *that still live solicitous to see this duty performed; these have had a power to perswade me to undertake it; which, truly, I have not done, but with some distrust of mine own Abilities, and yet so far from despair, that I am modestly confident my humble language shall be accepted, because I present all Readers with a Commixture of truth, and* Sir Henry Wotton's *merits.*

* Mr. i. ii. Ou-dert, and others.

This being premised, I proceed to tell the Reader, that the father of Sir *Henry Wotton* was twice married, first to *Elizabeth,* the Daughter of Sir *John Rudstone* Knight; after whose death, though his inclination was averse to all Contentions; yet, necessitated he was to several Suits in Law: in the prosecution whereof, (which took up much of his time, and were the occasion of many Discontents) he was by divers of his friends earnestly perswaded to a *re-marriage;* to whom he as often answered, That if ever he did put on a resolution to marry, *he was seriously resolved to avoid three sorts of persons:*

namely, those $\begin{cases} \text{that had } Children. \\ \text{that had } Law\text{-}suits. \\ \text{that were of his } Kindred. \end{cases}$

B　　　　And

And yet, following his own Law-suits, he met in *Westminster-Hall* with one Miftrefs *Morton*, Widow to —— *Morton* of *Kent* Efquire: who was alfo engaged in feveral fuits in Law, and, he obferving her Comportment at the time of hearing one of her Caufes before the Judges, could not but at the fame time, both compaf-fionate her Condition, and yet, fo affect her Perfon, that although there were in her a con-currence of all thofe accidents, againft which he had fo ferioufly refolved ; yet his affection to her grew then fo ftrong, that he refolved to folicite her for a Wife ; and did ; and obtain-ed her.

By her (who was the Daughter of Sir *Wil-liam Finch* of *Eaftwell* in *Kent*) he had *Henry* his youngeft fon. His Mother undertook to be Tutorefs unto him during much of his Child-hood ; for whofe care and pains, he paid her each day w th fuch vifible fignes of future per-fection in Learning, as turned her imployment into a pleafing-trouble : which fhe was content to continue, till his Father took him into his own particular care, and difpofed of him to a Tutor in his own Houfe at *Bocton*.

And, when time and diligent inftruction, had made him fit for a removal to an higher Form, (which was very early) he was fent to *Winche-fter-School*: a place of ftrict Difcipline and Or-der: that fo, he might in his youth be mould-ed into a Method of living by Rule ; which his
                                                    wife

wife Father knew to be the moft neceffary way, to make the future part of his life, both happy to himfelf, and ufeful for the difcharge of all bu- fnefs, whether publick or private.

And, that he might be confirmed in this *re- gularity*, he was at a fit age removed from that *School*, to *New-Colledge* in *Oxford*; both being founded by *William Wickham* Bifhop of *VVin- chefter*.

There he continued, till about the eighteenth year of his Age: and was then tranfplanted into *Queens-Colledge*; where within that year, he was by the chief of that Colledge, perfwa- fively injoyned to write a play for their pri- vate ufe: (it was the Tragedy of *Tancredo*) which was fo interwoven with Sentences, and for the Method and exact perfonating thofe humours, paffions, and difpofitions, which he propofed to reprefent, fo performed; that the graveft of that fociety declared, he had in a fleight imployment, given an early, and a folid teftimony of his future abilities. And, though there may be fome fower difpofitions, which may think this not worth a *memorial*; yet, that wife Knight *Baptifta Guarini* (whom learned *Italy* accounts one of her ornaments) thought it neither an uncomely, nor an unprofitable im- ployment for his Age.

But I pafs to what will be thought more fe- rious.

About the nineteenth year of his Age, he
pro-

proceeded Master of *Arts*; and at that time
read in Latine three Lectures *de Oculo*: wherein, he having described the *Form*, the *Motion*,
the curious *compofure* of the *Eye*; and, demonstrated, how of those very many, every *humour*
and *nerve* performs its distinct Office, so as the
God of Order hath appointed, without mixture
or confusion; and all this, to the advantage of
man, to whom it is given; not onely as the bodies guide: but, whereas all other of his fen-
fes require time to inform the Soul: this, in
an inftant apprehends and warns him of *danger*;
teaching him in the very *eyes* of others to difcover *wit, folly, love*, and *hatred*. After thefe obfervations he fell to difpute this Optique queftion, *Whether we fee by the Emiffion of the
Beams from within; or Reception of the Species
from without?* and after that, and many other
like learned difquifitions, in the Conclufion of
his *Lectures,* he took a fair occafion to beautifie
his difcourfe with a Commendation of the bleffing and benefit of *Seeing:* By which, we do
not only difcover *Natures Secrets:* but, with a
continued content (for the eye is never weary
of feeing) behold the great *Light* of the *World,*
and by it difcover the Fabrick of the *Heavens,*
and both the Order and Motion of the *Celeftial Orbs*; nay, that if the *eye* look but down-
ward, it may rejoyce to behold the bofome
of the *Earth*, our common Mother, *embroi-
dered* and *adorned* with numberlefs and various

rious *Flowers*, which man fees daily grow up to
perfection; and then, filently moralize his own
condition, who in a fhort time (like thofe
ve:y *Flowers*) *decayes, withers*, and quickly returns again to that *Earth*, from which both had
their firft being.

Thefe were fo exactly debated, and fo Rhe-
torically heightned, as, among other admirers,
caufed that learned *Italian, Albericus Gentilis*
(then Profeffor of the *Civil Law* in *Oxford*)
to call him *Henrice mi ocelle*; which dear expreffion of his, was alfo ufed by divers of Sir *Henry*'s deareft Friends, and by many other perfons of Note, during his ftay in the Univerfity.

But his ftay there was not long; at leaft, not
fo long as his Friends once intended : for, the
year after Sir *Henry* proceeded Mafter of Arts,
his father (whom Sir *Henry* did never mention
without this, or fome like reverential expreffion; as, *That good man my father*; or, *My father
the beft of men:*) about that time, this good
man changed this for a better life; leaving to
Sir *Henry*, as to his other younger fons, a rentcharge of an hundred Mark a year, to be paid
for ever, out of fome one of his Mannors of a
much greater value.

And here, though this good man be dead, yet
I wifh a Circumftance or two that concern him,
may not be buried without a Relation; which I
fhall undertake to do, for that I fuppofe, they

B 3   may

may so much concern the Reader to know, that I may promise myself a pardon for a short Digression.

IN the year of our Redemption, 1553. *Nicholas Wotton* Dean of *Canterbury* (whom I formerly mentioned) being then Ambassador in *France*, dream'd, that his Nephew, this *Thomas Wotton*, was inclined to be a party in such a project, as, if he were not suddenly prevented, would turn both to the loss of his life, and ruine of his *Family*.

Doubtless, the good Dean did well know, that common Dreams are but a senseless paraphrase on our waking thoughts; or, of the business of the day past; or, are the result of our over ingaged affections, when we betake our selves to rest; and, that the observation of them, may turn to silly Superstitions, as they too often do: But, though he might know this, and, might also believe that Prophesies are ceased; yet, doubtless he could not but consider, that all Dreams are not to be neglected or cast away; and did therefore rather lay this Dream aside, than intend totally to lose it; for that dreaming the same again the Night following, when it became a double Dream; like that of *Pharaoh* (of which dreams, the learned have made many observations) and that, it had no dependance on his waking thoughts, much less on the desires of his heart; then, he did more seriously oufly confider it, and remembred that Almighty God was pleafed in a Dream to reveal and to affure * *Monica* the Mother of St. *Auftin,* that he, her fon (for whom fhe wept fo bitterly, and prayed fo much) fhould at laft become a Chriftian: This the good Dean confidered; and, confidering alfo, that Almighty God (though the caufes of Dreams be often unknown) hath even in thefe latter times, by a certain *illumination* of the foul in fleep, difcovered many things that humane wifdom could not forefee: Upon thefe confiderations, he refolved to ufe fo prudent a remedy by way of prevention, as might introduce no great inconvenience to either party. And to that end, he wrote to the *Queen* ('twas Queen *Mary*) and befought her, *That fhe would caufe his Nephew* Thomas Wotton, *to be fent for out of* Kent: *and, that the Lords of her Council might interrogate him in fome fuch feigned queftions, as might give a colour for his Commitment into a favourable* Prifon; *declaring, that he would acquaint her Majefty with the true reafon of his requeft, when he fhould next become fo happy as to fee, and fpeak to her Majefty.*

'Twas done as the *Dean* defired: and in Prifon I muft leave Mr. *Wotton,* till I have told the Reader what followed.

At this time a Marriage was concluded betwixt our *Queen Mary*, and *Philip King* of *Spain:* And though this was concluded with
the

* St. Auftin's confeffion.

the advice, if not by the perfuafion of her Privy Council, as having many probabilities of advantage to this Nation: yet, divers perfons of a contrary perfwafion, did not onely declare againft it, but alfo raifed Forces to oppofe it; believing (as they faid) it would be a means to bring *England* under fubjection to *Spain*, and make thofe of this Nation flaves to *ftrangers*.

And of this number Sir *Thomas Wyat* of *Boxley-Abby* in *Kent* (betwixt whofe Family, and the Family of the *Wottons*, there had been an ancient and intire friendfhip) was the principal Actor; who having perfwaded many of the Nobility and Gentry (efpecially of *Kent*) to fide with him; and, being defeated, and taken Prifoner, was legally arraigned, condemned, and loft his life: So did the Duke of *Suffolk*, and divers others, efpecially many of the Gentry of *Kent*, who were there in feveral places executed as *Wyats* affiftants.

And of this number, in all probability, had Mr. *Wotton* been, if he had not been confin'd: for, though he was not ignorant that another mans Treafon, ma es it mine by concealing it; yet, he durft confefs to his Uncle, when he returned into *England* and came to vifit him in Prifon, that he had more than an intimation of *Wyats* intentions; and, thought he had not continued actually *innocent*, if his Uncle had not fo happily dream'd him into a *Prifon*; out of

of which place, when he was delivered by the
fame hand that caufed his Commitment, they
both confidered the Dream more ferioufly; and
then, both joyned in praifing God for it; *That
God, who tyes himfelf to no Rules, either in preventing of evil, or in fhewing of mercy to thofe,
whom of his good pleafure he hath chofen to
love.*

And this Dream was the more confiderable,
becaufe many of the Dreams of this *Thomas
Wotton* did moft ufually prove true, both in
foretelling things to come, and difcovering
things paft: of which I will give the Reader but
one particular more, namely this; This *Thomas,*
a little before his death, dream'd that the *Univerfity Treafury* was robbed by *Townfmen,* and
poor *Scholars*; and, that the number was five:
And being that day to write to his Son *Henry*
at *Oxford,* he thought it worth fo much pains, as
by a Poftfcript in his Letter, to make a flight
inquiry of it; the Letter (which was writ out
of *Kent,* and dated three dayes before) came
to his Sons hands the very morning after the
night in which the Robbery was committed;
and when the City and Univerfity were both in
a perplext Enqueft of the Thieves, then did Sir
H. Wotton fhew his fathers Letter, and by it fuch
light was given of this work of *darknefs,* that
the five guilty perfons were prefently difcovered, and apprehended, without putting the *Univerfity* to fo much trouble, as the cafting of a
Figure.
　　　　　　　　　　　　　　　　　　And

And it may yet be more confiderable, that this *Nicholas* and *Thomas Wotton* fhould both (being men of holy lives, of even tempers, and much given to fafting and prayer) forefee and foretell the very dayes of their own death: *Nicholas* did fo, being then Seventy years of age, and in perfect health. *Thomas* did the like in the 65 year of his age ; who being then in *London* (where he dyed) and forefeeing his death there, gave direction that his Body fhould be carried to *Boston* ; and though he thought his Uncle *Nicholas* worthy of that noble Monument which he built for him in the *Cathedral Church* of *Canterbury* ; yet, this humble man gave direction concerning himfelf, to be buried privately, and efpecially without any pomp at his Funeral.

BUt it may now feem more then time that I return to Sir *Henry Wotton* at *Oxford* ; where, after his optick Lecture, he was taken into fuch a bofom friendfhip with the learned *Albericus Gentilis* (whom I formerly named) that if it had been poffible, *Gentilis* would have breathed all his excellent knowledge both of the *Mathematicks* and *Law*, into the breaft of his dear *Harry* (for fo *Gentilis* ufed to call him :) and though he was not able to do that, yet, there was in Sir *Henry* fuch a propenfity and connaturalnefs to the *Italian* Language, and thofe Studies whereof *Gentilis* was a great Mafter, that
this

this friendſhip between them did daily in-creaſe, and proved daily advantagious to Sir *Henry*, for the improvement of him in ſeveral Sciences, during his ſtay in the Uni-verſity.

From which place, before I ſhall invite the Reader to follow him into a forreign Nation; though I muſt omit to mention divers perſons that were then in *Oxford*, of memorable note for Learning, and Friends to Sir *Henry Wotton*, yet I muſt not omit the mention of a love that was there begun betwixt him and Dr. *Donne* (ſometimes Dean of St. *Pauls*) a man, of whoſe abilities I ſhall forbear to ſay any thing, becauſe he who is of this *Nation*, that pretends to Learn-ing or Ingenuity, and is ignorant of Dr. *Donne*, deſerves not to know him. The friendſhip of theſe two, I muſt not omit to mention, being ſuch a friendſhip as was generouſly elemented: And as it was begun in their Youth, and in an Univerſity, and there maintained by cor-reſpondent Inclinations and Studies, ſo it laſted till Age and Death forced a Sepa-ration.

In *Oxford* he ſtayed till about two years after his fathers death: at which time, he was about the two and twentieth year of his Age; and having to his great Wit, added the ballaſt of Learning, and knowledge of the Arts, he then laid aſide his Books, and betook himſelf to the uſeful Library of Travel, and a more general
Conver-

Converſation with Mankind, employing the remaining part of his Youth, his induſtry and fortune to adorn his mind, and to purchaſe the rich
treaſure of forreign knowledge ; of which, both
for the ſecrets of Nature, the diſpoſitions of
many Nations, their ſeveral Laws and Languages, he was the poſſeſſor in a very large meaſure,
as I ſhall faithfully make to appear, before I take
my Pen from the following Narration of his
Life.

In his Travels, which was almoſt nine years
before his return into *England*, he ſtayed but
one year in *France*, and moſt of that in *Geneva* ;
where he became acquainted with *Theodor Beza*
(then very aged) and with *Iſaac Cauſabon*, in
whoſe fathers houſe (if I be rightly informed)
Sir *Henry Wotton* was lodged, and there contraƈt-
ed a moſt worthy friendſhip with him and his
moſt learned Son.

Three of the remaining eight years, were
ſpent in *Germany*, the other five in *Italy* (the
Stage on which God appointed he ſhould aƈt a
great part of his life) where both in *Rome* ,
Venice, and *Florence*, he became acquainted with
the moſt eminent men for Learning, and all
manner of Arts, as *Piƈture*, *Sculpture* , *Chy-
miſtry* , *Architeƈture* , and divers other ma-
nual Arts ; even Arts of inferiour nature ;
of all which, he was a moſt dear Lover, and a
moſt excellent Judge.

He

He returned out of *Italy* into *England* about the Thirtieth year of his Age, being then noted by many, both for his person and comportment; for indeed he was of a choice shape, tall of stature, and of a most perswasive behaviour; which was so mixed with sweet Discourse, and Civilities, as gained him much love from all persons with whom he entred into an acquaintance.

And whereas he was noted in his Youth to have a sharp wit, and apt to jest; that, by Time, Travel, and Conversation, was so polish'd, and made so useful, that his company seemed to be one of the delights of Mankind; insomuch, as *Robert Earl of Essex* (then one of the darlings of fortune, and in greatest favour with *Queen Elizabeth*) invited him first into a friendship, and after a knowledge of his great abilities, to be one of his Secretaries; the other being Mr. *Henry Cuffe*, sometimes of *Merton* Colledge in *Oxford* (and there also the acquaintance of Sir *Henry Wotton* in his Youth) Mr. *Cuffe* being then a man of no common note in the University for his Learning; nor after his removal from that place, for the great abilities of his mind; nor indeed, for the *fatalness* of his end.

Sir *Henry Wotton* being now taken into a serviceable friendship with the Earl of *Essex*, did personally attend his Counsels and Employments in two Voyages at Sea against the *Spaniard*,

ard, and also in that (which was the Earls last) into *Ireland*; that Voyage wherein he did so much provoke the Queen to anger then, and worse at his return into *England*; upon whose immovable favour he had built such sandy hopes, as incouraged him to those undertakings which (with the help of a contrary Faction) suddenly caused his Commitment to the Tower.

Sir *Henry Wotton* observing this, though he was not of that Faction (for the *Earls* followers were also divided into their several interests) which incouraged the *Earl* to those undertakings which proved so fatal to him, and divers of his Confederation: yet, knowing *Treason* to be so comprehensive, as to take in even Circumstances, and out of them to make such Conclusions as subtle States-men shall project, either for their revenge or safety; considering this, he thought prevention by absence out of *England*, a better security than to stay in it, and plead his innocency in a *Prison*. Therefore did he, so soon as the Earl was apprehended, very quickly, and as privately glide through *Kent* to *Dover*, without so much as looking toward his native and beloved *Bocton*; and was by the help of favourable winds, and liberal payment, within Sixteen hours after his departure from *London*, set upon the *French* shore; where he heard shortly after, that the *Earl* was Arraign'd, Condemned, and Beheaded; that

his

his Friend Mr. *Cuffe* was hang'd, and divers other persons of Eminent Quality executed.

The Times did not look so favourably upon Sir *Henry Wotton*, as to invite his return into *England*; having therefore procured of his elder brother (the Lord *Wotton*) an assurance that his Annuity should be paid him in *Italy*, thither he went, happily renewing his intermitted friendship and interest, and indeed, his great content, in a new conversation with his old acquaintance in that Nation; and more particularly in *Florence*, which City is not more eminent for the great Dukes Court, then for the great recourse of men of choicest note for Learning and Arts; in which number he there met with his old Friend, Seignior *Vietta*, (a Gentleman of *Venice*, and) then taken to be *Secretary* to the Great Duke of *Tuscany*.

After some stay in *Florence*, he went the 4th time to visit *Rome*, where in the *English Colledge* he had very many Friends (their humanity made them really so, though they knew him to be a dissenter from many of their Principles of Religion;) and having enjoyed their company, and satisfied himself concerning some Curiosities that did partly occasion his Journey thither, he returned back to *Florence*, where a most notable accident befell him; an accident, that did not onely find new employment for his choice
Abili-

Abilities, but introduce him a knowledge and an interest with our King *James*, then King of *Scotland*; which I shall proceed to relate.

But first, I am to tell the Reader, That though Queen *Elizabeth* (or she and her Council) were never willing to declare her *Successor*; yet, *James* then King of the *Scots*, was confidently believed by most to be the man upon whom the sweet trouble of Kingly Government would be imposed; and the *Queen* declining very fast, both by age, and visible infirmities, those that were of the *Romish* perswasion in point of Religion (even *Rome* it self, and those of this Nation) knowing that the death of the *Queen*, and the establishing of her *Successor*, were taken to be *critical* dayes for destroying or establishing the *Protestant* Religion in this Nation, did therefore improve all opportunities for preventing a Protestant Prince to succeed Her. And, as the *Pope*'s Excommunication of *Queen Elizabeth*, had both by the judgement and practice of the Jesuited Papist, exposed Her to be warrantably destroyed; so (if we may believe an angry Adversary, * *Watson in his Quodlibets.* (a * *secular Priest* against a *Jesuite*) you may believe, that about that time there were many endeavours, first to excommunicate, and then to shorten the life of King *James.*

Immedi-

Immediately after Sir *Henry Wotton*'s return from *Rome* to *Florence* (which was about a year before the death of Queen *Elizabeth*) *Ferdinand* the great Duke of *Florence* had intercepted certain Letters that difcovered a defign to take away the life of the then King of *Scots*. The Duke abhorring the Fact, and refolving to endeavour a prevention of it, advifed with his Secretary *Vietta*, by what means a caution might be beft given to that King ; and after confideration, it was refolved to be done by Sir *Henry Wotton*, whom *Vietta* firft commended to the *Duke*, and the *Duke* had noted and approved of above all the *English* that frequented his Court.

Sir *Henry* was gladly called by his Friend *Vietta* to the *Duke*, who after much profeffion of truft and friendfhip, acquainted him with the fecret ; and being well inftructed, difparched him into *Scotland* with Letters to the King, and with thofe Letters, fuch *Italian* Antidotes againft poyfon, as the *Scots* till then had been ftrangers to.

Having parted from the *Duke*, he took up the name and language of an *Italian* ; and thinking it beft to avoid the line of *English* intelligence and danger, he pofted into *Norway*, and through that Country towards *Scotland*, where he found the King at *Sterling* ; then he ufed means (by *Bernard Lindfey*, one of the Kings Bed-Chamber) to procure him a fpeedy and

C   pri-

private conference with His Majesty ; assuring him, *That the businefs which he was to negotiate, was of such consequence, as had caused the great Duke of* Tuscany, *to enjoyn him suddenly to leave his Native Countrey of* Italy, *to impart it to his King.*

This being by *Bernard Lindsey* made known to the King, the King after a little wonder, (mixt with jealousie) to hear of an *Italian* Ambassador, or Messenger, required his name, (which was said to be *Octavio Baldi*) and appointed him to be heard privately at a fixed hour that Evening.

When *Octavio Baldi* came to the Presence-Chamber-door, he was requested to lay aside his long *Rapier* (which *Italian*-like he then wore) and being entred the Chamber, he found there with the King three or four *Scotch* Lords standing distant in several corners of the Chamber. At the fight of whom, he made a stand ; which the King observing, *bad him be bold, and deliver his Message, for he would undertake for the secrefie of all that were present.* Then did *Octavio Baldi* deliver his Letters and his Message to the King in *Italian*; which, when the King had graciously received, after a little pause, *Octavio Baldi* steps to the Table, and whispers to the King in his own Language, that he was an *English* man, befeeching Him for a more private conference with His Majesty; and, that he might be concealed during his stay in that Nation;

tion; which was promi ed, and really performed by the King, during all his abode there;
(which was about three M nths) all which
time was fpent with much pleafantnefs to the
King, and, with as much to *Octavio Baldi* himfelf, as that Countrey could afford; from
which he departed as true an *Italian* as he
came thither.

To the *Duke* at *Florence* he retu n'd with a
fair and grateful account of his employment,
and within fome few Months a ter his return,
there came certain News to *Florence*, that
Queen *Elizabeth* was dead, and *James* King
of the *Scots* proclaimed King of *England*. I he
Duke knowing travel and bufinefs to be the
beft Schools of wifdom, and that Sir *Henry*
Wotton had been tutor'd in both, advis'd him
to return prefently to *England*, and joy the
King with his new and better Title, and
there wait upon Fortune for a better employment.

When King *James* came into *England*, he
found, amongft other of the late Queens Officers, the Lord *Wotton*, Comptroller of the
Houfe, of whom he demanded, *If he knew one*
Henry Wotton, *that had fpent much time in*
forreign Travel? The Lord replied, he knew
him well, and that he was his Brother; then the
King asking where he then was, was anfwered,
at *Venice*, or *Florence*; but by late Letters from
thence, he underftood, he would fuddenly be at

C 2 *Paris.*

Paris. Send for him, said the King, and when he shall come into England, bid him repair to me. The Lord *Wotton* after a little wonder, asked the King, If he knew him? to which the King answered, *You must rest unsatisfied of that, till you bring the Gentleman to me.*

Not many Months after this Discourse, the Lord *Wotton* brought his brother to attend the King, who took him in His Arms, *and bade him welcome by the name of* Octavio Baldi, *saying, he was the most honest, and therefore the best Dissembler that ever he met with:* And said, *Seeing I know you neither want Learning, Travel, nor Experience, and that I have had so real a Testimony of your faithfulness and abilities to manage an Embassage, I have sent for you to declare my purpose; which is, to make use of you in that kind hereafter:* And indeed the King did so most of those two and twenty years of his Raign; but before he dismist *Octavio Baldi* from his present attendance upon him, he restored him to his old name of *Henry Wotton,* by which he then knighted him.

Not long after this, the King having resolved, according to his Motto (*Beati pacifici*) to have a friendship with his Neighbour-Kingdoms of *France* and *Spain,* and also for divers weighty reasons, to enter into an Alliance with the State of *Venice,* and to that end to send Ambassadors to those several places, did propose the choice of these Employments to Sir *Henry Wotton* ;

Wotton; who confidering the fmallnefs of his own Eftate (which he never took care to augment) and knowing the Courts of great Princes to be fumptuous, and neceffarily expenfive, inclined moft to that of *Venice*, as being a place of more retirement, and beft fuiting with his *Genius*, who did ever love to joyn with Bufinefs, Study, and a tryal of natural Experiments; for both which fruitful *Italy*, that *Darling of Nature, and Cherifher of all Arts, is fo juftly famed* in all parts of the *Chriftian World*.

Sir *Henry* having after fome fhort time and confideration, refolved upon *Venice*, and a large allowance being appointed by the *King* for his voyage thither, and a fetled maintenance during his ftay there, he left *England*, nobly accompanied through *France* to *Venice*, by Gentlemen of the beft families and breeding that this Nation afforded; they were too many to name, but thefe two, for following reafons may not be omitted; Sir *Albertus Morton* his Nephew, who went his Secretary, and *William Bedel*, a man of choice Learning, and fanctified Wifdom, who went his Chaplain. And, though his dear friend Dr. *Donne* (then a private Gentleman) was not one of that Number that did perfonally accompany him in this Voyage, yet the reading of this following Letter fent by him to Sir *Henry Wotton*, the morning before he left *England*, may teftifie he wanted not his friends beft wifhes to attend him.

C 3 SIR,

SIR,

After those reverend papers, whose soul is (name,
Our good, and great Kings lou'd hand, and feard
By which to you he derives much of his;
And how he may, makes you almost the same;

A Taper of his Torch, a Copy writ
From his Original, and a fair Beam
Of th' same warm and dazling Sun, though it
Must in another Sphere his vertue stream;

After those Learned Papers which your hand
Hath stor'd with notes of use and pleasure too;
From which rich treasury you may command
Fit matter whether you will write or do.

After those oving Papers where Friends send
With glad grief to your Sea-ward-steps farewel,
Which thicken on you now as prayers ascend
To heaven on troops at a good mans passing-bell.

Admit this honest Paper, and allow
It such an audience as your self would ask;
What you would say at Venice, this sayes now,
And has for nature what you have for task.

To swear much love; nor to be chang'd before
Honour alone will to your fortune fit,
Nor shall I then honour your fortune more,
Than I have done your honour-wanting-wit.

                                        But

But 'tis an eafier load (though both opprefs)
  To want, than govern greatnefs ; for we are
In that, our own, and onely bufinefs ;
  In this, we muft for others vices care.

'Tis therefore well, your fpirits now are plac'd
  In their laft furnace, in activity ;   (ore-paft
Which fits them : Schools, and Courts, *and* Wars
  To touch and tafte in any beft degree.

For me ! *(if there be fuch a thing as I)*
  Fortune *(if there be fuch a thing as fhe)*
Finds that I bear fo well her tyrannie,
  That fhe thinks nothing elfe fo fit for me.

But, though fhe part us, to hear my oft prayers.
  For your increafe, *God is as near me here ;*
And, to fend you what I fhall beg, his ftairs
  In length, *and* eafe, *are alike every where.*

J. Donne.

SIR *Henry Wotton* was received by the State of *Venice*, with much honour and gladneſs, both for that he delivered his Embaſſage moſt elegantly in the *Italian* Language, and came alſo in ſuch a Juncture of time, as his Maſters friendſhip ſeem'd uſeful for that Republick: the time of his coming thither was about the year 1604. *Leonardo Donato* being then Duke; a wiſe and reſolv'd man, and to all purpoſes ſuch (Sir *Henry VVotton* would often ſay it) as the State of *Venice* could not then have wanted; there having been formerly in the time of *Pope Clement* the eighth, ſome conteſts about the priviledges of church-men, and the power of the Civil Magiſtrate; of which, for the information of common Readers, I ſhall ſay a little, becauſe it may give light to ſome paſſages that follow.

About the year 1603. the Republick of *Venice* made ſeveral Injunctions againſt Lay-perſons giving Lands or Goods to the Church, without Licence from the Civil-Magiſtrate; and in that inhibition, they expreſt their reaſons to be, *For that when it once came into the hands of the Eccleſiaſticks, it was not ſubject to alienation; by reaſon whereof, (the lay people being at their death charitable even to exceſs) the Clergy grew every day more numerous, and, pretending*

ex

*exemption from all publick service and taxes, the
burthen did grow too heavy to be born by the
Laity.*

Another occasion of difference was, That
about this time complaints were justly made by
the *Venetians* against two Clergy-men, the *Abbot* of *Nervesa*, and a *Canon* of *Vicenza*; for
committing such sins, as I think not fit to
name; nor are these mentioned with an Intent to fix a Scandal upon any Calling; (for
holiness is not tyed to Ecclesiastical Orders, and
Italy is observed to breed the most vertuous,
and most vicious men of any Nation) these
two having been long complained of at *Rome* in
the name of the State of *Venice*, and no satisfaction being given to the *Venetians*, they seised their persons, and committed them to
prison.

The justice, or injustice of such power, then
used by the *Venetians*, had formerly had some
calm debates betwixt the present Pope *Clement*
the Eighth, and that *Republick* : for he did
not excommunicate them; considering (as I
conceive) that in the late *Council of Trent* it
was at last (after many Politique disturbances,
and delayes, and indeavours to preserve the
Popes present power) declar'd, in order to a
general reformation of those many Errours
which were in time crept into the Church :
that though *Discipline*, and especial *Excommunication* be one of the chief sinews of Church
Go-

government; and intended to keep men in obedience to it: for which end, it was declar'd to be very profitable; yet it was alfo declar'd, and advifed to be ufed with great fobriety and care: becaufe experience had info med them, that when it was pronounced unadvifedly, or rafhly, it became more *contemn'd* then *fear'd.* And, though this was the advice of that Council at the Conclufion of it, which was not many years before this quarrel with the *Venetians:* yet this prudent, patient Pope *Clement* dying: *Pope Paul* the fi r, who fucceeded him, being a man of a much hotter temper, brought this difference with the *Ven tians* to a much higher Contention: objecting thofe late acts of that State, to be a diminution of his juft power, and limited a time for their revocation; threatning, if he were not obeyed, to proceed to excommunication of the *Republick*; who ftill offered to fhew both reafon and ancient cuftom to warrant their Actions. But this *Pope,* contrary to his Predeceffors moderation, required abfolute obedience without difputes.

Thus it continued for about a year; the Pope ftill threatning Excommunication, and the *Venetians* ftill anfwering him with fair fpeeches, and no performance, till at laft, the Popes zeal to the *Apoftolick Sea,* did make him to excommunicate the *Duke,* the whole *Senate,* and all their Dominions; and then fhut up all their *Churches*; charging the whole Clergy to forbear

bear all sacred Offices to the *Venetians*, till
their Obedience should render them capable of
Absolution.

But this act of the Popes did the more confirm
the *Venetians* in their resolution not to obey
him; *And to that end, upon the hearing of his
Interdict, they presently* published by sound *of
Trumpet, a Proclamation to this effect.*

   " That whosoever hath received from *Rome*
" any Copy of a Papal interdict, publish'd there, ~b
" well against the Law of God, as against the
" Honour of this Nation, shall presently ren-
" der it to the Councel of *Ten*, upon pain of
" death.

Then was the *Inquisition* presently suspended
by Order of the State; and the Flood-gates
being thus set open, any pleasant or scoffing
wit might safely vent it self against the *Pope*, either by free speaking, or in Print.

Matters thus heightned, the State advised
with Father *Paul*, a holy and Learned Fryer
(the Authour of the *History of the Council of
Trent*) whose advice was, *Neither to Provoke
the Pope, nor lose their own Right*; he declaring
publickly in Print, in the name of the State,
That the Pope was trusted to keep two Keyes; one
of Prudence, *and the other of* Power; *And that
if they were not both used together,* Power a-
lone

lone is not effectual in an Excommunication.

And thus it continued, till a report was blown abroad, that the *Venetians* were all turned *Proteſtants:* which was believed by many, for that it was obſerv'd, the *Engliſh* Ambaſſadour was ſo often in conference with the *Senate*, aud his Chaplain Mr. *Bedel*, more often with Father *Paul:* And alſo, for that the *Republick* of *Venice* was known to give Commiſſon to *Gregory Juſtiniano*, then their Ambaſſadour in *England*, to make all theſe proceedings known to the King, and to crave a Promiſe of his aſſiſtance, if need ſhould require: and in the mean time, the *King*'s advice and judgment; which was the ſame that he gave to *Pope Clement* at his firſt coming to the Crown of *England*; (that Pope then moving him to an Union with the *Roman Church*) namely; *To endeavour the calling of a free Council, for the ſettlement of peace in Chriſtendom: And that he doubed not, but that the French King, and divers other Princes would joyn to aſſiſt in ſo good a work; and in the mean time, the ſin of this Breach, both with his, and the* Venetians *Dominions, muſt of neceſſity lie at the* Pope's *door.*

In this contention (which laſted ſeveral years) the *Pope* grew ſtill higher, and the *Venetians* more reſolv'd and careleſs; ſtill acquainting King *James* with their proceedings, which was done by the help of Sir *Henry Wotton,*

ton, Mr. *Bedel*, and *Padre Paulo*, whom the *Venetians* did then call to be one of their Confultors of State, and with his Pen to defend their Caufe: which was by him fo performed, that the *Pope* faw plainly, he had weakned his Power by exceeding it, and offered the *Venetians* Abfolution upon very eafie terms; which the *Venetians* ftill flighting did at laft obtain, by that which was fcarce fo much as a fhew of acknowledging it: For they made an order, that in that day. in which they were abfolv'd, there fhould be no publick rejoycing: nor any *Bonefires* that night; left the Common people might judg they were abfolved for committing a fault.

Thefe Contefts were the occafion of *Padre Paulo* his knowledge and intereft with King *James*, for whofe fake principally *Padre Paul* compiled that eminent Hiftory of the remarkable Council of *Trent*; which Hiftory was, as faft as it was written, fent in feveral fheets in Letters by Sir *Henry Wotton*, Mr *Bedel*, and Mr. *Bedel*, and others, unto King *James*, and the then Bifhop of *Canterbury* in *England*; and there firft made publick both in *Englifh*, and in the univerfal Language.

For eight years after Sir *Henry Wottons* going into *Italy*, he ftood fair, and highly valued in the Kings opinion, but at laft became much clouded by an accident, which I fhall proceed to relate.

At

At his firſt going Embaſſadour into *Italy*, as he paſſed through *Germany*, he ſtayed ſome dayes at *Auguſta*; where having been in his former Travels, well known by many of the beſt note for Learning and Ingeniouſneſs, (thoſe that are eſteemed the *Virtuoſi* of that Nation) with whom he paſſing an evening in merriments, was requeſted by *Chriſtopher Flecamore* to write ſome Sentence in his *Albe*; (a Book of white paper, which, for that purpoſe many of the *German* Gentry uſually carry about them) and Sir *Henry Wotton* conſenting to the motion, took an occaſion from ſome accidental diſcourſe of the preſent Company, to write a pleaſant definition of an Embaſſadour, in theſe very words.

> *Legatus eſt vir bonus peregrè miſſus ad mentiendum Reipublicæ cauſâ.*

Which Sir *Henry Wotton* could have been content ſhould have been thus Engliſhed:

> *An Ambaſſadour is an honeſt man, ſent to* lie *abroad for the good of his Country.*

But the word for *lye* being the hinge upon
which

which the Conceit was to turn) was not so
expre s'd in Latine as would admit(in the hands
of an enemy especial'y) so fair a constructi-
on as Sir *Henry* thought in *English*. Yet as
it was, it slept quietly among other Sentences
in this *Albo,* almost *eight years,* till by accident
it fell into the hands of *Jasper Scioppius*; a Ro-
manist, a man of a restless spirit, and a malicious
Pen : who with Books against King *James,*
prints this as a Principle of that Religion professed by the King and his Embassadour Sir
Henry Wotton , then at *Venice* ; and in *Venice*
it was presently after written in several Glass-
Windowes, and spitefully declared to be Sir
Henry VVottons.

This coming to the knowledge of King
James, he apprehended it to be such an over-
sight, such a weakness, or worse, in Sir *Henry*
VVotton, as caused the King to express much
wrath against him; and this caused Sir *Henry*
VVotton to write two Apologies, one to *Vel-*
serus (one of the Chiefs of *Augusta*) in the
Universal Language, which he caus'd to be
printed , and given, and scattered in the most
remarkable places both of *Germany* and *Italy ,*
as an Antidote against the venemous books of
Scioppius : and another Apology to King *James,*
which were both so ingenious, so clear, and so
choicely Eloquent, that his Majesty (who was
a pure Judge of it) could not forbear at the re-
ceit thereof, to declare publickly, *That Sir Hen-*
ry

ry VVotton had commuted sufficiently for a greater offence.

And now, as broken bones well set become stronger ; so Sir *Henry Wotton* did not only recover, but was much more confirmed in his Majesties estimation and favour then formerly he had been.

And as that man (his friend) of great wit * Dr. and useful fancy, gave in a Will * of his (a *Will* Donne. *of conceits*) his *Reputation* to his *Friends*, and his *Industry* to his *Foes*, because from thence he received both: so those friends, that in this time of tryal labored to excuse this facetious freedom of Sir *Henry Wottons*, were to him more dear, and by him more highly valued ; and those acquaintance that urged this as an advantage against him : caused him by this errour, to grow both more wise, and which is the best fruit errour can bring forth) for the future to become more industriously watchful over his tongue and pen.

I have told you a part of his imployment in *Italy*, where (notwithstanding the accusation of *Scioppius*) his interest still increas'd with this Duke *Leonardo Donato* ; after whose death (as though it had been an intail'd love) it was still found living in the succeeding Dukes, during all the time of his imployment to that State : (which was almost Twenty years.) All which time he studied the dispositions of those *Dukes*, and the other *Consultors* of State ; well know-

knowing, that he who negotiates a continued bufinefs, and neglects the ftudy of difpofitions, ufually fails in his propofed ends: But this Sir *Henry Wotton* did not, for by a fine forting of fit Prefents, curious, and not coftly entertainments, alwayes fweetned by various and pleafant difcourfe; with which, and his choice application of ftories, and his fo elegant deliver'd of all thefe, even in their *Italian* Language, he firft got, and ftill preferv'd fuch intereft in the State of *Venice,* that it was obferv'd (fuch was either his merit or his modefty) they never denyed him any requeft.

But all this fhewes but his abilities, and his fitnefs for that Imployment: 'Twill therefore be needful to tell the Reader, what ufe he made of the Intereft which thefe procured him; and that indeed was, rather to oblige others, then to enrich himfelf; he ftill endeavouring that the reputation of the *Englifh* might be maintain'd, both in the *German* Empire, and in *Italy*; where many Gentlemen, whom Travel had invited into that Nation, received from him chearfull Entertainments, advice for their behaviour, and fhelter, or deliverance from thofe accidental ftorms of adverfity, which ufually attend upon Travel.

And becaufe thefe things may appear to the Reader to be but Generals, I fhall acquaint him with two particular Examples; one, of his merciful difpofition, and one, of the Noblenefs

D

blenefs of his Mind: which fhall follow.

There had been many *Englifh* Souldiers brought by Commanders of their own Country, to ferve the *Venetians* for pay againft the *Turk*: and thofe *Englifh*, having by Irregularities, or Improvidence, brought themfelves into feveral Gallies and Prifons, Sir *Henry Wotton*, became a Petitioner to that State for their Lives, and Inlargement; and his requeft was granted; fo that thofe (which were many hundreds, and there made the fad Examples of humane mifery, by hard imprifonment, and unpitied poverty in a ftrange Nation) were by his means releafed, relieved, and in a comfortable Condition fent to thank God and him for their Lives and Libertyes, in their own Country.

And this I have obferved as one teftimony of the compaffionate Nature of him, who was (during his ftay in thofe parts) as a City of Refuge for the Diftreffed of this and other Nations.

And for that which I offer as a Teftimony of the Noblenefs of his mind: I fhall make way to the Readers clearer underftanding of it, by telling him that Sir *Henry Wotton* was fent thrice Embaffadour to the Republick of *Venice*; and that at his fecond going thither, he was employed Embaffador to feveral of the *German* Princes, and to the Emperour *Ferdinando* the fecond; and, that his employment to him, and thofe
Prin-

Princes, was to incline them to equitable Conditions, for the reſtauration of the Queen of *Bohemia* and her Deſcendents to their Patrimonial Inheritance of the *Palatinate.*

This was by his eight months conſtant endeavours and attendance upon the *Emperour*, his Court and Counſel) brought to the probability of a ſucceſful Concluſion without bloodſhed, there being at that time two oppoſite armies in the field but, as they were treating, the Armies met; and there was a battle fought, the managery whereof was ſo full of miſerable errours on the one ſide (ſo Sir *Henry Wotton* expreſſes it in a diſpatch to the King) and ſo advantagious to the Emperour, as put an end to all Hopes of a ſucccceſsful Treaty : ſo that *Sir Henry* ſeeing the face of Peace altered by that Victory, prepared for a Removal from that Court ; and at his departure from the *Emperour*, was ſo bold as to remember him, *That the Events of every Battel move en the unſeen wheels of Fortune, which are this moment up, and down the next ; and therefore', humbly adviſed him to uſe his Victory ſo ſoberly, as ſtill to put on thoughts of Peace.* Which advice, though it ſeemed to be ſpoke with ſome Paſſion, his dear Miſtreſs the *Queen* of *Bohemia*, being concerned in it, was yet taken in good part, by the *Emperour*, who was much pleaſed with his carriage , all the time that he reſided in his Court; and ſaid, *That the King his Maſter was look'd on as an*

Abet-

Abettor of his Enemy the Palfgrave, but yet, he took him to be a Perfon of much *Honour* and *Merit,* and did therefore defire him to accept of that *Jewel,* as a Teftimony of his good opinion of him; which was a *Jewel* of Diamonds, of more value then a thoufand pounds.

This was received with all Circumftances and terms of Honour, by Sir *Henry Wotton*; but the next morning, at his departing from *Vienna,* at his taking leave of the Countefs of *Sabrina* (an *Italian* Lady) in whofe Houfe the Emperour had appointed him to be lodg'd, and honourably entertained: *He acknowledged her Merits, and befought her to accept of that Jewel, as a teftimony of his gratitude for her Civilities:* prefenting her with the fame that was given him by the *Emperour*; which being fuddenly difcovered by the *Emperour,* was by him taken for a high affront, and Sir *Henry Wotton* told fo: To which he replyed, *That though he received it with thankfulnefs; yet he found in himfelf an indifpofition to be the better for any gift that came from an Enemy to his Royal Miftrefs the Queen of Bohemia,* for fo fhe was pleafed, he fhould alwayes call her.

Many other of his fervices to his Prince, and this Nation, might be infifted upon, as namely his procuration of Priviledges, and courtefies with the *German* Princes, and the Republick of *Venice,* for the *Englifh* Merchants, and,

and what he did by direction of *King James*
with the *Venetian* State, concerning the Bishop of *Spalato's* return to the Church of *Rome*.
But for the particulars of these, and many
more, that I mean to make known; I want a
view of some papers that might inform me,
(his late Majesties *Letter-Office* having suffe-
red a strange alienation) and, indeed I want
time too; for, the Printers Press stayes; so
that I must haste to bring Sir *Henry Wotton* in
an instant from *Venice* to *London*, leaving the
Reader to make up what is defective in this
place, by this small supplement of the inscription under his Armes, which he left at all
those houses where he rested, or lodged,
when he returned from his last Embassie into
England.

Henricus Wottonius Anglo-Cantia-
nus, Thomæ optimi viri filius natu
minimus, a serenissimo Jacobo I. Mag.
Britt. *Rege, in equestrem titulum ad-*
scitus, ejusdemque ter ad Rempubli-
cam Venetam *Legatus Ordinarius, se-*
mel ad confæderatarum Provinciarum
Ordines in Juliacensi *negotio.* Bis ad
Carolum Emanuel, *Sabaudiæ* Ducem;
semel ad unitos superioris G rmaniæ

Principes in Conventu Heilbrunenſi, *poſtremo ad Archiducem* Leopoldum, Ducem Wittembergenſem, *Civitates imperiales*, *Argentinam*, *Ulmamque*, & *ipſum Romanorum Imperatorem* Ferdinandum ſecundum, *Legatus Extraordinarius*, *tandem hoc didicit*,

Animas fieri ſapientiores quieſcendo.

To *London* he came that year in which King *James* dyed; who having for the reward of his forreign ſervice, promiſed him the reverſion of an Office which was fit to be turned into preſent money, for a ſupply of his preſent neceſſities, and alſo granted him the reverſion of the *Maſter of the Rolls* place, if he out-lived charitable Sir *Julius Cæſar*, who then poſſeſſed it: and then, grown ſo old, that he was ſaid to be kept alive beyond Natures Courſe, by the prayers of thoſe many poor which he daily relieved.

But, theſe were but in hope; and his condition required a preſent ſupport: For in the beginning of theſe imployments he ſold to his elder brother the Lord *Wotton*, the Rentcharge left by h's good Father, and (which is worſe) was now at his return indebted to
ſeve-

several persons, whom he was not able to satisfie, but by the Kings payment of his Arrears
due for his forreign Imployments: He had
brought into *England* many servants, of which
some were *German* and *Italian* Artists; this
was part of his condition, who had many times
hardly sufficient to supply the occasions of the
day. (For it may by no means be said of his
providence, as himself said of Sir *Philip Sidney*'s
wit, *That it was the very measure of congruity*)
He being alwayes so careless of money, as
though our Saviours words, *Care not for to mor-*
row, were to be literally understood.

But it pleased God, that in this juncture of
time, the Provostship of His Majesties Colledge
of *Eaton* became void by the death of--*Murray*,
for which there were (as the place deserv'd)
many earnest and powerful Suiters to the *King*.
Sir *Henry* who had for many years (like *Sici-*
phus) rolled the restless stone of a State imployment; and knowing experimentally, that
the great blessing of sweet content was not to
be found in multitudes of men or business; and,
that a *Colledge* was the fittest place to nourish
holy thoughts, and to afford rest both to his body
and mind , which his age (being now almost
threescore years) seemed to require, did therefore use his own, and the interest of all his friends
to procure it. By which means, and quitting the
King of his promised reversionary Offices, and
a piece of honest policy (which I have not

D 4   time

time to relate) he got a Grant of it from His Majesty.

And this was a fair settlement for his *mind:* but *money* was wanting to furnish him with those necessaries which attend removes, and a settlement in such a place; and to procure that, he wrote to his old friend Mr. *Nicholas Pey*, for his assistance; of which *Nicholas Pey*, I shall here say a little, for the clearing of something that I shall say hereafter.

He was in his youth a Clerk, or in some such way, a servant to the Lord *Wotton*, Sir *Henry*'s brother; and by him, when he was Comptroller of the Kings Houshold, was made a great Officer in His Majesties house. This, and other favours being conferred upon Mr. *Pey* (in whom was a radical honesty) were alwayes thankfully acknowledged by him, and his gratitude exprest by a willing and unwearied serviceableness to that Family even till his death. To him Sir *Henry Wotton* wrote, to use all his interest at Court, to procure Five hundred pounds of his Arrears (for less would not settle him in the Colledge) and the want of it, *wrinkled his face with care*; ('twas his own expression) and that being procured, he should the next day after find him in his *Colledge,* and *Invidia remedium* writ over his *Study* door.

This money, being part of his Arrears, was by his own, and the help of honest *Nicholas Pey*'s interest in Court, quickly procured him;
and

and he as quickly in the *Colledge*, the place where indeed his happiness then seemed to have its beginning, the *Colledge* being to his mind, as a quiet Harbor to a Sea-faring-man after a tempestuous voyage; where, by the bounty of the pious Founder, his very *Food* and *Rayment* were plentifully provided for him in kind; where he was freed from all corroding cares, and seated on such a Rock, as the waves of want could not probably shake, where he might sit in a *Calm*, and looking down, behold the busie multitude turmoyl'd and tossed in a tempestuous Sea of dangers! And (as Sir *William Davenant* has happily exprest the like of another person)

Laugh at the graver business of the State,
Which speaks men rather wise than fortunate.

Being thus setled according to the desires of his *heart*, his first *study* was the Statutes of the *Colledge*: by which, he conceiv'd himself bound to enter into *Holy Orders*, which he did; being made *Deacon* with convenient speed, shortly after, as he came in his *Surplice* from the *Church-service*, an old Friend, a person of Quality, met him so attired, and joyed him of his new habit; to whom Sir *Henry Wotton* replied, *I thank* God *and the* King, *by whose goodness I now am in this condition; a condition, which that* Emperor *Charles the Fifth, seem'd to approve: who, after so many remarkable*

remarkable Victories, when his glory was great in the eyes of all men, freely gave up his Crown, *and the many cares that attended it, to* Philip *his son, making a holy retreat to a Cloysteral life, where he might by devout* meditations *consult with* God, (which the rich or busie men seldom do) *and have leisure both to examine the errors of his life past, and prepare for that great day , wherein all flesh must make an account of their actions : And after a kind of tempestuous life, I now have the like advantage from him,* that makes the out-goings of the morning to praise him ; *even from my* God, *whom I daily magnifie for this particular mercy, of an exemption from business, a quiet mind, and a liberal maintenance, even in this part of my life, when my* age *and* infirmities *seem to sound me a retreat from the pleasures of this world, and invite me to contemplation, in which I have ever taken the greatest felicity.*

And now to speak a little of the employment of his *time:* After his customary publick Devotions, his use was to retire into his *Study,* and there to spend some hours in reading the Bible, and Authors in Divinity, closing up his meditations with private prayer ; this was, for the most part, his employment in the Forenoon : But, when he was once sate to Dinner, then nothing but chearful thoughts possess'd his mind ; and, those still increased by constant company at his Table, of such persons as brought thither additions both of Learning and Pleasure ;

sure ; but some part of most dayes was usually spent in *Philosophical Conclusions*. Nor did he forget his innate pleasure of *Angling*, which he would usually call, *his idle time, not idely spent*; saying, he would rather live five *May-months*, than *forty Decembers*.

He was a great lover of his Neighbours, and a bountiful entertainer of them very often at his Table, where his meat was choice, and his discourse better.

He was a constant Cherisher of all those youths in that School, in whom he found either a constant diligence, or a *genius* that prompted them to Learning ; for whose encouragement, he was (beside many other things of necessity and beauty) at the charge of setting up in it two rowes of *Pillars*, on which he caused to be choicely drawn, the pictures of divers of the most famous *Greek* and *Latin Historians*, *Poets*, and *Orators* ; perswading them not to neglect *Rhetorick*, because *Almighty God has left Mankind affections to be wrought upon:* And he would often say, *That none despised Eloquence, but such dull souls as were not capable of it.* He would also often make choice of some Observations out of those *Historians* and *Poets :* and would never leave the School, without dropping some choice *Greek* or *Latin Apothegm* or sentence, that might be worthy of a room in the memory of a growing Scholar.

He

He was pleafed conftantly to breed up one or more hopeful Youths, which he picked out of the *School*, and took into his own Domeftick care, and to attend him at his Meals ; out of whofe *Difcourfe* and *Behaviour*, he gathered obfervations for the better compleating of his intended work of *Education :* of which, by his ftill ftriving to make the whole better, he lived to leave but part to Pofterity.

He was a great Enemy to *wrangling Difputes* of *Religion,* concerning which, I fhall fay a little, both to teftifie that, and to fhew the readinefs of his Wit.

Having in *Rome* made acquaintance with a pleafant *Prieft*, who invited him one Evening to hear their Vefper *Mufick* at *Church* ; the Prieft feeing Sir *Henry* ftand obfcurely in a corner, fends to him by a Boy of the Quire this queftion, writ in a fmall piece of paper, *Where was your Religion to be found before* Luther *?* To which queftion Sir *Henry* prefently under-writ, *My Religion was to be found* then, *where yours is not to be found* now, *in the written Word of* God.

The next Vefper, Sir *Henry* went purpofely to the fame Church, and fent one of the Quire-boyes with this Queftion, to his honeft, pleafant friend, the Prieft ; *Do you believe all thofe many Thoufands of poor Chriftians were damn'd, that were Excommunicated, becaufe the* Pope, *and the* Duke of Venice, *could not agree about their temporal power ?* Speak your Confcience. To which
he

he under-writ in *French* , *Monsieur* , *excusay moy.*

To one that asked him, *Whether a Papist may be saved ?* he replyed, *You may be saved without knowing that.* Look to your self.

To another, whose earnestness exceeded his knowledge, and was still railing againk the *Papists*, he gave this advice, *Pray Sir forbear , till you have studied the Points better ; for the wise* Italians *have this Proverb, He that understands amiss, concludes worse :* And take heed of thinking, *The farther you go from the Church of* Rome, *the nearer you are to God.*

And to another that spake indiscreet, and bitter words against *Arminius*, I heard him reply to this purpose :

In my travel towards Venice, *as I past through* Germany, *I rested almost a year at* Leyden, *where I entred into an acquaintance with* Arminius *(then the Professor of* Divinity *in that University)* a *man much talk'd of in this Age, which is made up of opposition and* Controversie *: And indeed, if I mistake not* Arminius *in his expressions (as so weak a brain as mine is may easily do) then I know I differ from him in some points ; yet, I profess my judgement of him to be, that he was a man of most rare* Learning, *and I knew him to be of a most strict life, and of a most meek spirit. And that he was so mild, appears by his Proposals to our Master* Perkins *of* Cambridge, *from whose Book, of the* Order and Causes of Salvation *(which was first*
writ

writ in Latin) Arminius *took the occasion of writing some* Queries *to him concerning the consequents of his* Doctrine, *intending them* ('*tis said*) *to come privately to Mr.* Perkin's *own hands , and to receive from him, a like private, and a like loving* Answer: *But, Mr.* Perkins *dyed before those* Queries *came to him; and 'tis thought* Arminius *meant them to dye with him; for though he lived long after, I have heard he forbore to publish them,* (*but since his death, his sons did not:*) *And 'tis pity* (*if God had been so pleased*) *that Mr.* Perkins *did not live to see, consider, and answer those proposals himself; for he was also of a most meek* spirit, *and of great and sanctified* Learning: *And though since their deaths, many* (*of high parts and piety*) *have undertaken to clear the* Controversie*; yet, for the most part, they have rather satisfied themselves, than convinced the dissenting party. And doubtless, many middle-witted men* (*which yet may mean well*) *many Scholars that are not in the highest Form for Learning* (*which yet may preach well*) *men that shall never know, till they come to Heaven, where the questions stick betwixt* Arminius *and the Church of* England, *will yet in this world be tampering with, and thereby perplexing the* Controversie, *and do therefore justly fall under the reproof of St.* Jude, *for being* Busie-bodies, *and for* medling with things they understand not.

And here it offers it self (I think not unfitly) to tell the Reader, that a friend of Sir *Henry ry Wottons*, being defigned for the imployment of an *Ambaffador*, came to *Eaton*, and requefted from him fome experimental Rules for his prudent and fafe carriage in his Negotiations ; to whom he fmilingly gave this for an infallible *Aphorifm* ; *That, to be in fafety himfelf, and ferviceable to his* Countrey, *he fhould alwayes, and upon all occafions fpeak the* truth *(it feems a* State-Paradox *) for, fayes Sir* Henry Wotton, *you fhall never be believed; and by this means, your truth will fecure your felf, if you fhall ever be called to any account; and'twill alfo put your Adverfaries (who will ftill hunt counter) to a lofs in all their difquifitions, and undertakings.*

Many more of this nature might be obferved, but they muft be laid afide; for I fhall here make a little ftop, and invite the Reader to look back with me, whil'ft (according to my promife) I fhall fay a little of Sir *Albertus Morton,* and Mr. *William Bedel*, whom I formerly mentioned.

I have told you that are the Readers, that at Sir *Henry Wottons* firft going Ambaffador into *Italy*, his Cofin, Sir *Albert Morton*, went his Secretary; and am next to tell you, that Sir *Albertus* dyed, *Secretary of State* to our late King; but cannot, am not able to exprefs the forrow that poffeft Sir *Henry Wotton* at his firft hearing the news that Sir *Albertus* was by death loft to him and this world; and yet, the Reader may partly guefs by thefe following expreffions :

ons: The firſt in a Letter to his *Nicholas Pey*, of which this that followeth is a part.

———*And* My dear Nick, *When I had been here almoſt a fortnight, in the midſt of my great contentment, I received notice of Sir* Albertus Morton *his departure out of this World, who was dearer to me, than mine own being in it; what a wound it is to my heart, you that knew him, and knew me, will eaſily believe : but, our Creators Will muſt be done, and unrepiningly received by his own Creatures, who is the Lord of all Nature, and of all Fortune, when he taketh to himſelf now one, and then another, till that expected day, wherein it ſhall pleaſe him to diſſolve the whole, and wrap up even the Heaven it ſelf as a Scrole of parchment : This is the laſt* Philoſophy *that we muſt ſtudy upon Earth ; let us therefore that yet remain here, as our dayes and friends waſte, reinforce our love to each other; which of all vertues, both* ſpiritual *and* moral, *hath the higheſt* priviledge, *becauſe death it ſelf cannot end it. And my good* Nick, &c.

This is a part of his ſorrow thus expreſt to his *Nick Pey*; the other part is in this following Elogy, of which the Reader may ſafely conclude, 'twas too hearty to be diſſembled.

Tears

Tears wept at the Grave of Sir *Albertus Morton*, by *Henry Wotton*.

Silence in truth, would speak my sorrow best,
   For deepest wounds, can least their feelings tell;
Yet let me borrow from mine own unrest,
A time to bid him whom I lov'd, farewell.

Oh my unhappy Lines, you that before
Have serv'd my youth to vent some wanton cryes,
And now congeal'd with grief, can scarce implore
Strength to accent, Here my *Albertus* lies.

This is that Sable stone, this is the Cave
And womb of earth, that doth his Corps embrace;
While others sing his praise, let me ingrave
These bleeding numbers to adorn the place.

Here will I paint the Characters of woe:
Here will I pay my tribute to the dead;
And here, my faithful tears in showres shall flow
To humanize the flints on which I tread.

Where, though I mourn my matchless loss alone,
And none between my weakness judge and me;
              E   Yet,

Yet, even these pensive walls allow my moan,
Whose doleful Echoes to my plaints agree.

But is he gone ? and live I riming here,
As if some Muse would listen to my lay ?
When all dis-tun'd sit waiting for their dear,
And bathe the Banks where he was wont to play.

Dwell then in endless bliss with happy souls,
Discharg'd from natures, *and from* tortunes *trust :*
Whil'st on this fluid Globe, my Hour-glass rowls,
And runs the rest of my remaining dust.

H. Wotton.

This concerning his Sir *Albertus Morton.*

And for what I shall say concerning Mr. *William Bedel,* I must prepare the Reader, by telling him, That when King *James* sent Sir *Henry Wotton* Ambassador to the State of *Venice,* he sent also an Ambassador to the King of *France,* and another to the King of *Spain*; with the Ambassador of *France,* went *Joseph Hall* (late *Bishop* of *Norwich*) whose many and useful works, speak his great merit; with the Ambassador of *Spain,* went *Ja. Wadsworth*; and with Sir *Henry Wotton* went *William Bedel.*

These three Chaplains, to these three Ambassadors, were all bred in one University, all of one * Colledge, all Benefic'd in one Diocess, and all most dear and intire Friends : But in *Spain,* Mr. *Wadsworth* met with temptations, or reasons,

Emanuel Colledge in Cambridge.

reasons, such as were so powerful, as to perswade him (who of the three, was formerly observ'd to be the most averse to that Religion that calls it self *Catholick*) to disclaim himself a Member of the Church of *England,* and declare himself for the Church of *Rome*, discharging himself of his attendance on the Ambassadoi, and betaking himself to a Monasterial life ; in which he lived very regularly, and so dved.

When Dr. *Hall* (the late *Bishop* of *Norwich*) came into *England*, he wrote to Mr. *Wadsworth*, ('tis the first Epistle in his printed Decads) to perswade his return, or the reason of his Apostasie ; the Letter seemed to have in it many sweet expressions of love, and yet, there was something in it that was so unpleasant to Mr. *Wadsworth*, that he chose rather to acquaint his old friend Mr. *Bedel* with his motives ; by which means, there past betwixt Mr. *Bedel*, and Mr. *Wadsworth* very many Letters, which be extant in Print, and did well deserve it ; for in them there seems to be a controversie, not of Religion only, but, who should answer each other with most love and meeknefs ; which I mention the ra her, because it seldom falls out so in a Book-War.

There is yet a little more to be said of Mr. *Bedel*, for the greatest part of which, the Reader is referred to this following Letter of Sir *Henry Wottons*, writ to our late King *Charles*.

May

May it please Your most Gracious Majesty,

HAving been informed that certain persons have, by the good wishes of the Archbishop of Armagh, been directed hither, with a most humble Petition unto Your Majesty, that You will be pleased to make Mr. William Bedel (now resident upon a small Benefice in Suffolk) Governor of your Colledge at Dublin, for the good of that Society; and my self being required to render unto Your Majesty some testimony of the said William Bedel, who was long my Chaplain at Venice, in the time of my first imployment there; I am bound in all Conscience and Truth (so far as Your Majesty will vouchsafe to accept my poor judgement) to affirm of him, That I think hardly a fitter man for that Charge, could have been propounded unto Your Majesty in Your whole Kingdom, for singular Erudition and Piety, Conformity to the Rites of the Church, and Zeal to advance the Cause of God; wherein his Travels abroad, were not obscure, in the time of the Excommunication of the Venetians.

For it may please Your Majesty to know, that this is the man whom Padre Paulo took, I may say, into his very soul, with whom he did communicate the inwardest thoughts of his heart, from whom he professed to have received more knowledge in all Divinity, both Scholastical and Positive, than from any that he had ever practised in his dayes; of which, all the passages were well known to the King

Your

Your Father, of most blessed memory. And, so with Your Majesties good favour, I will end this needless Office; for the general Fame of his Learning, his Life, and Christian temper, and those Religious Labours which himself hath dedicated to Your Majesty, do better describe him than I am able.

Your MAJESTIES

Most humble and faithful Servant,

H. WOTTON.

———————————

TO this Letter, I shall add this; That he was (to the great joy of Sir *Henry Wotton*) made Governor of the said Colledge; and that after a fair discharge of his duty and trust there, he was thence removed to be, *Bishop* of *Kilmore:* In both which places, his life was so holy, as seemed to equal the primitive Christians; for as they, so he kept all the *Ember-weeks*, observed (besides his private devotions) the *Canonical* hours of Prayer very strictly; and so he did all the Feasts, and Fast-dayes of his

E 3   Mother,

Mother, the Church of *England*; his Patience and Charity were both such, as shewed his affections were set upon *things that are above*; for indeed his whole life brought forth the *fruits of the spirit*; there being in him such a remarkable meekness, that as St. *Paul* advised his *Timothy* in the Election of a *Bishop*, * *That he have a good report of those that be without*; so had he: for those that were without. even those that in point of Religion, were of the *Roman* perswasion (of which there were very many in his Diocess) did yet ever look upon him with respect and reverence; and, testified it, by a concealing, and safe protecting him in the late horrid Rebellion in *Ireland*, when the fury of the wild *Irish* knew no distinction of persons; and yet there, and then, he was protected and cherished by those of a contrary perswasion; and there, and then he dyed, though not by violence: And with him was lost many of his learned Writings, which were thought worthy of preservation; and amongst the rest, was lost the *Bible*, which by many years labour, and conference, and study, he had translated into the *Irish* Tongue, with an intent to have printed it for publick use.

More might be said of Mr. *Bedel*, who (I told the Reader) was Sir *Henry Wotton's* first Chaplain; and much of his second Chaplain, *Isaac Bargrave*, Doctor in *Divinity*, and the late learned and hospitable Dean of *Canterbury*; as also,

* 1 Tim. 3. 7.

alfo, of the Merit of many others, that had the happiness to attend Sir *Henry* in his forreign imployments: But, the Reader may think that in this digreffion, I have already carried him too far from *Eaton-Colledge*, and therefore I fhall lead him back as gently, and as orderly as I may to that place, for a further conference concerning Sir *Henry Wotton*.

Sir *Henry Wotton* had propos'd to himfelf, before he entred into his Collegiate life, to write the life of *Martin Luther* ; and in it, the Hiftory of the Reformation, as it was carried on in *Germany :* For the doing of which, he had many advantages by his feveral Embaffies into thofe parts, and his intereft in the feveral Princes of the *Empire;* by whofe means he had accefs to the Records of all the *Hans Towns*, and the knowledge of many fecret paffages that fell not under common view; and in thefe he had made a happy progrefs, as is well known to his worthy friend Dr. *Duppa*, the late Reverend Bifhop of *Salisbury;* but in the midft of this defign, His late Majefty (King *Charles*) that knew the value of Sir *Henry Wottons* Pen) did by a perfwafive loving violence (to which may be added a promife of 500 *l.* a year) force him to lay *Luther* afide, and betake himfelf to write the Hiftory of *England*; in which he proceeded to write fome fhort Characters of a few Kings, as a foundation upon which he meant to build; but, for the prefent, meant to be more

E 4   large

large in the story of *Henry* the *sixth*, the Founder of that Colledge, in which he then enjoy'd all the worldly happiness of his present being ; but Sir *Henry* dyed in the midst of this undertaking, and the footsteps of his labours are not recoverable by a more than common diligence.

This is some account both of his inclination, and the employment of his time in the Colledge, where he seemed to have his *Youth* renewed by a continual conversation with that Learned Society, and a daily recourse of other Friends of choicest breeding and parts, by which that great blessing of a chearful heart was still maintained ; he being alwayes free, even to the last of his dayes, from that peevishness which usually attends Age.

And yet his mirth was sometimes damp'd by the remembrance of divers old Debts, partly contracted in his forreign Employments, for which his just Arrears due from the *King*, would have made satisfaction ; but, being still delayed with Cou.t-promises, and finding some decayes of health, he did (about two years before his death) out of a Christian desire, that none should be a loser by it, make his last *Will*; concerning which, a doubt still remains, whether it discovered more *holy wit*, or *conscionable policy :* But there is no doubt, but that his chief design was a *Christian* endeavour that his Debts might be satisfied.

And

And that it may remain as such a Testimony, and a Legacy to those that lov'd him, I shall here impart it to the Reader, as it was found writ with his own hand.

IN the Name of God Almighty and All-merciful, I Henry Wotton, Provost of His Majesties Colledge by Eaton, being mindful of mine own mortality, which the sin of our first Parents did bring upon all flesh, Do by this last Will and Testament, thus dispose of my self, and the poor things I shall leave in this World. My Soul, I bequeath to the Immortal God my Maker, Father of our Lord Jesus Christ, my blessed Redeemer, and Mediator, through his all-sole sufficient satisfaction for the sins of the whole World, and efficient for his Elect; in the number of whom, I am one by his meer grace, and thereof most unremoveably assured by his holy Spirit, the true Eternal Comforter. My Body I bequeath to the Earth, if I shall end my transitory dayes at, or near Eaton, to be buried in the Chappel of the said Colledge, as the Fellows shall dispose thereof, with whom I have liv'd (my God knows) in all loving affection; or if I shall dye near Boston Malherb, in the County of Kent, then I wish to be laid in that Parish Church, as near as may be to the Sepulchre of my good Father, expecting a joyful Resurrection with him in the Day of Christ.

After

After this account of his *Faith*, and this Sur-
render of his *Soul* to that God that infpir'd it ;
and this direction for the difpofal of his body ;
he proceeded to appoint that his *Executours*
fhould lay over his grave a Marble ftone, plain,
not coftly: And confidering that time moul-
* Juven. ders even Marble to duft; (for * *Monuments
themfelves muft die.*) therefore did he (waving
the common way) think fit rather to preferve
his name (to which the Son of *Sirac* advifeth
all men) by an ufeful *Apothegm,* then by a large
enumeration of his defcent or merits, (of both
which he might juftly |have boafted:) but, he
was content to forget them, and did chufe
onely this prudent, pious, Sentence, to difcover his Difpofition, and preferve his *Memory*.
'Twas directed by him, to be thus infcribed:

Hic jacet hujus Sententiæ primus Author.

DISPUTANDI PRURITUS, ECCLE-
SIARUM SCABIES.

Nomen aliàs quære.

Which may be Englifhed thus,

Here lies the firft Author of this Sentence.

THE ITCH OF DISPUTATION,
WILL PROVE THE SCAB OF
THE CHURCH.

Iuquire his name elfewhere.

And

And if any shall object (as I think some
have) That Sir *Henry Wotton* was not the
first Authour of this Sentence ; but, that this,
or a Sentence like it, was long before his time;
To him I answer, that *Solomon* sayes , *Nothing
can be spoken that hath not been spoken ; for there
is no new thing under the Sun.* But grant, that
in his various reading, he had met with this ,
or a like Sentence ; yet reason will perswade all
Readers to believe, That Sir *Henry Wotton*'s
mind was then so fix'd on that part of the Communion of *Saints* which is above, that an holy
Lethargy did surprize his *Memory.* For doubtlefs, if he had not believed himself to be the
first Authour of — what he said, he was too
prudent first to own, and then expose it to the
publick view, and censure of every *Critick*
(with which that Age abounded, and this
more.) And questionless, 'twill be Charity in
all Readers, to think his mind was then so fix'd
on Heaven, that a holy zeal did transport him;
and in this Sacred Extasie, his thoughts being
onely of the Church Triumphant, (into which
he daily expected his admission) Almighty God
was pleased to make him a *Prophet,* to tell the
Church Militant, (and particularly that part of
it in this Nation) where the weeds of contro-
vefie grow to be daily both more numerous, and
more destructive to humble Piety ; where men
have Consciences which boggle at Ceremonies, and scruple not to speak and act such sins

as

as the ancient humble Chriftians believed to be a fin to think ; where (as our Revered *Hooker* fayes) former *Simplicity*, and foftnefs of Spirit, is not now to be found ; becaufe *Zeal* hath drowned *Charity*, and *Skill Meeknefs*.) Thefe fad changes have proved this *Epitaph* to be a ufeful Caution unto us of this Nation ; and the fad effects thereof in *Germany* have prov'd it to be a mournful *Truth.*

This by way of Obfervation concerning his *Epitaph:* The reft of his *Will* followes in his own words.

Further, I the faid Henry Wotton, *do conftitute and ordain to be joynt Executors of this my laft* Will *and* Teftament, *my two Grand-Nephews,* Albert Morton, *fecond fon to Sir* Robert Morton *Knight, late deceafed, and* Thomas Bargrave, *eldeft fon to Dr* Bargrave, *Dean of* Canterbury, *Husband to my Right Vertuous and onely Neece. And I do pray the forefaid Dr.* Bargrave *, and Mr.* Nicholas Pey *, my moft faithful and chofen friends, together with Mr.* John Harrifon *one of the Fellowes of* Eaton Colledge, *beft acquainted with my Books and Pictures, and other Utenfils, to be Supervifors of this my laft* Will *and* Teftament. *And I do pray the forefaid Dr.* Bargrave, *and Mr.* Nicholas Pey, *to be Solicitors for fuch Arrearages as fhall appear due unto me from his Majefties Exchequer at the time of my death ; and to affift my fore-named* Execu-

Executors in some reasonable and conscientious satisfaction of my Creditours, and discharge of my Legacies now specified; or, that shall be hereafter added unto this my Testament, *by any Codicil or Schedule, or left in the hands, or in any Memorial with the aforesaid Mr.* John Harison. *And first, To my most dear Soveraign and Master of incomparable* Goodnes, (*in whose gracious opinion, I have ever had some portion, as far as the interest of a plain honest man) I leave four Pictures at large of those Dukes of* Venice, *in whose time I was there imployed, with their names written on the back side, which hang in my great ordinary Dining-room, done after the Life by* Edoardo Fialetto. *Likewise a Table of the* Venetian Colledge, *where Ambassadours had their Audience, hanging over the Mantle of the Chimney in the said Room, done by the same hand, which containeth a draught in little, well resembling the famous D.* Leonardo Donato, *in a time which needed a wise and constant man.* It' *The Picture of a Duke of* Venice *hanging over against the door, done either by* Titiano, *or some other principal hand long before my time.* Most humbly beseeching his Majesty, *that the said Pieces may remain in some corner of any of his Houses, for a poor Memorial of his most humble vassal.*

It' *I leave his said Majesty all the Papers and Negotiations of Sir* Nich. Throgmorton *Knight, during his famous imployment under* Queen Elizabeth, *in* Scotland *and in* France, *which contain*

tain divers *secrets of State, that perchance his Majesty will think fit to be preserved in his Paper-Office, after they have been perused and sorted by* Mr. *Secretary* Windebanck, *with whom I have heretofore, as I remember, conferred about them. They were committed to my disposal by Sir* Arthur Throgmorton *his son, to whose worthy memory I cannot better discharge my faith, then by assigning them to the highest place of trust.* It *I leave to our most Gracious and Vertuous Queen* Mary, Dioscorides, *with the Plants naturally colored, and the Text translated by* Matthiolo, *in the best Language of* Tuscany, *whence her said Majesty is lineally descended. for a poor token of my thankful devotion, for the honour she was once pleased to do my private study with her presence. I leave to the most hopeful Prince, the Picture of the elected and crowned Queen of* Bohemia, *his Aunt, of clear and resplendent vertues through the clouds of her Fortune. To my Lords* Grace of Canterbury *now being, I leave my Picture of Divine* Love, *rarely copied from one in the Kings Galleries, of my presentation to his Majesty: beseeching him to receive it as a pledge of my humble reverence to his great* Wisdom. And *to the most worthy* Lord Bishop *of* London, Lord high Treasurer *of* England, *in true admiration of his Christian simplicity, and contempt of earthly pomp; I leave a Picture of* Heraclitus *bewailing, and* Democritus *laughing at the world: Most humbly beseeching the said Lord Arch-*
bishop

shop his Grace, *and the Lord Bishop of* London, *of both whose favours I have tasted in my life time, to intercede with our most gracious Soveraign after my death, in the bowels of* Jesus Chrift, *That out of compassionate memory of my long Services (wherein I more studied the publick Honour, then mine own Utility) some Order may be taken out of my Arrears due in the Exchequer, for such satisfaction of my Creditors, as those whom I have Ordained Supervisors of this my last* Will *and* Teftament *shall present unto their Lordships, without their farther trouble: Hoping likewise in his Majesties most indubitable Goodness, that he will keep me from all prejudice, which I may otherwise suffer by any defect of formality in the Demand of my said Arrears.* To —— *for a poor addition to his Cabinet, I leave as Emblems of his attractive Vertues, and Obliging Nobleness, my great* Load-stone ; *and a piece of* Amber *of both kindes naturally united, and onely differing in degree of* Concoction, *which is thought somewhat rare.* Item, *A piece of* Chriftal Sexangular, *(as they grow all) grasping divers several things within it, which I bought among the Rhætian* Alps, *in the very place where it grew: recommending most humbly unto his Lordship, the reputation of my poor Name in the point of my debts, as I have done to the forenamed Spiritual Lords; and am heartily sorry, that I have no better token of my humble thankfulness*

to

to his honoured Person. It' I leave to Sir Francis Windebank, one of his Majesties principall Secretaries of State, (whom I found my great friend in point of Neceßity) the four Seasons of old Baßano, to hang near the Eye in his Parlour, (being in little form) which I bought at Venice, where I first entred into his most worthy Acquaintance.

To the above named Doctor Bargrave Dean of Canterbury, I leave all my Italian Books not disposed in this Will. I leave to him likewise my Viol de Gamba, which hath been twice with me in Italy, in which Country I first contracted with him an unremovable Affection. To my other Supervisor Mr. Nicholas Pey, I leave my Chest, or Cabinet of Instruments and Engines of all kinds of uses: in * the lower box whereof, are some fit to be bequeathed to none but so entire an honest man as he is. I leave him likewise forty pound for his pains in the solicitation of my

* In it were Italian locks, picklocks, screws to force open doors; and things of worth and rarity, that he had gathered in his foreign Travel.

Arrears, and am sorry that my ragged Estate can reach no further to one that hath taken such care for me in the same kind, during all my forreign Imployments. To the Library at Eaton Colledg I leave all my Manuscripts not before disposed, and to each of the Fellows a plain Ring of Gold, enameld black; all save the verge,

verge, *with this Motto within*, Amor unit omnia.

This is my last Will *and* Testament, *save what shall be added by a Schedule thereunto annexed.* Writt-n *on the first of* October, *in the present year of our Redemption* 16‹7. *And subscribed by my self, with the Testimony of these Witnesses.*

H. Wotton.

Nich. Oudert.
Geo. Lash.

ANd now, becaufe the mind of man is beft fatisfied by the knowledge of *E-vents*, I think fit to declare, that every one that was named in his Will, did gladly receive their Legacies; by which, and his moft juft and paffionate defires for the payment of his debts, they joyned in affifting the Overfeers of his Will; and by their joynt endeavours to the King (then whom none was more willing) confcionable fatisfaction was given for his juft debts.

The next thing wherewith I fhall acquaint the Reader, is, That he went ufually once a year, if not oftner, to the beloved *Bocton-hall*, where he would fay, he found both cure for all cares, by the company (which he called the living furniture) of that place: and, a reftorative of his ftrength, by the Connatu-ralnefs of that, which he called his *genial* aire.

He yearly went alfo to *Oxford*. But the Summer before his death he changed that for a journey to *Winchefter*-Colledge; to which School he was firft removed from *Bocton*. And as he returned from *Winchefter*, towards *Eaton* Colledge, faid to a friend, his Companion in that Journey; " How ufefull " was that advice of a Holy *Monk*, who perfwaded

" swaded his friend to perform his Custo` "ry devotions in a constant place; because in " that place, we usually meet with those ve- " ry thoughts which possessed us at our last " being there; And I find it thus far expe- " rimentally true; that, at my now being in " that School, and seeing that very place " where I sate when I was a boy, occasioned " me to remember those very thoughts of " my youth which then possessed me; sweet " thoughts indeed, that promised my grow- " ing years numerous pleasures, without " mixtures of cares; and those to be en- " joyed, when time (which I therefore " thought slow pac'd) had changed my *youth* " into *manhood*. But age and experience " have taught me, that those were but em- " pty hopes. And though my dayes have " been many, and those mixt with more " pleasures, than the sons of men do usual- " ly enjoy: yet, I have alwayes found it " true, as my *Saviour* did fore-tell, *Suffici-* " *ent for the day is the evil thereof*. Never- " theless, I saw there a succession of boyes " using the same recreations; and questionless " possessed with the same thoughts that then " possessed me. Thus one generation succeeds " another, both in their *lives, recreations, hopes,* " *fears, and deaths*.

After his return from *Winchester* (which was about nine Moneths before his death)

he

he fell into a dangerous *Fever*, which weakned him much; he was then alfo much troubled with an *Afthma*, or continual fhort fpitting, but that infirmity he feemed to overcome in a good degree by leaving Tobacco, which he had taken fomewhat immoderately: And about two moneths before his *death* (in *October* 1639.) he again fell into a *Fever*, which though he feem'd to recover, yet, thefe ftil! left him fo weak, that thofe common infirmities, which were wont like civil Friends to vifit him, and after fome fhort time to depart; came both oftner, and at laft took up their conftant habitations with him, ftill weakning his body; of which he grew dayly more fenfible, retiring oftner into his Study, and making many Papers that had paft his Pen, both in the dayes of his *youth* and *bufinefs*, ufelefs by fire. Thefe, and feveral unufual expreffions to his Friends, feemed to foretell his death, for which he feemed to thofe many friends that obferved him, to be well prepared, and ftill free from all fear, and chearful; (as feveral Letters writ in his bed, and but a few dayes before his death may teftifie.) And in the beginning of *December* following, he fell again into a *Quartan Fever*, and in the tenth fit, his better part, that part of Sir *Henry Wotton* which could not dye, put off Mortality with as much content and chearfulnefs, as humane frailty is capable of: he

be-

being in perfect peace with God and man.

And thus the *Circle* of his *Life*, (that *Circle* which began at *Bocton*, and in the *Circumference* thereof, did first touch at *Winchester-School*, then at *Oxford*, and after upon so many remarkable parts and passages in *Christendom*;) That *Circle* of his *Life*, was by *Death* thus closed up and compleated, in the seventy and second year of his *Age*, at *Eaton Colledge*, where (according to his Will) he now lies buried, dying worthy of his Name and *Family*, worthy of the love and favour of so many *Princes*, and Persons of eminent *Wisdom* and *Learning*, worthy of the trust committed unto him, for the Service of his *Prince* and *Country*.

And all Readers are requested to believe, that he was worthy of a more worthy Pen, to have preserved his Memory, and commended his Merits to the imitation of Posterity.

AN
ELEGIE
ON
Sir HENRY WOTTON,
WRIT
By Mr *ABRAM COWLEY*.

*W*Hat *shall we say, since* silent *now is he,*
Who when he spoke *all things woul'd* silent *be.*
Who had so many languages *in store,*
That only fame *shall speak of him in more.*
Whom England *now no more return'd must see:*
He's gone to Heaven, *on his* fourth *Embassie.*
On Earth he travail'd often, not to say
H'ad been abroad to pass loose time *away :*
For, in what ever land he chanc'd to come,
He read the men *and* manners : *bringing home*
Their Wisdom, Learning, *and their* Pietie,
As if he went to Conquer, *not to* see.
So well he understood the most and best
Of Tongues, *that* Babel *sent into the West :*

Spoke

Spoke them so truly, that he had (you'd swear)
Not only liv'd, but, been born every where.
Justly each Nations *speech to him was known :*
Who, for the World *was made, not us alone.*
Nor, ought the Language *of that man be less*
Who in his brest had all things to express :
We say that Learning's *endless, and blame* Fate
For not alowing life a longer date :
He did the utmost bounds of Knowledg *finde ;*
And found them not so large as was his minde :
But, like the brave Pellean youth *did mone :*
Because that Art *had no more* Worlds *then one.*
And, when he saw that he through all had past,
He dy'd, *least he should* Idle *grow at last.*

A. Cowley.

FINIS.

The LIFE

OF

Mr. *RICH. HOOKER*,

THE

AUTHOR of thofe Learned Books

OF THE

𝕷𝖆𝖜𝖘 𝖔𝖋 𝕰𝖈𝖈𝖑𝖊𝖘𝖎𝖆𝖘𝖙𝖎𝖈𝖆𝖑 𝕻𝖔𝖑𝖎𝖙𝖞.

Pfal. 145. 4.
One generation fhall praife thy works to another:

Prov. 2. 15.
The tongue of the wife ufeth knowledge rightly.

LONDON,
Printed by *Tho: Newcomb*, for *Rich: Marriot*,
fold by moft *Bookfellers*. M.DC.LXX.

To his very Worthy Friend Mr. *Iſaac Walton*, upon his Writing and Publiſhing the Life of the Venerable and Judicious Mr. *Richard Hooker.*

I.

HAyle, *Sacred Mother*, Britiſh Church, *all hayle!*
  From whoſe fruitful Loyns have ſprung
  Of Pious Sons ſo great a throng,
  That Heav'n t'oppoſe their force of ſtrength did fail:
And, let the mighty Conquerors, o're Almighty arms prevail;
How art thou chang'd from what thou wert a late,
  When deſtitute, and quite forlorn,
(And ſcarce a Child of thouſands, with thee left to mourn)
  Thy veil all rent, and all thy garments torn :
With tears thou didſt bewail thine own, and childrens fate:
  Too much (alas !) thou didſt reſemble then
  Sion *thy pattern ;* Sion, *in aſhes laid,*
   Deſpis'd, Forſaken, and betray'd;
  Sion, *thou doſt reſemble once agen :*
And rais'd, like her, the glory of the World art made.
  Threnes only to thee could that time belong,
But now thou art the lofty Subject of my Song.

Begin,

II.

Begin *my Verſe, and where the doleful Mother ſate,*
　(*As it in Viſion was to* Eſdras *ſhown*
　　Lamenting, with the reſt, her deareſt Son,
　(*Bleſt* C H A R L E S, *who his Forefathers has outgon,*
And to the Royal, join'd the Martyrs brighter Crown)
　Let a new City riſe, with beautious ſtate :
And, beautious let its Temple be, and beautiful the Gate !
　Lo ! how the Sacred Fabrick up does riſe !
　　The Architects ſo skilful All,
　　So grave, ſo humble, and ſo wiſe :
　　The Axes, and the Hammers noiſe
Is drown'd in ſilence, or, in numbers Muſicall !
　　'Tis up ; and, at the Altar ſtand
　　The Reverend Fathers ; as of Old,
　　With Harps. *and* Incenſe *in their hand :*
Nor, let the pious ſervice grow or ſtiff, or cold.
　　Th'inferiour Prieſts, the while,
　To Praiſe continually imploy'd, or Pray,
　　Need not the weary hours beguile,
Eneugh's the ſingle Duty of each day.
Thou thy ſelf, Woodford, *on thy humbler Pipe muſt play ;*
　And, tho but lately entred there,
　So gracious thoſe thou honour'ſt all appear,
　　So ready and attent to hear
An eaſie part, proportion'd to thy skill, may'ſt bear.

III.

　But where (alas !) where wilt thou fix thy choice ?
　　The Subjects are ſo noble all,
　　So great their beauties, and thy art ſo ſmall,

They'll

They'll judge, I fear, themselves disparag'd by thy voyce:
Yet try, and since thou canst not take
A name so despicably low,
But 'twill exceed what thou canst do,
Tho thy whole Mite thou away at once shouldst throw,
Thy Poverty a vertue make ;
And, what thou may'st Immortal live,
(Since Immortality thou canst not give)
From one, who has enough to spare, be ambitious to receive!
Of Reverend, and Judicious Hooker *sing ;*
Hooker, *does to th' Church belong,*
The Church, *and* Hooker *claim thy Song,*
And inexhausted Riches to thy Verse will bring :
So far, beyond it self, will make it grow,
That life, his gift to thee, thou shalt again on him bestow.

IV.

How great, blest Soul, must needs thy Glories be,
Thy Joyes how perfect, and thy Crown how fair,
Who mad'st the Church thy chiefest care ;
This Church, which owes so much to thee,
That all Her Sons are studious of thy memory ?
'Twas a bold work the Captiv'd to redeem,
And not so only, but th'Oppre(s'd to raise,
(Our aged Mother) to that due Esteem
She had, and merited in her younger dayes ;
When Primitive Zeal, and Piety,
Were all her Laws, and Policy :
And decent Worship kept the mean,
It's too wide stretch't Extreams between,
The rudely scrupulous, and extravagantly vain.

A 3

This

This was the work of Hookers *Pen;*
With Judgement, Candor, and such Learning writ,
Matter, and Words so exactly fit,
That, were it to be done agen,
Expected 'twould be, as its Answer hitherto has been.

RITORNATA.

To Chelsea, *Song; there, tell Thy Patrons Friend*
The Church is Hookers *Debtor :* Hooker *His;*
And strange 'twould be, if he should Glory miss,
For whom two such most powerfully contend.
   Bid him, chear up, the Day's his own :
      And, he shall never die
   Who after Seventy's past and gone,
   Can all th' Assaults of Age desie :
Is, master still, of so much youthful heat,
A Child, so perfect, and so sprightly to beget.

Bensted Hants.   *Sam: Woodford.*
   Mar. 10. 16⁶⁹⁄₇₀.

THE

THE LIFE
O F
Mr. RICHARD HOOKER.

The Introduction.

I Have been perfwaded, by a Friend whom I reverence, and ought to obey, to write The Life of RICHARD HOOKER, the happy Author of Five (if not more) of the Eight learned Books of the Laws of Ecclefiaftical Polity. And, though I have undertaken it, yet it hath been with fome unwillingnefs ; becaufe I forefee that it muft prove to me, and efpecially at this time of my Age, a work of much labour to enquire, confider, refearch, and determine what is needful to be known concerning him: For, I knew him not in his Life, and muft therefore not only look back to his Death, now 64 years paft ; but, almoft 50 years beyond that, even to his Childhood and Youth, and gather thence fuch Obfervations and Prognofticks, as may at leaft adorn, if not prove neceffary for the compleating of what I have undertaken.

This trouble I forefee ; and forefee alfo, that it is impoffible to efcape Cenfures ; againft which I

will

*will not hope my well-meaning and diligence can
protect me (for I consider the Age in which I live)
and shall therefore but intreat of my Reader a suspension of them, till I have made known unto him
some Reasons, which I my self would now fain believe do make me in some measure fit for this undertaking: and, if these Reasons shall not acquit
me from all Censures, they may at least abate of
their severity, and this is all I can probably hope
for.* My Reasons follow.

*About forty years past (for I am now past the
Seventy of my Age) I began a happy affinity with*
William Cranmer *(now with God) grand Nephew unto the great Archbishop of that name, a
Family of noted prudence and resolution; with him
and two of his Sisters, I had an entire and free
friendship: one of them was the Wife of Doctor*
Spencer, *a Bosom-friend, and sometime Com-pupil with Mr.* Hooker *in* Corpus-Christi Colledge *in* Oxford, *and after President of the same.
I name them here, for that I shall have occasion to
mention them in this following Discourse; as also*
George Cranmer *their Brother, of whose useful
abilities my Reader may have a more authentick
Testimony, than my Pen can purchase for him, by
that of our learned* Cambden, *and others.*

This William Cranmer, *and his two forenamed
Sisters, had some affinity, and a most familiar
friendship with M.* Hooker; *and, had had some part
of their Education with him in his house, when he
was Parson of* Bishops-Borne *near* Canterbury, *in
which*

which City their good father then lived. They had
(I say) a part of their Education with him , as
my self since that time a happy Cohabitation with
them ; and having some years before read part of
Mr. Hookers Works with great liking and satisfaction, my affection to them made me a diligent In-
quisitor into many things that concerned him ; as
namely, of his Person, his Nature, the management
of his Time, his Wife, his Family, and the Fortune
of him and his. Which inquiry hath given me
much advantage in the knowledge of what is now
under my consideration, and intended for the satisfaction of my Reader.

I had also a friendship with the Reverend Dr.
Usher, the late learned Archbishop of Armagh, and
with Dr. Morton, the late learned and charitable
Bishop of Durham ; as also with the learned John
Hales of Eaton-Colledge; and with them also
(who loved the very name of Mr. Hooker) I have
had many discourses concerning him : and from
them, and many others that have now put off Mortality, I might have had more Informations, if I
could then have admitted a thought of any fitness
for what by perswasion I have now undertaken. But,
though that full Harvest be irrecoverably lost, yet,
my Memory hath preserved some gleanings, and my
Diligence made such additions to them, as I hope
will prove useful to the completing of what I intend, In the discovery of which I shall be faithful,
and with this assurance put a period to my Introduction.

B THE

The Life.

IT is not to be doubted but that *Richard Hooker* was born at *Heavy-tree* near or within the Precincts, or in the City of *Exeter*; a City which may juftly boaft, that it was the Birth place of him, and Sir *Tho. Bodley*; as indeed the County may in which it ftands, that it hath furnifhed this Nation with Bifhop *Jewel*, Sir *Francis Drake*, Sir *Walter Raleigh*, and many others, memorable for their Valour and Learning. He was born ab ut the Year of our Redemption 1553, and of Parents that were not fo remarkable for their Extraction or Riches, as for their Virtue and Induftry, and Gods bleffing upon both; by which they were enabled to educate their Children in fome degree of Learning, of which our *Richard Hooker* may appear to be one fair teftimony; and that Nature is not fo partial, as alwayes to give the great bleffings of Wifdom and Learning, and with them the greater bleffings of Virtue and Government, to thofe only that are of a more high and honourable Birth.

His

His Complexion (if we may guefs by him at the age of Forty) was Sanguine, with a mixture of Choler; and yet, his Motion was flow even in his Youth, and fo was his Speech, never expreffing an Earneftnefs in either of them, but a Gravity futable to the Aged. And 'tis obferved (fo far as Inquiry is able to look back at th's diftance of Time) that at his being a School-boy he was an early Queftionift, quietly inquifitive *Why this was, and that was not, to be remembred? Why this was granted and that denied?* This being mixt with a remarkable Modefty, and a fweet ferene quietnefs of Nature, and with them a quick apprehenfion of many perplext parts of Learning impofed then upon him as a Scholar, made his Mafter and others to believe him to have an inward bleffed Divine Light, and therefore to confider him to a little wonder. For in that, Children were lefs pregnant, lefs confident, and more malleable, than in this wifer, but not better, Age.

This Meeknefs and conjuncture of Knowledge, with Modefty in his Converfation, being obferved by his Schoolmafter, caufed him to perfwade his Parents (who intended him for an Apprentice) to continue him at School, till he could find out fome means, by perfwading his rich Uncle, or fome other charitable perfon, to eafe them of a part of their care and charge; affuring them, that their fon was fo enriched

B 2   with

with the bleffings of Nature and Grace, that God feemed to fingle him out as a fpecial Inftrument of his Glory. And the good man told them alfo, that he would double his diligence in inftructing him, and would neither expect nor receive any other Reward, than the content of fo hopeful and happy an employment.

This was not unwelcome News, and efpecially to his Mother, to whom he was a dutiful and dear Child; and all Parties were fo pleafed with this propofal, that it was refolved fo it fhould be. And in the mean time his Parents and Mafter laid a foundation for his future happinefs, by inftilling into his Soul *the feeds of Piety,* thofe confcientious principles of *loving and fearing God;* of *an early belief that he knows the very fecrets of our Souls; That he punifheth our Vices, and rewards our Innocence; That we fhould be free from hypocrifie, and appear to man what we are to God, becaufe firft or laft the crafty man is catch't in his own fnare.* Thefe feeds of Piety were fo feafonably planted, and fo continually watered with the daily dew of Gods bleffed Spirit, that his Infant vertues grew into fuch holy habits, as did make him grow daily into more and more favour both with God and man, which with the great Learning that he did attain to, hath made *Richard Hooker* honour'd in this, and will continue him to be fo to fucceeding Generations.

This

This good Schoolmaster, whose Name I am not able to recover (and am sorry , for that I would have given him a better memorial in this humble Monument, dedicated to the memory of his Scholar) was very sollicitous with *John Hooker*, then Chamberlain of *Exeter*, and Uncle to our *Richard*, to take his Nephew into his care , and to maintain him for one Year in the University, and in the mean time to use his endeavours to procure an admission for him into some Colledge ; still urging and assuring him, that his Charge would not continue long , for the Lads Learning and Manners were both so remarkable, that they must of necessity be taken notice of ; and that doubtless God would provide him some second Patron , that would free him and his Parents from their future care and charge.

These Reasons, with the affectionate Rhetorick of his good Master, and Gods blessing upon both, procured from his Uncle a faithful promise, that he wou'd take him into his care and charge before the expiration of the Year following, which was performed by the assistance of the Learned *John Jewell*, who left, or was about the first of Queen *Maries* Reign, expell'd out of *Corpus-Christi* Colledge in *Oxford* (of which he was a Fellow) for adhering to the Truth of those Principles of Religion , to which he had assented in the dayes of her Brother and Predecessor *Edward* the Sixth ; and

B 3   he

he having now a juft caufe to fear a more heavy
punifhment than Expulfion, was forced, by for-
faking this, to feek fafety in another Nation;
and, with that fafety the enjoyment of that
Doctrine and Worfhip, for which he fuffer'd.

But the Cloud of that Perfecution and Fear
ending with the Life of Queen *Mary*, the Affairs of the Church and State did then look
more clear and comfortable; fo that he, and
with him many others of the fame judgement,
made a happy return into *England* about the firft
of Queen *Elizabeth*; in which Year, this *John
Jewell* was fent a Commiffioner or Vifitor of
the Churches of the Weftern parts of this
Kingdom, and efpecially of thofe in *Devon-
fhire*, in which County he was born, and then
and there he contracted a friendfhip with *John
Hooker*, the Uncle of our *Richard*.

In the fecond or third Year of her Reign, this
John Jewell was made Bifhop of *Salisbury*, and
there being alwayes obferved in him a willing-
nefs to do good, and to obliege his Friends, and
now a power added to it, *John Hooker* gave him
a Vifit in *Salisbury*, *and befought him for Charity's
fake to look favourably upon a poor Nephew of his,
whom Nature had fitted for a Scholar, but the
Eftate of his Parents was fo narrow, that they were
unable to give him the advantage of Learning;
and that the Bifhop would therefore become his Patron, and prevent him from being a Tradefman;*
for

for he was a Boy of remarkable hopes. And though the Bifhop knew men do not ufually look with an indifferent eye upon their own Children and Relations yet he affented fo far to *John Hooker*, that he appointed the Boy and his Schoolmafter fhould attend him about *Eafter* next following at that place, which was done accordingly; and then after fome Queftions and obfervations of the Boyes learning and gravity, and behaviour, the Bifhop gave his Schoolmafter a reward, and took order for an annual Penfion for the Boyes Parents. promifing alfo to take him into his care for a future preferment, which was performed; for about the Fifteenth Year of his age, which was *Anno* 1567, he was by the Bifhop appointed to remove to *Oxford*, and there to attend Dr. *Cole*, then Prefident of *Corpus-Chrifti* Colledge. Which he did; and Dr. *Cole* had (according to a promife made to the Bifhop) provided for him both a Tutor (wh'ch was faid to be the learned Dr. *John Reynolds*) and a Clerks place in that Colledge: which place, though it were not a full maintenance, yet with the contribution of his Uncle, and the continued Penfion of his Patron the good Bifhop, gave him a comfortable fubfiftence. And in this condition he continued unto the Eighteenth Year of his age, ftill increafing in Learning and Prudence, and fo much in Humility and Piety, that he feemed to be filled with the Holy Ghoft, and even like St. *John*

B 4 *Baptift,*

Baptist, to be sanctified from his Mothers womb, who did often bless the day in which she bare him.

About this time of his age he fell into a dangerous Sickness; which lasted two Months; all which tim his Mother, having notice of it, did in her hourly prayers as earnestly beg his life of God, as the Mother of St. *Augustine* did that he might become a true Christian; and their prayers were both so heard as to be granted. Which Mr. *Hooker* would often mention with much joy *and as often pray that he might never live to occasion any sorrow to so good a Mother, of whom he would often say, he loved her so dearly, that he would endeavour to be good even as much for hers, as for his own sake.*

As soon as he was perfectly recovered from this Sickness, he took a journey from *Oxford* to *Exeter*, to satisfie and see his good Mother, being accompanied with a Countreyman and Companion of his own Colledge, and both on foot; which was then either more in fashion, or want of money, or their humility made it so : But on foot they went, and took *Salisbury* in their way, purposely to see the good Bishop, who made Mr. *Hooker* and his Companion dine with him at his own Table; which Mr. *Hooker* boasted of with much joy and gratitude when he saw his Mother and Friends: And at the Bishops parting with him, the Bishop gave him good Counsel, and his Benediction, but forgot to give him money ; which when the Bishop had considered, he sent a Servant in all haste to call *Richard* back to him, and at *Richards* return, the Bishop said to him, *Richard, I sent for you back to lend you a Horse, which hath carried me many a Mile, and I thank God with much ease* ; and presently delivered into his hand a Walking-staff, with which he professed he had travelled through many parts of *Germany* ; and he said, *Richard, I do not give, but lend you my Horse ; be sure you be honest, and bring my Horse back to me at your return this way to* Oxford. *And I do now give you Ten Groats to bear your charges to* Exeter ; *and here is Ten Groats more, which I charge you to deliver to your Mother, and tell her, I send her a Bishops Benediction with it, and beg the continuance of her prayers for me. And if you bring my Horse back to me, I will give you Ten Groats more to carry you on foot to the Colledge, and so God bless you, good* Richard.

And this, you may believe, was performed by both Parties. But, alas! the next News that followed Mr. *Hooker* to *Oxford*, was, that his learned and charitable Patron had changed this for a better life. Which may be believed, for that as he lived, so he dyed, in devout meditation and prayer ; and in both so zealously, that it became a religious question, Whether his last Ejaculations, or his Soul, did first enter into Heaven?

And

And now Mr. *Hooker* became a man of sorrow and fear; of sorrow, for the loss of so dear and comfortable a Patron; and of fear, for his future subsistence: But Dr. *Cole* raised his spirits from this dejection, by bidding him go chearfully to his Studies, and assuring him he should neither want food nor rayment (which was the utmost of his hopes) for he would become his Patron.

And so he was for about nine months, and not longer; for about that time, this following accident did befall Mr. *Hooker.*

Edwin Sandys (then Bishop of *London,* and after Archbishop of *York*) had also been in the dayes of Queen *Mary* forced, by forsaking this, to seek safety in another Nation; where for some Years Bishop *Jewell* and he were Companions at Bed and Board in *Germany,* and where in this their Exile they did often eat the bread of sorrow; and by that means they there began such a friendship, as lasted till the death of Bishop *Jewell,* which was in *September* 1571. A little before which time, the two Bishops meeting, *Jewell* began a story of his *Richard Hooker,* and in it gave such a Character of his Learning and Manners, that though Bishop *Sandys* was educated in *Cambridge,* where he had obliged and had many Friends; yet his resolution was, that his Son *Edwin* should be sent to *Corpus-Christi* Colledge in *Oxford,* and by all means be Pupil to Mr. *Hooker,* though his

his Son *Edwin* was not then much yonger : for, the Bishop said , *I will have a Tutor for my Son that shall teach him Learning by Instruction, and Vertue by Example*; *and my greatest care shall be of the last. and* (*God willing*) *this* Richard Hooker *shall be the Man into whose hands I will commit my* Edwin. And the Bishop did so about twelve moneths, or not much longer after this resolution.

And doubtless as to these two a better choice could not be made; for Mr. *Hooker* was now in the nineteenth year of his age , had spent five in the University, and had by a constant unwearied diligence attained unto a perfection in all the learned Languages; by the help of which, an excellent Tutor, and his unintermitted Study, he had made the subtilty of all the Arts easie and familiar to him, and usefull for the discovery of such Learning as lay hid from common Searchers; so that by these added to his great Reason, and his Industry added to both, *He did not onely know more, of Causes and effects, but what he knew , he knew better then other men.* And with this Knowledge he had a most blessed and clear Method of Demonstrating what he knew, to the great advantage of all his Pupils, (which in rime were many) but especially to his two first, his dear *Edwin Sandys* , and his as dear *George Cranmer*, of which there will be a fair Testimony in the ensuing Relation.

This

This for his Learning. And for his Behaviour, amongſt other Teſtimonies this ſtill remains of him, That in four years, he was but twice abſent from the Chappel prayers; and that his Behaviour there was ſuch as ſhewed an awful reverence of that God which he then worſhipped and prayed to; giving all outward teſtimonies that his Affections were ſet on heavenly things. This was his Behaviour towards God; and for that to Man, it is obſervable that he was never known to be angry, or paſſionate, or extream in any of his Deſires; never heard to repine or diſpute with Providence, but by a quiet gentle ſubmiſsion and reſignation of his will to the Wiſdome of his Creator, bore the burthen of the day with patience; never heard to utter an uncomly word: and by this and a grave Behaviour, which is a Divine Charm, he begot an early Reverence unto his Perſon, even from thoſe that at other times, and in other companies, took a liberty to caſt off that ſtrictneſs of Behaviour and Diſcourſe that is required in a Collegiate Life. And when he took any liberty to be pleaſant, his Wit was never blemiſht with Scoffing, or the utterance of any Conceit that border'd upon, or might beget a thought of Looſeneſs in his hearers. Thus milde, thus innocent and exemplary was his Behaviour in his Colledge, and thus this good man continued till his death, ſtill increaſing in Learning, in Patience, and Piety.

In

In this nineteenth year of his age, he was *December* 24. 1573, admitted to be one of the twenty Scholars of the Foundation, being elected and so admitted as born in *Devon* or *Hantshire*, out of which Countries a certain number are to be elected in Vacancies by the Founders Statutes. And now, as he was much encouraged, so now he was perfectly incorporated into this beloved Colledg, which was then noted for an eminent Library, strict students, and remarkable Scholars. And indeed it may glory, that it had Cardinal *Poole,* Bishop *Jewel,* Doctor *John Reynolds,* and Doctor *Thomas Jackson* of that Foundation: The First, famous for his Learned Apology for the Church of *England,* and his Defence of it against *Harding.* The Second, for the learned and wise Menage of a publique Dispute with *John Hart* (of the *Romish* perswasion) about the Head and Faith of the Church, and then printed by consent of both parties. And, the Third, for his most excellent Exposition of the Creed, and other Treatises: All such as have given greatest satisfaction to men of the greatest Learning. Nor was this man more Noteworthy for his Learning, than for his strict and and pious Life, testified by his abundant love and charity to all men.

And in the year 1576. *Febr.* 23. Mr. *Hookers* Grace was given him for *Inceptor* of Arts, Doctor *Herbert Westphaling,* a man of note for Learning,

Learning, being then Vice-chancellour. And
the Act following he was compleated Master,
which was *Anno* 1577. his Patron Doctor *Cole*
being Vice-chancellour that year, and his dear
friend *Henry Savill* of *Merton Colledge* being
then one of the Proctors. 'Twas that *Henry
Savill*, that was after Sir *Henry Savill*, Warden
of *Merton Colledge*, and Provost of *Eaton*: He
which founded in *Oxford* two famous Lectures, and endowed them with liberal maintenance.

'Twas that Sir *Henry Savil*, that translated
and enlightned the History of *Cornelius Taci-
tus*, with a most excellent Comment; and enriched the world by his laborious and chargeable collecting the scattered pieces of S. *Chry-
sostome*, and the publication of them in one entire Body in Greek; in which Language he
was a most judicious Critick. 'Twas this Sir
Henry Savill, that had the happiness to be a
Contemporary, and familiar friend to Mr. *Hooker*; and let Posterity know it.

And in this year of 1577. He was admitted
Fellow of the Colledge; happy also in being
the Contemporary and Friend of Dr. *John Reynolds*, of whom I have lately spoken; and of
Dr. *Spencer*: both which were after, and successively, made Presidents of *Corpus-Christi*
Colledge; men of great Learning and Merit,
and famous in their Generations.

Nor was Mr. *Hooker* more happy in his Contemporaries

temporaries of his Time and Colledge, than in the Pupillage and Friendſhip of his *Edwin Sandys* and *George Cranmer*; of whom my Reader may note, that this *Edwin Sandys* was after Sir *Edwin Sandys*, and as famous for his *Speculum Europæ*, as his brother *George* for making Poſterity beholden to his Pen by a learned Relation and Comment on his dangerous and remarkable *Travels*; and for his harmonious Tranſlation of the *Pſalms of David*, the Book of *Job*, and other Poetical parts of Holy Writ, into moſt high and elegant Verſe. And for *Cranmer*, his other Pupil, I ſhall refer my Reader to the printed Teſtimonies of our learned Mr. *Cambden*, of *Fines Moriſon*, and others.

    " This *Cranmer*, whoſe Chriſten name was
" *George*, was a Gentleman of ſingular hopes,
" the eldeſt Son of *Thomas Cranmer*, Son of
" *Edmund Cranmer*, the Archbiſhops brother :
" he ſpent much of his youth in *Corpus-Chriſti*
" Colledge in *Oxford*, where he continued
" Maſter of Arts for many years before he re-
" moved, and then betook himſelf to Tra-
" vel, accompanying that worthy Gentleman
" Sir *Edwin Sandys* into *France*, *Germany*, and
" *Italy*, for the ſpace of three years ; and after
" their happy return he betook himſelf to an
" Imployment under a Privy Counſellour of
" note, for an unhappy undertaking, after
" whoſe Fall, he went in place of Secretary
             " with

" with Sir *Henry Killegrew* in his Embaffage in-
" to *France*: and after his death he was fought
" after by the moft Noble Lord *Mount-Joy*,
" with whom he went into *Ireland* where he
" remained untill in a battel againft the Re-
" bels, near *Carlingford*, an unfortunate wound
" put an end both to his Life, and the great
" Hopes that were conceived of him: he being
" then but in the 36 year of his age.

Betwixt Mr. *Hooker* and thefe his two Pupils, there was a facred Friendfhip, a Friendfhip
made up of Religious Principles, which increafed dayly by a fimilitude of Inclinations to the
fame Recreations and Studies; a Friendfhip
elemented in Youth, and in an Univerfity,
free from felf-ends, which the Friendfhips of
Age ufually are not: and in this fweet, this
bleffed, this fpiritual Amity they went on for
many years; and as the Holy Prophet faith,
fo *they took fweet counfel together, and walked in
the Houfe of God as Friends*. By which means
they improved it to fuch a degree of Amity as
as bordered upon Heaven; a Friendfhip fo
facred, that when it ended in this world, it
began in the next, where it fhall have no
end.

And, though this world cannot give any degree of Pleafure equal to fuch a Friendfhip: yet,
Obedience to Parents, and a defire to know the
Affairs, Manners, Lawes, and Learning of
other Nations, that they might thereby become

come the more ferviceable unto their own, made them put off their Gowns, and leave the Colledge and Mr. *Hooker* to his Studies, in which he was daily more affiduous: ftill, enriching his quiet and capacious Soul with the precious Learning of the Philofophers, Cafuifts, and Schoolmen ; and with them the foundation and reafon of all Laws, both Sacred and Civil: and with fuch other Learning as lay moft remote from the track of common Studies. And as he was diligent in thefe, fo he feemed reftlefs in fearching the fcope and intention of Gods Spirit revealed to Mankind in the Sacred Scripture: for the underftanding of which, he feemed to be affifted by the fame Spirit with which they were written: He *that regardeth truth in the inward parts*, making him to underftand *wifdom fecretly:* And the good man would often fay, that the Scripture was not writ to beget *Difputations*, and *Pride*, and *Oppofition* to *Government*; but, *Charity* and *Humility*, *Moderation*, *Obedience* to *Authority*, and peace to Mankind: of which vertues, no man did ever repent himfelf at his death. And, that this was really his judgment, did appear in his future writings, and in all the actions of his life: Nor was this excellent man a ftranger to the more light and airy parts of Learning, as *Mufick* and *Poetry*; all which he had digefted, and made ufeful: and of all which, the Reader will have a fair teftimony, in what will follow.

C   In

o by letter from AW of Oxon.

In the Year 1579. the Chancellor of the University was given to understand, that the publick *Hebrew Lecture* was not read according to the Statutes; nor could be, by reason of a distemper that had seiz'd the brain of Mr. *Kingsmill*, who was to read it; so that, it lay long unread, to the great detriment of those that were studious of that language: Therefore, the *Chancellor* writ to his *Vice-chancellor*, and the *University*, that he had heard such commendations of the excellent knowledge of Mr. *Richard Hooker* in that tongue, that he desired he might be procured to read it: And he did, and continued to do so, till he left *Oxford*.

Within three months after his undertaking this Lecture (namely in *October* 1579.) he was with Dr. *Reynolds*, and others expell'd his *Colledge*; and this Letter transcrib'd from Dr. *Reynolds* his own hand, may give some account of it.

To Sir *Francis Knolles*.

I *Am sorry, Right Honourable, that I am enforced to make unto you such a suit, which, I cannot move, but I must complain of the unrighteous dealing of one of our* Colledge; *who hath taken upon him against all Law and Reason, to expell out of our house, both me and Mr.* Hooker, *and three other of our Fellows, for doing that which by Oath we were bound to do. Our matter must be heard*
before

before the Bishop of Winchester, *with whom I do not doubt, but we shall find equity. Howbeit, forasmuch as some of our adversaries have said, that the* Bishop *is already forestalled and will not give us such audience as we look for; therefore I am humbly to beseech your Honour, that you will desire the* Bishop, *by your Letters, to let us have Justice; though it be with rigour, so it be Justice: our Cause is so good that I am sure we shall prevail by it. Thus much I am bold to request of your Honour for* Corpus Christ Colledge *sake, or rather for* Chrifts *sake; whom I beseech to bless you with daily encrease of his manifold gifts, and the blessed graces of his holy Spirit.*

London,
Octob. 9.
1579.

Your HONOURS
in Christ to command,
JOHN REYNOLDS.

This Expulsion was by Dr. *John* Barfoote, Chaplain to *Ambrose* Earl of *Warwick*, and then Vice-president of the Colledge: I cannot learn the pretended cause; but, that they were restor'd the same Month is most certain.

I return to Mr. *Hooker* in his *Colledge*, where he continued his studies with all quietness, for the space of three years; about which time, he enter'd into Sacred Orders, and was made Deacon and Priest; and, not long after, was appointed to preach at St. *Pauls Crofs*.

C 2   In

In order to which Sermon to *London* he came, and immediately to the *Shunamites houfe*; which is a Houfe fo called, for that, befides the Stipend paid the Preacher, there is provifion made alfo for his Lodging and Dyet two days before, and one day after his Sermon ; this houfe was then kept by *John Churchman* , fometimes a Draper of good Note in *Watling-ftreet*, upon whom Poverty had at laft come like an armed man, and brought him into a neceffitous condition; which, though it be a punifhment , is not alwayes an argument of Gods disfavour, for he was a vertuous man: I fhall not yet give the like teftimony of his Wife, but leave the Reader to judge by what follows. But to this houfe Mr. *Hooker* came fo wet, fo weary, and weatherbeaten, that he was never known to exprefs more paffion, than againft a Friend that diffuaded him from footing it to *London*, and for finding him no eafier an Horfe ; fuppofing the Horfe trotted, when he did not: And at this time alfo, fuch a faintnefs and fear poffeft him, that he would not be perfwaded two dayes quietnefs, or any other means could be ufed to make him able to preach his Sundayes Sermon ; but a warm Bed, and Reft, and Drink, proper for a Cold, given him by Mrs. *Churchman*, and her diligent attendance added unto it, enabled him to perform the office of the day, which was in or about the Year 1581.

And

And in this firſt publick appearance to the World, he was not ſo happy as to be free from Exceptions againſt a point of Doctrine deliver-ed in his Sermon, which was, *That in God there were two Wills, an Antecedent, and a Conſequent Will; his firſt Will, that all Mankind ſhould be ſa-ved; but his ſecond Will was, that thoſe only ſhould be ſaved, that did live anſwerable to that degree of Grace which he had offered, or afforded them.* This ſeemed to croſs a late Opinion of Mr. *Calvins*, and then taken for granted by ma-ny that had not a capacity to examine it, as it had been by him, and hath been ſince by Dr. *Jackſon*, and Dr. *Hammond*, and others of great Learning, who believe that a contrary Opinion trenches upon the Honour and Juſtice of our merciful God. How he juſtified this, I will not undertake to declare, but it was not excepted againſt (as Mr. *Hooker* declares in an Orational Anſwer to Mr. *Travers*) by *John Elmer*, then Biſhop of *London*, at this time one of his Audi-tors, and at laſt one of his Advocates too, when Mr. *Hooker* was accuſed for it.

But the juſtifying of this Doctrine did not prove of ſo bad conſequence, as the kindneſs of Mrs. *Churchmans* curing him of his late Di-ſtemper and Cold; for that was ſo gratefully ap-prehended by Mr. *Hooker*, that he thought him-ſelf bound in conſcience to believe all that ſhe ſaid; ſo that the good man came to be perſwa-ded by her, *that he was a man of a tender conſti-*

C 3   *tion,*

tion, and *that it was best for him to have a Wife, that might prove a Nurse to him ;* such an one as *might both prolong his life, and make it more comfortable ; and such a one she could and would provide for him, if he thought fit to marry.* And he not considering, that *the children of this world are wiser in their generation, than the children of light ;* but, like a true *Nathanael,* fearing no guile, because he meant none, did give her such a power as *Eleazar* was trusted with, when he was sent to choose a Wife for *Isaac ;* for even so he trusted her to choose for him, promising upon a fair Summons to return to *London,* and accept of her choice ; and he did so in that or the year following. Now the Wife provided for him, was her Daughter *Joan,* who brought him neither Beauty nor Portion ; and for her Conditions, they were too like that Wife's which is by *Solomon* compar'd to a *dripping house ;* so that he had no reason to *rejoyce in the Wife of his Youth,* but too just cause to say with the holy Prophet, *Woe is me that I am constrained to have my habitation in the tents of Kedar.*

This choice of Mr. *Hookers* (if it were his choice) may be wondred at ; but let us consider that the Prophet *Ezekiel* sayes, *There is a wheel within a wheel,* a secret Sacred wheel of Providence (especially in Marriages) guided by his hand, that *allows not the race to the swift,* nor *bread to the wise,* nor good wives to good men: and he that can bring good out of evil,
(for

(for Mortals are blind to this Reason) only knows why this blessing was denied to patient *Job*, to meek *Moses*, and to our as meek and patient Mr. *Hooker*. But so it was; and, let the Reader cease to wonder, for *Affliction is a Divine dyet*, which though it be not pleasing to Mankind, yet Almighty God hath often, very often imposed it as good, though bitter Physick to those children whose Souls are dearest to him.

And by this means the good man was drawn from the tranquillity of his Colledge, from that Garden of Piety, of Pleasure, of Peace, and a sweet Conversation, into the thorny Wilderness of a busie World, into those corroding cares that attend a married Priest, and a Countrey Parsonage, which was *Draiton Beauchamp* in *Buckinghamshire*, not far from *Alesbury*, and in the Diocese of *Lincoln*, to which he was presented by *John Cheny* Esquire, then Patron of it, the 9th of *December* 1584. where he behaved himself so as to give no occasion of evil, but (as St. *Paul* adviseth a Minister of God) *in much patience, in afflictions, in anguishes, in necessities; in poverty, and no doubt in long-suffering :* yet troubling no man with his discontents and wants.

And in this condition he continued about a year, in which time his two Pupils, *Edwin Sandys* and *George Cranmer*, took a journey to see their Tutor, where they found him with a Book

in

in his hand (it was the *Odes* of *Horace*) he being then like humble and innocent *Abel*, tending his small allotment of sheep in a common field, which he told his Pupils he was forced to do then, for that his servant was gone home to Dine, and assist his Wife to do some necessary houshold business. When his servant returned and released him, his two Pupils attended him unto his house, where their best entertainment was his quiet company, which was presently denied them, for *Richard was call'd to rock the Cradle*; and the rest of their welcome was so like this, that they staid but till next morning, which was time enough to discover and pity their Tutors condition; and having in that time remembred and pa aphrased on many of the innocent recreations of their younger dayes, and other like diversions, given him as much present comfort as they were able, they were forced to leave him to the company of his wife *Joan*, and seek themselves a quieter Lodging : But at their parting from him, Mr. *Cranmer* said, *Good Tutor, I am sorry your lot is fall'n in no better ground as to your Parsonage*; *and, more sorry that your Wife proves not a more comfortable Companion after you have wearied your self in your restless studies.* To whom the good man replied, *My dear* George, *If Saints have usually a double share in the miseries of this life, I that am none, ought not to repine at what my wise Creator hath appointed for me, but labour, as indeed I do daily, to submit mine*

mine to his Will, and possess my soul in patience, and peace.

At their return to *London*, *Edwin Sandys* acquaints his father. who was then Bishop of *London*, and after Archbishop of *York*, with his Tutors sad condition, and follicits for his removal to some Benefice that might give him a more comfortable subsistence ; which his father did most willingly grant him, when it should next fall into his power. And not long after this time, which was in the year 1585, Mr. *Alvie* (Master of the Temple) dyed, who was *a man of a strict Life, of great Learning, and of so venerable Behaviour, as to gain so high a degree of love and reverence from all men, that he was generally known by the name of* Father Alvie. At the Temple-Reading , next after the death of this *Father Alvie*, he the said -Archbishop of *York* being then at Dinner with the *Judges*, the *Reader*, and *Benchers* of that Society, met with a Condolement for the death of *Father Alvie*, an high commendation of his Saint-like life, and of his great merit both to God and man : and as they bewail'd his death, so they wish't for a like pattern of Virtue and Learning to succeed him. And here came in a fair occasion for the Bishop to commend Mr. *Hooker* to *Father Alvies* place, which he did with so effectual an earnestness, and that seconded with so many other Testimonies of his worth, that Mr. *Hooker* was sent for from *Draiton Beauchamp* to *London*, and there

the

the Maſterſhip of the Temple propoſed unto
him by the Biſhop, as a greater freedom from his
Countrey cares, and the advantage of a better
Society, and a more liberal Penſion than his
Countrey Parſonage did afford him. But theſe
Reaſons were not powerful enough to incline
him to a willing acceptance of it; his wiſh was
rather to gain a better Countrey living, where
he might *ſee Gods bleſſings ſpring out of the
Earth, and be free from Noiſe* (ſo he expreſt the
deſire of his heart) *and eat that bread which he
might more properly call his own in privacy and
quietneſs.* But, notwithſtanding this averſneſs,
he was at laſt perſwaded to accept of the Biſhops
proposal, and was by * Patent for Life, made
Maſter of the Temple the 17*th* of *March* 1585.
he being then in the **34**th year of his age.

** This
you may
find in
the Tem-
ple Re-
cords.*

William Ermſtead *was Maſter of the Temple at the Diſſolution of the Priory, and* dyed 2 Eliz.

Richard Alvey *Bat. Divinity*, Pat. 13 Febr. 2 Eliz. *Magiſter ſi-
ve Cuſtos Domûs & Eccleſiæ novi Templi*, dyed 27 Eliz.

Richard Hooker *ſucceeded that year by Patent* in terminis, *as* Alvey
had it, and he left it, 33 Eliz.

That year Dr. Balgey *ſucceeded* Richard Hooker.

And, here I ſhall make a ſtop; and, that the
Reader may the better judge of what follows,
give him a character of the Times, and Temper
of the people of this Nation, when Mr. *Hooker* had his admiſſion into this place, a place
which he accepted, rather than deſired; and
yet here he promiſed himſelf a **virtuous** quietneſs,

ness, that blessed Tranquillity which he alwayes prayed and labour'd for; that so he might in peace bring forth the fruits of peace, and glorifie God by uninterrupted prayers and praises: for this he always thirsted, and yet this was denied him. For his admission into this place, was the very beginning of those oppositions and anxieties, which till then this good man was a stranger to, and of which the Reader may guess by what follows.

In this character of the Times, I shall, by the Readers favour, and for his information, look so far back as to the beginning of the Reign of Queen *Elizabeth*, a time in which *the many pretended Titles to the Crown, the frequent Treasons, the Doubts of her Successor, the late Civil War, and the sharp Persecution that raged to the effusion of so much blood in the Reign of Queen* Mary, were fresh in the memory of all men; and, begot fears in the most pious and wisest of this Nation, lest the like dayes should return again to them, or their present posterity. And the apprehension of these dangers, begot a hearty desire of a settlement in the Church and State, believing there was no other probable way left to make them sit quietly under their own Vines and Fig-trees, and enjoy the desired fruit of their Labours. But, *Time,* and *Peace,* and *Plenty,* begot *Self-ends,* and these begot *Animosities, Envy, Opposition,* and *Unthankfulness* for those very blessings for which they lately thirsted, being
then

then the very utmoſt of their deſires, and even beyond their hopes.

This was the temper of the Times in the beginning of her Reign, and thus it continued too long; for thoſe very people that had enjoyed the deſires of their hearts in a Reformation from *Rome*, became at laſt ſo like the grave, as never to be ſatisfied; but were ſtill thirſting for more and more, neglecting to pay that Obedience, and perform thoſe Vows which they made in their dayes of adverſities and fear: ſo that in ſhort time, there appeared three ſeveral Intereſts, each of them fearleſs and reſtleſs in the proſecution of their deſigns; they may for diſtinction be called, The active *Romaniſts*, The reſtleſs *Non-conformiſts* (of which there were many ſorts) and, The paſſive *peaceable Proteſtant*. The Counſels of the firſt conſidered, and reſolved on in *Rome*: the ſecond in *Scotland*, in *Geneva*, and in divers ſelected, ſecret, dangerous Conventicles, both there, and within the boſom of our own Nation: the third pleaded and defended their Cauſe by eſtabliſht Laws, both Eccleſiaſtical and Civil; and if they were active, it was to prevent the other two from deſtroying what was by thoſe known Laws happily eſtabliſht to them and their Poſterity.

I ſhall forbear to mention the very many and dangerous Plots of the Romaniſts againſt the Church and State, becauſe what is principally intended in this digreſſion, is an account of the

Opinions

Opinions and Activity of the Non-conformists; against whose judgement and practice, Mr. *Hooker* became at last, but most unwillingly, to be ingaged in a Book-war; a War, which he maintained not as against an Enemy, but with the spirit of meeknefs and reafon.

In which number of Non-conformists, though fome might be fincere, well-meaning men, whofe *indifcreet Zeal* might be fo like *Charity*, as thereby to cover a multitude of their Errours; yet, of this party, there were many that were poffeft with a high degree of *fpiritual wickednefs*, I mean, with an innate reftlefs *pride*, and *malice*. I do not mean the vifible carnal fins of *Gluttony*, and *Drunkennefs*, and the like (from which good Lord deliver us) but, fins of a higher nature, becaufe they are more unlike God, who is the God of *love* and *mercy*, and *order*, and *peace*; and more like the *Devil*, who is not a *Glutton*, nor can be *drunk*, and yet is a Devil; but I mean thofe fpiritual wickedneffes of *malice* and *revenge*, and an *oppofition* to *Government*. Men that joyed to be the Authors of mifery, which is properly his work that is *the enemy and difturber of Mankind*; and, greater fins than *Gluttony* or *Drunkennefs*, though fome will not believe it. And of this party, there were alfo many, whom prejudice and a furious Zeal had fo blinded, as to make them neither to hear reafon, nor adhere to the wayes of peace. Men, that were the dregs of Mankind, whom *Pride* and *Self-conceit*, had made

made to overvalue their own pitiful, crooked wifdom fo much, as not to be afham'd to hold foolifh and unmannerly Difputes againft thofe men whom they ought to reverence ; and, thofe Laws which they ought to obey. Men, that labour'd and joyed to find out the faults , and to fpeak evil of Government ; and then, to be the Authors of Confufion. Men, whom Company, and Converfation, and Cuftom, had at laft fo blinded, and made fo infenfible that thefe were fins ; that, like thofe that perifht in the *gainfaying of Core*, fo thefe dyed without repenting of thefe *fpiritual wickednefjes :* of which the practifes of *Copinger*, and *Hacket* in their lives ; and, the death of them and their adherents, are God knows too fad examples ; and, ought to be cautions to thofe men that are inclin'd to the like *fpiritual wickednefjes.*

And in thefe Times which tended thus to Confufion , there were alfo many others that pretended a tendernefs of Confcience, refufing to take an Oath before a lawful Magiftrate ; and yet thefe men, in their fecret Conventicles, did covenant and fwear to each other, to be affiduous and faithful in ufing their beft endeavours to fet up the *Presbyterian Doctrine* and *Difcipline*; and, both in fuch a manner as they themfelves had not yet agreed on. To which end , there were many that wandred up and down, and were active in fowing Difcontents and Sedition , by venemous and fecret murmurings, and a difper-

fion

sion of scurrilous Pamphlets and Libels against
the Church and State, but especially against the
Bishops ; by which means, together with indiscreet Sermons, the common people became so
phanatick, as to believe *the Bishops to be Antichrift*, and the only obstructers of Gods Discipline ; and then given over to such a desperate
delusion, as to find out a Text in the *Revelation*
of *St. John,* that *Antichrift was to be overcome
by the Sword.*   So that those very men, that began with tender and *meek Petitions,* proceeded
to *Admonitions,* then to *Satyrical Remonstrances;*
and at last, having numbred who was not, and
who was, for their Cause, they got a supposed
certainty of so great a Party, that they durst
threaten *first the Bishops,* then *the Queen and Parliament* ; to all which they were secretly encouraged by the *Earl of Leicester,* then in great favour with Her Majesty, and the reputed Cherisher and Patron general of these pretenders to
Tenderness of Conscience; his design being, by
their means, to bring such an *odium* upon the
Bishops, as to procure an Alienation of their
Lands, and a large proportion of them for himself: which avaritious desire had so blinded his
reason, that his ambitious and greedy hopes had
almost put him into a present possession of *Lam-
beth-house.*

And to these undertakings, the Non-conformists of this Nation were much encouraged and
heightned by a Correspondence and Confedera-
cy

cy with that Brotherhood in *Scotland*; so that
here they became so bold, that * one told the
Queen openly in a Sermon, *She was like an unta-
med Heyfer, that would not be ruled by Gods people,
but obstructed his Discipline.* And in *Scotland* they
were more confident, for there * they declared
Her an *Atheist*, and grew to such an height, as
not to be accountable for any thing spoken
against Her, *nor for Treason against their own
King, if spoken in the Pulpit*; shewing at last
such a disobedience to Him, that His Mother
being in *England*, and then in distress, and in
prison, and in danger of death, the Church denied the King their prayers for her: and at another time, when He had appointed a day of
Feasting, the Church declared for a general Fast,
in opposition to His Authority.

To this height they were grown in both Nations, and by these means there was distill'd into
the minds of the common people such other
venemous and turbulent principles, as were inconsistent with the safety of the Church and
State: and these vented so daringly, that, beside the loss of life and limbs, they were forced
to use such other severities as will not admit of
an excuse, if it had not been to prevent Confusion, and the perillous consequences of it;
which, without such prevention, would have
been Ruine and Misery to this numerous Nation.

Marginal notes:

* Mr. *Dering*.

* Vide Bishop *Spots-woods* History of the Church of *Scotland*.

These

These Errours and Animosities were so remarkable, that they begot wonder in an ingenious *Italian*, who being about this time come newly into this Nation, writ scoffingly to a friend in his own Countrey, to this purpose, *That the Common people of* England *were wiser than the wisest of his wiser Nation ; for, here the very Women and Shop-keepers, were able to judge of Predestination, and determine what Laws were fit to be made concerning Church-government ; and then, what were fit to be obeyed or abolisht. That they were more able (or at least thought so) to raise and determine perplext Cases of Conscience, than the wisest of the most learned Colledges in* Italy. *That men of the slightest Learning, and the most ignorant of the Common people, were mad for a new* or Super- *or* Re-reformation *of Religion ; and that in this* they appeared like that man, who would never cease to whet and whet his knife, till there was no steel left to make it useful. And he concluded his Letter with this observation, *That those very men that were most busie in Oppositions, and Disputations, and Controversies, of finding out the faults of their Governors, had usually the least of* Humility *and* Mortification, *or of the* power *of* Godliness.

And to heighten all these Discontents and Dangers, there was also sprung up a generation of Godless men ; men that had so long given way to their own lust of delusion, and so highly opposed the blessed motions of his Spirit, and

D   the

the inward light of their own Confciences, that
they had thereby finned themfelves into a belief which they would, but could not believe ;
into a belief which is repugnant even to humane
Natu e (for the Heathens believe that there
are many gods) but thefe had fin'd themfelves
into a belief that there was no God; To, finding
nothing in themfelves but what was worfe than
nothing, began to wifh what they were not able
to hope for; that they fhould be like the beafts
that perifh: And wicked company (which is the
Atheifts Sanctuary, were fo bold as to fay fo,
though the worft of Mankind when he is left
alone at midnight, may wifh, but cannot then
think it a belief that there is no God. Into this
wretched, this reprobate condition, many had
then finned themfelves.

And now when the Church was peftered with
them, and with all thefe other Irregularities ;
when her Lands were in danger of Alienation,
her Power at leaft neglected, and her Peace torn
to pieces by feveral Schifms, and fuch Herefies
as do ufually attend that fin (for Herefies do
ufually out-live their firft Authors) when the
Common people feemed ambitious of doing
thofe very things that were attended with moft
dangers, that thereby they might be punifh'd,
and then applauded and pitied ; when they called the Spirit of oppofition a Tender Confcience, and complained of perfecution , becaufe
they wanted power to perfecute others ; when
                                           the

the giddy multitude raged, and became restless to find out misery for themselves and others; and the Rabble would herd themselves together, and endeavour to govern and act in spight of Authority. In this extremity of fear, and danger of the Church and State, when to suppress the growing evils of both, they needed a man of prudence and piety, and of an high and fearless fortitude, they were blest in all by *John Whitgift* his being made Archbishop of *Canterbury*; of whom Sir *Henry Wotton* (that knew him well, for he was his Pupil) gives this true Character: *That he was a man of Reverend and Sacred memory; and, of the primitive temper; such a temper, as when the Church by lowliness of Spirit did flourish in highest examples of Virtue.*

And though I dare not undertake to add to this excellent and true character of Sir *Henry Wotton*, yet I shall neither do right to this Discourse, nor to my Reader, if I forbear to give him a further and short account of the life and manners of this excellent man; and it shall be short, for I long to end this digression, that I may lead my Reader back to Mr. *Hooker*, where we left him at the *Temple*.

John Whitgift was born in the County of *Lincoln*, of a Family that was ancient, and noted to be both prudent, and affable, and Gentile by nature; he was educated in *Cambridge*, much of his Learning was acquired in *Pembroke Hall*,

D 2 (where

(where Mr. *Bradford* the Martyr was his **Tutor**)
from thence he was remov'd to *Peter-house*, from
thence to be Master of *Pembroke Hall*, and from
thence to the Mastership of *Trinity* Colledge:
About which time, the Queen made him Her
Chaplain and not long after Prebend of *Ely*,
and then Dean of *Lincoln* ; and having for many years past look't upon him with much reverence and favour, gave him a fair testimony of
both, by giving him the Bishoprick of *Wor-
cester*, and (which was not a usual favour) for-
giving him his First-fruits ; then by constituting
him Vice-president of the principality of *Wales*.
And having experimented his Wisdom, his Justice, and Moderation in the menage of Her affairs, in both these places ; She, in the 26*th* of
Her Reign, made him Archbishop of *Canterbury*, and not long after of Her Privy Council ,
and trusted him to manage all Her Ecclesiastical Affairs and Preferments. In all which Removes, he was like the Ark, which left a blessing upon the place where it rested ; and in all
his Imployments was like *Jehoida*, that did good
unto *Israel*.

These were the steps of this Bishops ascen-
sion to this place of dignity and cares ; in which
place (to speak Mr. *Cambdens* very words in
his Annals) *he devoutly consecrated both his
whole life to God, and his painful labours to the
good of his Church.* And yet in this place he
met with many oppositions in the regulation of
                                          Church-

Church-affairs, which were much difordered at his entrance, by reafon of the age and remifnefs of Bifhop *Grindall*, his immediate Predeceffor, the activity of the Non-conformifts, and their chief affiftant the *Earl* of *Leicefter*, and indeed by too many others of the like Sacrilegious principles. With thefe he was to encounter ; and, though he wanted neither courage, nor a good caufe, yet he forefaw, that without a great meafure of the Queens favour, it was impoffible to ftand in the breach that was made into the Lands and Immunities of the Church, or to maintain the remaining rights of it. And therefore by juftifiable facred Infinuations fuch as St. *Paul* to *Agrippa* (*Agrippa, believeft thou? I know thou believeft*) he wrought himfelf into fo great a degree of favour with Her, as by his pious ufe of it, hath got both of them a great degree of Fame in this World, and of Glory in that into which they are now entred.

His merits to the Queen, and Her favours to him were fuch, that *She called him Her little black Husband*, and *called his Servants Her Servants* : and She faw fo vifible and bleffed a fincerity fhine in all his cares and endeavours for the Churches, and for Her good, that She was fuppofed to truft him with the very fecrets of Her Soul, and to make him Her Confeffor ; of which She gave many fair teftimonies, and of which one was, that *She would never eat Flefh*

in Lent without obtaining a Licence from her lit-
tle black Husband: and would often say, *She*
pitied him because She trusted him, and had eased
Her self, by laying the burthen of all Her Clergy-
cares upon his shoulders , which he managed with
prudence and piety.

I shall not keep my self within the promised
Rules of brevity in this account of his Interest
with Her Majesty, and his care of the Churches
Rights, if in this digression I should enlarge to
particulars ; and therefore my desire is, that one
Example may serve for a Testimony of both.
And that the Reader may the better understand it , he may take notice, that not many
years before his being made Archbishop, there
passed an Act or Acts of Parliament, intending
the better preservation of Church-lands, by re-
calling a power which was vested in others to
Sell or Lease them by lodging and trusting the
future care and protection of them only in the
Crown : And amongst many that made a bad
use of this power or trust of the Queens , the
Earl of Leitester was one ; and the Bishop having
by his Interest with Her Majesty, put a stop to the
Earls sacrilegious designs, they two fell to a open
opposition before Her ; after which they both
quitted the Room, not friends in appearance ;
but the Bishop made a sudden and a seasonable
retu n to Her Majesty (for he found Her alone)
and spake to Her with great humility and reverence, and to this purpose.

I be-

I Beseech Your Majesty to hear me with patience, and to believe that Yours, and the Churches safety, are dearer to me than my Life ; but, my Conscience dearer than both : and therefore give me leave to do my Duty, and tell You, That Princes are deputed Nursing Fathers of the Church, and owe it a protection ; and therefore God forbid that You should be so much as Passive in her Ruines, when You may prevent it ; or that I should behold it without horrour and detestation, or should forbear to tell Your Majesty of the sin and danger of Sacriledge : And, though You and my self were born in an Age of Frailties, when the primitive piety and care of the Churches Lands and Immunities are much decayed ; yet (Madam) let me beg that you would first consider that there are such sins as Prophaneness and Sacriledge ; and, that if there were not, they could not have names in Holy Writ, and particularly in the New Testament. And I beseech You to consider, that though our Saviour said, He judged no man ; and to testifie it, would not judge nor divide the inheritance betwixt the two Brethren ; nor would judge the Woman taken in Adultery : yet, in this point of the Churches Rights he was so zealous, that he made himself both the Accuser, and the Judge, and the Executioner too, to punish these sins ; witnessed, in that he himself made the Whip to drive the Prophaners out of the Temple, overthrew the Tables of the Money-changers, and drove them out of it. And consider that it was St. Paul that said to those Christians of

D 4   his

his time that were offended with Idolatry, yet com-
mitted Sacriledge; Thou that abhorrest Idols,
dost thou commit Sacriledge?*Supposing(I think)*
Sacriledge the greater sin. This may occasion Your
Majesty to consider that there is such a sin as Sacriledge; *and to incline You to prevent the Curse that*
will follow it, I beseech You also to consider, that
Constantine *the first Christian Emperour, and*
Helena *his Mother; that King* Edgar, *and* Edward the Confessor, *and indeed many others of*
Your Predecessors, and many private Christians,
have also given to God, and to his Church, much
Land and many Immunities, which they might
have given to those of their own Families, and did
not : but, gave them as an absolute Right and
Sacrifice to God : *And, with these Immunities*
and Lands they have entail'd a Curse upon the
Alienators of them; *God prevent Your Majesty*
from being liable to that Curse.

And, to make You that are trusted with their pre-
servation, the better to understand the danger of it,
I beseech You forget not, that, besides these Curses,
the Churches Land and Power have been also en-
deavoured to be preserved, as far as Humane Rea-
son, and the Law of this Nation have been able to
preserve them, by an immediate and most sacred
Obligation on the Consciences of the Princes of this
Realm. For, they that consult Magna Charta, *shall*
find, that as all Your Predecessors were at their Co-
ronation, so You also were sworn before all the Nobi-
lity and Bishops then present, and in the presence
of

of God, and in his stead *to him that anointed* You, To maintain the Church-lands, and the Rights belonging to it ; *and this* testified *openly at the holy Altar, by laying* Your *hands on the Bible then lying upon it. And not only* Magna Charta , *but many modern* Statutes *have denounced a Curse upon those that break* Magna Charta : *A* Curse *like the* Leprosie, *that was* intail'd *on the* Jews ; *for, as that, so these* Curses *have and will cleave to the very* stones *of those buildings that have been consecrated to God ; and, the fathers* sin *of* Sacriledge, *will prove to be* intail'd *on his* Son *and* Family. *And now what account can be given for the breach of this* Oath *at the last great day, either by* Your Majesty, *or by me, if it be wilfully, or but negligently violated I know not ?*

And therefore, good Madam, *let not the late* Lords *Exceptions against the failings of some few* Clergy-men, *prevail with* You *to punish* Posterity, *for the Errors of this present Age ; let particular men suffer for their particular Errors, but let* God *and his Church have their right : And though I pretend not to Prophesie, yet I beg* Posterity *to take notice of what is already become visible in many Families,* That Church-land added to an ancient Inheritance, hath proved like a Moth fretting a Garment, and secretly consumed both : *Or like the Eagle that stole a coal from the* Altar, and thereby set her Nest on fire, which consumed both her young Eagles, and her self that stole it. *And though I shall forbear to speak reproachfully of*

Your

Your Father, yet I beg You to take notice, that a part of the Churches Rights, added to the vast Treasure left him by his Father, hath been conceived to bring an unavoidable Consumption upon both, notwithstanding all his diligence to preserve them.

And consider that after the violation of those Laws, to which he had sworn in Magna Charta, *God did so far deny him his restraining Grace, that as King* Saul *after he was forsaken of God, fell from one sin to another ; so he, till at last he fell into greater sins than I am willing to mention. Madam.* Religion is the Foundation and Cement of humane Societies: *and when they that serve at Gods Altar, shall be exposed to Poverty, then, Religion it self will be exposed to scorn, and become contemptible, as You may already observe in too many poor Vicaridges in this Nation. And therefore, as You are by a late Act or Acts of Parliament entrusted with a great power to preserve or waste the Churches Lands ; yet, dispose of them for* Jesus *sake, as the Donors intended ; let neither Falshood nor Flattery beguile You to do otherwise : but put a stop to Gods and the* Levites *portion (I beseech You) and to the approaching Ruines of his Church, as You expect comfort at the great day ; for,* Kings *must be judged ; Pardon this affectionate plainness, my most dear Soveraign, and let me beg still to be continued in Your favour, and the Lord still continue You in his.*

The

The Queens patient hearing this affectionate Specy, and her future Care to preserve the Churches Rights, which till then had been neglected, may appear a fair Testimony, that he made hers and the Churches Good the chiefest of his Cares, and that she also thought so. And of this there were such daily testimonies given, as begot betwixt them so mutual a joy and confidence, that they seemed born to believe and do good to each other; she not doubting his Piety to be more than all his Opposers, which were many ; nor his Prudence equal to the chiefest of her Council, who were then as remarkable for active Wisdome , as those dangerous Times did require, or this Nation did ever enjoy. And in this condition he continued twenty years; in which time he saw some Flowings, but many more Ebbings of her Favour towards all men that opposed him, especially the *Earl of Leicester:* so that God seemed still to keep him in her Favour, that he might preserve the remaining Church Lands and Immunities from Sacrilegious Alienations. And this Good man deserved all the Honour and Power with which she trusted him ; for he was a pious man, and naturally of Noble and Grateful Principles : he eased her of all her Church-cares by his wife Menage of them ; he gave her faithful and prudent Counsels in all the Extremities and Dangers of her Temporal Affairs, which were many; he lived to be

the

the Chief Comfort of her Life in her Declining age, to be then moſt frequently with her,
and her Aſſiſtant at her private Devotions, to
be the greateſt Comfort 'of her Soul upon her
Death-bed, to be preſent at the Expiration of
her laſt Breath, and to behold the cloſing of
thoſe Eyes that had long looked upon him
with Reverence and Affection. And let this
alſo be added, that he was the Chief Mourner
at her ſad Funeral ; nor let this be forgotten,
that within a few hours after her death, he
was the happy Proclaimer, that King _James_
(her peaceful Succeſſour) was Heir to the
Crown.

Let me beg of my Reader to allow me to
ſay a little, and but a little, more of this good
Biſhop, and I ſhall then preſently lead him back
to Mr. _Hooker_ ; and, becauſe I would haſten, I
will mention but one part of the Biſhops Charity and Humility, but this of both : He built
a large Almes-houſe near to his own Palace at
Croyden in _Surry_, and endowed it with Maintenance for a Maſter and twenty eight poor
Men and Women ; which he viſited ſo often,
that he knew their Names and Diſpoſitions ,
and was ſo truly humble, that he called them
Brothers and Siſters : and whenſoever the
Queen deſcended to that lowlines to dine with
him at his Palace in _Lambeth_, (which was very
often) he would uſually the next day ſhew the
like lowlineſs to his poor Brothers and Siſters

at

at *Croydon*, and dine with them at his Hofpital; at which time, you may believe, there was Joy at the Table. And at this place he built alfo a fair Free-School, with a good Accommodation and Maintenance for the Mafter and Scholars; Which gave juft occafion for *Boyfe Sifi*, then Embaffadour for the French King, and Refident here, at the Bifhops death to fay, *The Bifhop had publifhed many learned Books, but a Free-fchool to train up Youth, and an Hofpital to lodge and maintain aged and poor People, were the beft Evidences of Chriftian Learning that a Bifhop could leave to Pofterity*. This good Bifhop lived to fee King *James* fettled in Peace, and then fell fick at his Palace in *Lambeth*; of which when the King had notice, he went to vifit him, and found him in his Bed in a declining condition, and very weak; and after fome fhort difcourfe betwixt them, the King, at his departure affured him, *He had a great Affection for him, and a very high value for his Prudence and Vertues, and would indeavour to beg his life of God*. To which the good Bifhop replied, *Pro Ecclefia Dei, Pro Ecclefia Dei*. which were the laft words he ever fpake; therein teftifying, that as in his Life, fo at his Death, his chiefeft care was of Gods Church.

This *John Whitgift* was made Archbifhop in the year 1583. In which bufie place, he continued twenty years and fome moneths; and in which time, you may believe, he had many Try-als

als of his Courage and Patience; but his Motto was, *Vincit, qui patitur.*

And he made it good. Many of his many Trials were occasioned by the then powerful *Earl of Leicester*, who did still (but secretly) raise and cherish a Faction of Non-conformists to oppose him; especially one *Thomas Cartwright*, a man of noted Learning, sometime Contemporary with the Bishop in *Cambridge*, and of the same Colledge, of which the Bishop had been Master; in which place there began some Emulations (the particulars I forbear) and at last open and high Oppositions betwixt them; and in which you may believe Mr. *Cartwright* was most faulty, if his Expulsion out of the University can incline you to it.

And in this discontent after the Earls death (which was 1588) Mr. *Cartwright* appeared a chief Cherisher of a Party that were for the *Geneva* Church-government; and to effect it, he ran himself into many dangers both of Liberty and Life; appearing at the last to justifie himself and his Party in many Remonstrances, which he caused to be printed, and to which the Bishop made a first Answer, and *Cartwright* replyed upon him; and then the Bishop having rejoyned to his first Reply, Mr. *Cartwright* either was, or was perswaded to be, satisfied: for he wrote no more, but left the Reader to be judge which had maintained their

Cause

Caufe with moft Charity and Reafon. After fome filence, Mr. *Cartwright* received from the Bifhop many perfonal Favours, and retired himfelf to a more private Living, which was at *Warwick*, where he was made Mafter of an Hofpital, and lived quietly, and grew rich, and where the Bifhop gave him a Licence to Preach, upon prom fes not to meddle with Controverfies, but incline his Hearers to Piety and Moderation; and this Promife he kept during his Life, which ended 1602, the Bifhop furviving him but fome few moneths: each, ending his daies in perfect Charity with the other.

And now after this long Digreffion made for the Information of my Reader concerning what follows, I bring him back to venerable Mr. *Hooker*, where we left him in the *Temple*, and where we fhall find him as deeply engaged in a Controverfie with *Walter Trevers*, a Friend and Favorite of Mr. *Cartwrights*, as the Bifhop had ever been with Mr. *Cartwright* himfelf; and of which I fhall proceed to give this following account.

And firft this; That though the Pens of Mr. *Cartwright* and the Bifhop were now at reft, yet there was fprung up a new Generation of reftlefs men, that by Company and Clamours became poffeft of a Faith which they ought to have kept to themfelves, but could not; men that were become pofitive in afferting,

ing, *That a Papeſt cannot be ſaved*: inſomuch that about this time, at the Execution of the Queen of Scots, the Biſhop that preached her Funeral Sermon (which was Doctor *Howland*, then Biſhop of *Peterborough*) was reviled for not being poſitive for her Damnation. And beſide this Boldneſs of their becoming Gods, ſo far as to ſet limits to his Mercies; there was not onely one *Martin Mar-prelate*, but other venemous Books daily printed and diſperſed; Books that were ſo abſurd and ſcurrilous, that the graver Divines diſdained them an Anſwer. And yet theſe were grown into high eſteem with the Common people, till *Tom Naſh* appeared againſt them all, who was a man of a ſharp wit, and the Maſter of a ſcoffing Satyrical merry Pen, which he imployed to diſcover the Abſurdities of thoſe blind malitious ſenſleſs Pamphlets, and Sermons as ſenſleſs as they; *Naſh* his Anſwer being like his Books, which bore theſe Titles, *An Almond for a Parrot. A Fig for my God-ſon. Come crack me this Nut*, and the like: ſo that his merry Wit made ſuch a diſcovery of their Abſurdities, as (which is ſtrange) he put a greater ſtop to theſe malicious Pamphlets, than a much wiſer man had been able.

And now the Reader is to take notice, That at the Death of *Father Alvie*, who was Maſter of the *Temple*, this *Walter Travers* was Lecturer

rer there for the Evening Sermons, which he preach'd with great approbation, especially of the younger Gentlemen of that Society; and for the most part approved by Mr. *Hooker* himself, in the midst of their oppositions. For he continued Lecturer a part of his time, Mr. *Travers* being indeed a man of a Competent Learning, of a winning Behaviour, and of a blameless Life. But he had taken Orders by the Presbytery in *Antwerp,* (and with them some opinions, that could never be eradicated) and if in any thing he was transported, it was in an extreme desire to set up that Government in this Nation: For the promoting of which, he had a correspondence with *Theodore Beza* at *Geneva,* and others in *Scotland*; and was one of the chiefest assistants to Mr. *Cartwright* in that Design.

Mr. *Travers* had also a particular hope to set up this Government in the *Temple,* and to that end used his endeavours to be Master of it, and his being disappointed by Mr. *Hookers* admittance, proved some occasion of opposition betwixt them, in their Sermons. Many of which were concerning the Doctrine, and Ceremonies of this Church: Insomuch that, as Saint *Paul* withstood Saint *Peter* to his face, So did they, for as one hath pleasantly exprest it, *The Forenoon Sermon spake Canterbury, and the Afternoons, Geneva.*

In these Sermons there was little of bitter-

E   ness,

ness, but each party brought all the Reasons he was able to prove his Adversaries Opinion erroneous. And thus it continued a long time, till the Oppositions became so visible, and the Consequences so dangerous, especially in that place, that the prudent Archbishop put a stop to Mr. *Travers* his Preaching by a positive Prohibition: Against which Mr. *Travers* Appeal'd and Petition'd Her Majesties Privy Council to have it recalled: and where he met with many assisting Friends; but they were not able to prevail with or against the Arch-bishop, whom the Queen had intrusted with all Church-power: and he had received so fair a Testimony of Mr. *Hookers* Principles, and of his Learning and Moderation, that he withstood all Sollicitations. But the denying this Petition of Mr. *Travers* was unpleasant to divers of his Party; and, the Reasonableness of it became at last to be so magnified by them and many others of that party, as never to be answered; so that intending the Bishops and Mr. *Hookers* disgrace, they procured it to be privately printed, and scattered abroad: and then Mr. *Hooker* was forced to appear publickly, which he did, and Dedicated it to the Archbishop; and it proved so full an Answer, an answer that had in it so much of clear Reason, and writ with so much Meekness and Majesty of Style, that the Bishop began to wonder at the Man, to rejoyce that he had appeared in

his

his Caufe, and difdained not earneftly to beg his Friendfhip, even a familiar Friendfhip, with a man of fo much *quiet Learning* and *Humility.*

To enumerate the many particular points, in which Mr. *Hooker* and Mr. *Travers* diffented, (all or moft of which, I have feen written) would prove at leaft tedious; and therefore, I fhall impofe upon my Reader no more then two, which fhall immediately follow, and by which he may judge of the reft.

Mr. *Travers* excepted againft Mr. *Hooker*, for that in one of his Sermons he declared, *That the affurance of what we believe by the Word of God, is not to us fo certain as that which we perceive by fenfe.* And Mr. *Hooker* confeffeth he faid fo; and endeavours to juftifie it by the Reafons following.

Firft, I taught, That the things which God promifes in his Word are furer than what we touch, handle or fee; but are we fo fure and certain of them? if we be, why doth God fo often prove his Promifes to us, as he doth, by Arguments drawn from our fenfible Experience? For we muft be furer of the Proof than of the things Proved; otherwife it is no Proof. For Example: *How is it that many men looking on the Moon at the fame time, every one knoweth it to be the Moon, as certainly as the other doth: but many believing one and the fame Promife, have not all one and the fame Fulnefs of Perfwafion? For how falleth it out, that men being affured of any thing by Senfe, can*

E 2 *be*

be no surer of it than they are; when as the strong-
est in Faith that liveth upon the Earth, hath al-
wayes need to labour, strive and pray, that his
Assurance concerning Heavenly and Spiritu-
al things may grow, increase, and be aug-
mented?

The Sermon that gave him the cause of this
his Justification makes the Case more plain, by
declaring *that there is besides this Certainty of*
Evidence, a Certainty of Adherence: in which
having most excellently demonstrated what the
Certainty of Adherence is, he makes this comfortable use of it, *Comfortable* (he sayes) *as to*
weak Believers, who suppose themselves to be
faithless, not to believe, when notwithstanding
they have their Adherence ; *the Holy Spirit hath*
his private operations, *and worketh secretly in*
them, and effectually too, though they want the in-
ward Testimony of it.

Tell this to a man that hath a mind too
much dejected by a sad sense of his sin ; to one
that by a too severe judging of himself, concludes that he wants Faith, because he wants
the comfortable Assurance of it ; and his Answer will be, *Do not perswade me against my*
knowledge, against what I finde and feel in my
self; I do not, I know, I *do not believe.* (Mr.
Hookers own words follow) *Well then, to favour*
such men a little in their weakness, Let that be
granted which they do imagine ; be it that they
adhere not to Gods Promises, but are faithless and
with-

without belief; but are they not grieved for their unbelief? they confess they are; do they not wish it might, and also strive that it may be otherwayes? we know they do; whence cometh this, but from a secret Love and Liking that they have of those things believed? For, no man can love those things which in his own opinion are not; *and, if they think those things to be, which they shew they love when they desire to believe them; then must it be that by desiring to believe, they prove themselves true believers; For,* without Faith no man thinketh that things believed are: *which argument all the Subtilties of infernal powers will never be able to dissolve.* This is an abridgement of part of the Reasons he gives for his Justification of this his Opinion for which he was excepted against by Mr. *Travers.*

Mr. *Hooker* was also accused by Mr. *Travers,* for that he in one of his Sermons had declared, that *he doubted not but that God was merciful to many of our fore-fathers living in Popish Superstition, for as much as they Sinned ignorantly:* and Mr. *Hooker* in his answer professeth it to be his Judgment, and declares his Reasons for this Charitable opinion to be as followeth.

But first he states the question about *Justification* and *Works,* and how the *Foundation of Faith is overthrown;* and then he proceeds to discover that way which *Natural men* and some others have mistaken to be the way by which
E 3   they

they hope to attain true and everlasting happiness; and having discovered the mistaken, he proceeds to direct to that True way, by which and no other, everlasting life and blessedness is attainable; and, these two wayes he demonstrates thus: (they be his own words that follow) "That, the way of Nature, This, the way "of Grace; the end of that way, Salvation me-"rited, presupposing the righteousness of mens "works; their Righteousness, a Natural ability "to do them; that ability, the goodness of God "which created them in such perfection. But the "end of this way, Salvation bestowed upon men "as a gift: presupposing not their righteousness, "but the forgiveness of their Unrighteousness, "Justification; their Justification, not their "Natural ability to do good, but their hearty "Sorrow for not doing, and unfeigned belief in "him for whose sake not doers are accepted, which "is their vocation; their Vocation, the Election "of God, taking them out of the number of lost "Children; their Election a Mediator in whom "to be elected; this mediation inexplicable mer-"cy; this mercy, supposing their misery for whom "he vouchsafed to dye, and make himself a Me-"diator.

And he also declareth, There is no meritorious cause for our Justification but Christ, no effectual but his Mercy; and sayes also, We deny the Grace of our Lord Jesus Christ, we abuse, disanul, and annihilate the benefit of his Passion, if

by

by a proud imagination we believe we can merit everlasting life, or can be worthy of it. This belief (he declareth) is to deftroy the very effence of our Juftification, and he makes all opinions that border upon this, to be very dangerous. *Yet neverthelefs,* (and for this he was accufed) ' *Confidering how many vertuous* ' *and juft men, how many Saints and Martyrs* ' *have had their dangerous opinions , amongft* ' *which this was one, that they hoped to make God* ' *fome part of amends by voluntary punifhments* ' *which they laid upon themfelves* ; becaufe by ' this or the like erroneous opinions which do ' by confequence overthrow the merits of ' Chrift , fhall man.be fo bold as to write on ' their Graves, *fuch men are damned, there is for* ' *them no Salvation ?* St. Auftin faies, *errare pof-* ' *fum, Hæreticus effe nolo.* And except we put ' a difference betwixt them that err Ignorant- ' ly, and them that Obftinately perfift in it , ' how is it poffible that any man fhould hope to ' be faved ; give me a Pope or a Cardinal , ' whom great afflictions have made to know ' himfelf , whofe heart God hath touched with ' true forrow for all his Sins, and filled with a ' Love of Chrift and his Gofpel, whofe eyes ' are willingly open to fee the truth, and his ' mouth ready to renounce all errour, this one ' opinion of merit excepted, which he thinketh ' God will require at his hands, and becaufe he ' wanteth, trembleth, and is difcouraged, and

yet

' yet can fay, *Lord cleanfe me from all my fe-*
' *cret fins,* fhall I think becaufe of this or a like
' errour fuch men touch not fo much as the
' Hem of Chrifts Garment; if they do, where-
' fore fhould I doubt but that vertue may pro-
' ceed from Chrift to fave them ? no, I will not
' be afraid to fay to fuch a one, *you err in your*
' *opinion, but be of good comfort, you have to do*
' *with a merciful God who will make the beft of*
' *that little which you hold well and not with a cap-*
' *tious Sophifter, who gathereth the worft out of*
' *every thing in which you are miftaken.*

But it will be faid, *The admittance of Merit*
in any degree, overthroweth the foundation, exclu-
deth from the hope of mercy, from all poffibility
of Salvation. (And now Mr. *Hookers* own
words follow.)

'What though they hold the truth fincerely
' in all other parts of Chriftian Faith; although
' they have in fome meafure all the Vertues and
' Graces of the Spirit ? although they have
' all other tokens of Gods Children in them; al-
' though they be far from having any proud o-
' pinion that they fhall be faved by the wor-
' thinefs of their deeds; although the onely
' thing that troubleth and molefteth them be
' a little too much dejection, fomewhat too
' great a fear arifing from an erroneous con-
' ceit, that God will require a worthinefs in
' them, which they are grieved to finde want-
' ing in themfelves ? although they be not ob-
ftinate

'ftinate in this opinion? although they be wil-
'ling and would be glad to forfake it, if any one
'reafon were brought fufficient to difproye it?
'although the onely caufe why they do not
'forfake it ere they dye, be their Ignorance
'of that means by which it might be difproved?
'although the caufe why the Ignorance in this
'point is not removed, be the want of know-
'ledge in fuch as fhould be able, and are not
'to remove it; *Let me dye* (fayes Mr. *Hook-*
er) *if it be ever proved, that fimply an Errour*
doth exclude a Pope or Cardinal in fuch a cafe ut-
terly from hope of life. Surely I muft confefs,
that if it be an Errour to think that God may be
mercifull to fave men even when they err; my
greateft comfort is my error: were it not for
the love I bear to this error, I would never wifh
to fpeak or to live.

I was willing to take notice of thefe two
points, as fuppofing them to be very material;
and that as they are thus contracted, they may
prove ufeful to my Reader; as alfo for that the
anfwers be arguments of Mr. *Hookers* great and
clear reafon, and equal Charity. Other exceptions were alfo made againft him, as, *That he*
prayed before and not after his Sermons; that in
his Prayers he named Bifhops; that he kneeled both
when he prayed and when he received the Sacra-
ment, and (fayes Mr. *Hooker* in his defence) *other*
exceptions fo like thefe, as but to name, I fhould
have thought a greater fault then to commit them.
And

And 'tis not unworthy the noting, that in the manage of so great a controversie, a sharper reproof than this, and one like it, did never fall from the happy pen of this Humble man. That like it was upon a like occasion of exceptions, to which his answer was, *Your next argument consists of railing and of reasons ; to your Railing, I say nothing, to your Reasons, I say what follows.* And I am glad of this fair occasion, to testifie the Dove-like temper of this meek, this matchless man ; and doubtless if Almighty God had blest the Dissenters from the Ceremonies and Discipline of this Church, with a like measure of Wisdom and Humility, instead of their pertinacious zeal, then Obedience and Truth had kissed each other ; then Peace and Piety had flourished in our Nation, and this Church and state had been blest like *Jerusalem* that is at unity with it self ; But this can never be expected, till God shall bless the common people with a belief that Schism is a Sin, and *That there may be offences taken which are not given,* and, *That Laws are not made for private men to dispute, but to Obey.*

And this also may be worthy of noting, That these Exceptions of Mr. *Travers* against Mr. *Hooker,* were the cause of his Transcribing several of his Sermons, which we now see printed with his Books ; of his Answer to Mr. *Travers,* his Supplication, and of his most learned and useful discourse of *Justification* of *Faith*

Faith and *Works*; and by their Tranfcription they fell into the hands of others, and have been thereby preferved from being loft, as too many of his other matchlefs writings were, and from thefe I have gathered many obfervations in this Difcourfe of his Life.

After the publication of his Anfwer to the Petiton of Mr. *Travers*, Mr. *Hooker* grew dayly into greater repute with the moft learned and wife of the Nation; but it had a contrary ef-fect in very many of the Temple that were zealous for Mr. *Travers* and for his Church Difcipline: infomuch that though Mr. *Travers* left the place, yet the feeds of Difcontent could not be rooted out of that Society, by the great Reafon, and as great Meeknefs of this humble man: for though the chief Ben-chers gave him much Reverence and Incou-ragement, yet he there met with many neglects and oppofitions by thofe of Mafter *Travers* Judgment; in fo much that it turned to his extreme grief and that he might unbeguile and win them, he defigned to write a deliberate fober Treatife of the Churches power to make Canons for the ufe of Ceremonies, and by Law to impofe an obedience to them, as upon her Children; and this he propofed to do in *eight Books of the Laws of Ecclefiaftical Polity*; intending therein to fhew fuch Ar-guments as fhould force an affent from all men, if Reafon, delivered in fweet Language,

guage and void of any provocation, were able to do it; And that he might prevent all prejudice, he wrote before it a large Preface or Epiftle to the *Diffenting Brethren*, wherein there were fuch Bowels of Love, and fuch a Commixture of that *Love* with *Reafon*, as was never exceeded but in Holy Writ, and particularly by that of St. *Paul* to his dear Brother and fellow Labourer *Philemon*, than which none ever was more like this Epiftle of Mr. *Hookers*; fo that his dear friend and Companion in his Studies Doctor *Spenfer* might after his death juftly fay, *What admirable height of Learning and depth of Judgment dwelt in the lowly mind of this truly humble man, great in all wife mens eyes except his own; with what gravity and Majefty of fpeech his Tongue and Pen uttered Heavenly Myfteries; whofe eyes in the Humility of his Heart were alwayes caft down to the ground; how all things that proceeded from him were breathed as from the Spirit of Love, as if he, like the Bird of the Holy Ghoft, the Dove, had wanted Gall, let thofe that knew him not in his Perfon, judge by thefe living Images of his foul, his Writings.*

The foundation of thefe Books was laid in the Temple; but he found it no fit place to finifh what he had there defigned; and therefore folicited the Arch-Bifhop for a remove, to whom he fpake to this purpofe, My Lord, *When I loft the freedom of my Cell, which was my*
Col-

Colledge, yet I found some degree of it in my quiet Country Parsonage: but I am weary of the noise and oppositions of this place; and indeed, God and Nature did not intend me for Contentions, but for Study and quietness: My Lord, *My particular contests with* Mr. Travers *here, have proved the more unpleasant to me, because I believe him a good man, and that belief hath occasioned me to examine mine own Conscience concerning his opinions, and to satisfie that, I have consulted the Scripture, and other laws both humane and divine, whether the Conscience of him and others of his judgment ought to be so farr complyed with as to alter our frame of Church Government, our manner of Gods worship, our praising and praying to him, and our established Ceremonies as often as their tender Consciences shall require us, and in this examination, I have not onely satisfyed my self, but have begun a treatise, in which I intend the Justification of our Laws of Church-Government, and I shall never be able to finish it, but where I may Study, and pray for Gods blessing upon my indeavours, and keep my self in Peace and Privacy, and behold Gods blessing spring out of my Mother Earth, and eat my own bread without oppositions; and therefore if your Grace can Judge me worthy such a favour, let me beg it, that I may perfect what I have begun.*

About this time the Parsonage or Rectory of *Boscum*, in the Diocess of *Sarum*, and six miles from that City, became void. The Bishop

shop of *Sarum* is Patron of it, but in the vacancy of that See (which was three years betwixt the Translation of Bishop *Peirce* to the See of *York*, and Bishop *Caldwells* admission into it) the disposal of that and all Benefices belonging to that See, during this said vacancy, came to be disposed of by the Archbishop of *Canterbury*, and he presented *Richard Hooker* to it, in the year 1591: And *Richard Hooker* was also in the said year Instituted, *July* 17. to be a minor Prebend of *Salisbury*, the Corps to it being *Nether-Havin*, about ten miles from that City, which Prebend was of no great value, but intended chiefly to make him capable of a better preferment in that Church. In this *Boscum* he continued till he had finished four of his eight proposed Books of the Laws of Ecclesiastical Polity, and these were entered into the register Book in Stationers Hall, the 9. of *March* 1592. but not published till the year 1594. and then with the before-mentioned large and affectionate Preface, which he directs *to them that seek (as they term it) the Reformation of the laws and orders Ecclesiastical in the Church of England*; of which Books I shall yet say nothing more, but that he continued his laborious diligence to finish the remaining four during his life (of all which more properly hereafter) but at *Boscum* he finisht and publisht but onely the first four; being then in the 39*th* year of his Age.

He

He left *Boscum* in the year 1595. by a sur-
render of it into the hands of Bishop *Caldwell*,
and he presented *Benjamin Russel*, who was Instituted into it the 23. of *June* in the same
year.

The Parsonage of *Bishops Borne* in *Kent*,
three miles from *Canterbury*, is in that Arch-Bi-
shops gift, but in the latter end of the year
1594. Doctor *William Redman* the Rector of
it was made *Bishop* of *Norwich*, by which means
the power of presenting to it was *pro ea vice* in
the Queen; and she presented *Richard Hooker*,
whom she loved well, to this good living of
Borne the 7. of *July* 1595. in which living he
continued till his Death, without any addition
of Dignity or Profit.

And now having brought our *Richard Hook-*
er, from his Birth place to this where he found
a Grave, I shall onely give some account of his
Books, and of his behaviour in this Parsonage
of *Borne*, and then give a rest both to my self
and my Reader.

His first four Books and large Epistle have
been declared to be printed at his being at
Boscum, *Anno* 1594. Next I am to tell that
at the end of these four Books there is printed this Advertisement to the Reader. 'I have
' for some causes thought it at this time more
' fit to let go these first four Books by them-
' selves, than to stay both them and the rest,
' till the whole might together be published.
                                            Such

‘ Such generalities of the cause in question
‘ as are here handled, it will be perhaps not
‘ amiss to confider apart, by way of Introdu-
‘ ction unto the Books that are to follow con-
‘ cerning particulars, in the mean time the Rea-
‘ der is requested to mend the Printers errours, as
noted underneath.

And I am next to declare that his fifth
Book (which is larger than his first four) was
first also printed by it self *Anno* 1597. and
dedicated to his Patron (for till then he chose
none) the Archbishop. These Books were
read with an admiration of their excellency in
This, and their just fame spread it self into fo-
raign Nations.   And I have been told more
than forty years past, that either Cardinal *Allen*, or learned Doctor *Stapleton* (both English
men, and in *Italy* about the time when *Hookers*
four Books were first printed: meeting with
this general fame of them, were desirous to
read an Authour that both the Reformed and
the learned of their own Church did so much
magnifie, and therefore caused them to be sent
for; and after reading them, boasted to the
Pope (which then was *Clement* the eighth)
*that though he had lately said he never met with
an English Book whose Writer deserved the name
of Author;* yet there now appear'd a wonder
to them, and it would be so to his Holiness, if
it were in Latin, for *a poor obscure English Priest
had writ four such Books of Laws , and Church
Polity, and in a Style that exprest so Grave*
and

Card Allen
died in
1594

and such *Humble Majesty with clear demonstration of Reason*, that in all their readings they had not met with any that exceeded him; and this begot in the Pope an earneſt deſire that Doctor *Stapleton* ſhould bring the ſaid four Books, and looking on the Engliſh read a part of them to him in Latin, which Doctor *Stapleton* did, to the end of the firſt Book; at the concluſion of which, the Pope ſpake to this purpoſe; *There is no Learning that this man hath not ſearcht into, nothing too hard for his underſtanding: this man indeed deſerves the name of an Authour; his books will get reverence by Age, for there is in them ſuch ſeeds of Eternity, that if the reſt be like this, they ſhall laſt till the laſt fire ſhall conſume all Learning.*

Nor was this high, the onely teſtimony and commendations given to his Books; for at the firſt coming of King *James* into this Kingdom, he inquired of the Archbiſhop *Whitgift* for his friend Mr. *Hooker* that writ the Books of Church Polity; to which the anſwer was, that he dyed a *two years* year before Queen *Elizabeth*, who received the *above* ſad news of his Death with very much Sorrow; to which the King replyed, *and I receive it with no leſs, that I ſhall want the deſired happineſs of ſeeing and diſcourſing with that man, from whoſe Books I have received ſuch ſatisfaction: Indeed, my Lord, I have received more ſatisfaction in reading a leaf, or paragragh in* Mr. *Hooker*, though it were but about the *faſhion* of *Churches,* or

F *Church*

Church *mufick*, or the like, but *especially of the Sacraments, than I have had in the reading particular large Treatifes written but of one of thofe Subjects by others, though very learned men*; and, I obferve *there is in Mr.* Hooker *no affected language, but a grave, comprehenfive, clear manifeftation of Reafon, and that back't with the Authority of the* Scripture, *the* Fathers and Schoolmen, *and with all* Law *both* Sacred and Civil. *And, though many others write well, yet in the next age they will be forgotten*; *but doubtlefs there is in every page of* Mr. Hookers Book *the picture of a Divine Soul, fuch Pictures of* Truth *and* Reafon, *and drawn in fo facred Colours, that they fhall never fade, but give an immortal memory to the Author.* And it is fo truly true, that the King thought what he fpake, that as the moft learned of the Nation have and ftill do mention Mr. *Hooker* with reverence, fo he alfo did never mention him but with the Epithite of *Learned*, or *Judicious*, or *Reverend*, or *Venerable* Mr. Hooker.

Nor did his Son, our late King *Charles* the Firft, ever mention him but with the fame reverence, enjoining his Son, our now gracious King, to be ftudious in Mr. *Hookers* Books. And our * *In his* learned Antiquary Mr. *Cambden* * mentioning *Annals* the death, the modefty, and other vertues of *1599.* Mr. *Hooker*, and magnifying his Books, wifh't, *That for the honour of this, and benefit of other Nations, they were turn'd into the Univerfal Language.*

guage. Which work, though undertaken by many, yet they have been weary, and forsaken it; but the Reader may now expect it, having been long since begun, and lately fin'sht by the happy Pen of Dr. *Earl*, late Lord Bishop of *Salisbury*, of whom I may justly say (and let it not off.nd him, because it is such a truth as ought not to be conceal'd from Posterity, or those that now live,and yet know him not) that since Mr. *Hooker* dyed, none have liv'd whom God hath blest with more innocent Wisdom, more sanctified Learning, or a mo e pious, peaceable, primitive temper : so that this excellent person seems to be only like himself, and our veerbale *Rich. Hooker*; and only fit to make the learned of all Nations happy, in knowing what hath been too long confin'd to the language of our little Island.

There might be many more and just occasions taken to speak of his Books, which none ever did, or can commend too much, but I decline them, and hasten to an account of his Christian behaviour and death at *Borne*,in which place he continued his customary Ru'es of Mortification and Self-denial; was much in Fasting,frequent in Meditation and Prayers,enjoying those blessed returns, which only men of strict lives feel and know, and of which men of loose and godless lives, cannot be made sensible, for spiritual things are spiritually discern'd.

At

At his entrance into this place, his friendship was much fought for by Dr. *Hadrian Saravia,* then or about that time made one of the Prebends of *Canterbury,* a German by Birth , and fometimes a Paftor both in *Flanders* and *Holland,* where he had ftudied and well confidered the controverted points concerning Epifcopacy and Sacriledge ; and, in *England* had a juft occafion to declare his judgment concerning both, unto his Brethren Minifters of the Low Countreys, which was excepted againft by *Theodor Beza,* and others; againft whofe exceptions, he rejoyned, and thereby became the happy Author of many learned Tracts, writ in Latin, efpecially of three ; one, of the *Degrees of Minifters,* and *of the Bifhops fuperiority above the Presbytery*; a fecond againft *Sacriledge*; and, a third of *Chriftian Obedience to Princes* ; the laft being occafioned by *Gretzerus* the Jefuite. And it is obfervable, that when in a time of Churchtumults, *Beza* gave his reafons to the Chancellor of *Scotland* for the abrogation of Epifcopacy in that Nation, partly by Letters, and more fully in a Treatife of a threefold Epifcopacy (which he calls *Divine, Humane,* and *Satanical*) this Dr. *Saravia* had by the help of Bifhop *Whitgift* made fuch an early difcovery of their intentions, that he had almoft as foon anfwered that Treatife as it became publick ; and therein difcovered how *Beza's* opinion did contradict that of *Calvins,* and his adherents , leaving
them

them to interfere with themselves in point of *Episcopacy*; but of these Tracts it will not concern me to say more, than that they were most of them dedicated to his and the Church of *Englands* watchful Patron *John Whitgift* the Archbishop, and printed about the time in which Mr. *Hooker* also appeared first to the World in the publication of his first four Books of Ecclesiastical Polity.

This friendship being sought for by this learned Doctor, you may believe was not denied by Mr. *Hooker*, who was by fortune so like him, as to be engaged against Mr. *Travers*, Mr. *Cartwright*, and others of their judgement, in a Controversie too like Dr. *Saravia*'s ; so that in this year of 1595, and in this place of *Borne*, these two excellent persons began a holy friendship, increasing daily to so high and mutual affections, that their two wills seemed to be but one and the same, and their designs both for the glory of God, and peace of the Church, still assisting and improving each others vertues, and the desired comforts of a peaceable piety which I have willingly mentioned, because it gives a foundation to some things that follow.

This Parsonage of *Borne* is from *Canterbury* three miles, and near to the common Road that leads from that City to *Dover*, in which Parsonage Mr. *Hooker* had not been Twelve months, but his Books, and the innocency and sanctity of his life became so remarkable, that many

turn'd

turn'd out of the Road, and others (Scholars especially) went purposely to see the man, whose life and learning were so much admired; and alas, as our Saviour said of St. *John Baptist*, *What went they out to see, a man cloathed in purple and fine linnen?* no indeed, but an *obscure, harmless man, a man in poor Cloaths, his Loyns usually girt in a course Gown, or Canonical Coat; of a mean stature, and stooping, and yet more lowly in the thoughts of his Soul; his Body worn out, not with Age, but Study, and Holy Mortifications; his Face full of Heat-pimples, begot by his unactivity and sedentary life.* And to this true character of his person, let me add this of his disposition and behaviour; God and Nature blest with so blessed a bashfulness, that as in his younger dayes his Pupils might easily look him out of countenance; so neither then, nor in his age, *did he ever willingly look any man in the face; and was of so mild and humble a nature, that his poor Parish Clerk and he did never talk but with both their Hats on, or both off at the same time:* And to this may be added, that though he was not purblind, yet he was short or weak-sighted; and where he fixt his eyes at the beginning of his Sermon, there they continued till it was ended; and the Reader has a liberty to believe that his modesty and dim-sight, were some of the reasons why he trusted Mrs. *Churchman* to choose his Wife.

This

This Parifh-Clerk lived till the third or fourth year of the late Long Parliament, betwixt which time and Mr. *Hookers* death, there had come many to fee the place of his Burial, and the Monument dedicated to his memory by Sir *William Cooper* (who ftill lives) and the poor Clerk had many rewards for fhewing Mr. *Hookers* Grave-place, and his faid Monument, and did alwayes hear Mr. *Hooker* mentioned with commendations and reverence, to all which he added his own knowledge and obfervations of his humility and holinefs ; and in all which Difcourfes, the poor man was ftill more confirm'd in his opinion of Mr. *Hookers* vertues and learning ; but it fo fell out, that about the faid third or fourth year of the Long Parliament, the then prefent Parfon of *Borne* was Sequeftred (you may guefs why) and a *Genevian* Minifter put into his good Living ; this, and other like Sequeftrations, made the Clerk exprefs himfelf in a wonder, and fay, *They had Sequeftred fo many good men, that he doubted if his good Mafter Mr.* Hooker *had lived till now, they would have Sequeftred him too:*

It was not long, before this intruding Minifter had made a Party in and about the faid Parifh, that were defirous to receive the Sacrament as in *Geneva* ; to which end, the da was appointed for a felect Company, and Forms and Stools fet about the Altar or Communion-Table, for them to fit and eat, and drink ; but when they went about this work, there was a want of some Joint-stools, which the Minister sent the Clerk to fetch, and then to fetch Cushions; when the Clerk saw them begin to sit down, he began to wonder, but the Minister bad him *ceafe wondering, and lock the Church-door*; to whom he replied, *Pray take you the Keyes, and lock me out, I will never come more into this Church*; *for all men will fay, my Mafter* Hooker *was a good Man, and a good Scholar, and I am fure it was not ufed to be thus in his dayes :* And, the report fays, the old man went presently home, and dyed; I do not fay dyed immediately, but within a few dayes after.

But let us leave this grateful Clerk in his quiet Grave, and return to Mr. *Hooker* himself, continuing our obfervations of his Chriftian behaviour in this place, where he gave a holy Valediction to all the pleafures and allurements of Earth, poffeffing his Soul in a vertuous quietnefs, which he maintained by conftant Study, Prayers, and Meditations; his ufe was to preach once every *Sunday*, and he or his Curate to Catechife after the fecond Leffon in the Evening Prayer; his Sermons were neither long nor earneft, but uttered with a grave zeal, and an humble voice; his eyes alwayes fixt on one place to prevent his imagination from wandring, infomuch, that he feem'd to ftudy as he fpake; the defign of his Sermons (as indeed of all his Difcourfes) was to fhew Reafons for what he

fpake;

spake; and with thefe Reafons, fuch a kind of Rhetorick, as did rather convince and perfwade, than frighten men into piety; ftudying not fo much for matter (which he never wanted) as for apt illuftrations to inform and teach his unlearned Hearers by familiar Examples, and then make them better by convincing Applications; never labouring by hard words, and then by needlefs diftinctions and fub-diftinctions, to *amufe* his Hearers, and get glory to himfelf; but glory only to God. Which intention, he would often fay, was as difcernable in a Preacher, *as an Artificial, from a Natural beauty.*

He never failed the *Sunday* before every *Ember-week,* to give notice of it to his Parifhioners, perfwading them both to faft, and then to double their devotions for a learned and pious Clergy, but efpecially the laft, faying often, *That the life of a pious Clergy-man was vifible Rhetorick, and fo Convincing, that the moft Godlefs men, (though they would not deny themfelves the enjoyment of their prefent lufts) did yet fecretly wifh themfelves like thofe of the ftricteft lives:* And to what he perfwaded others, he added his own example of Fafting and Prayer; and did ufually every *Ember-week,* take from the Parifh-Clerk the Key of the Church-door; into which place he retir'd every day, and lockt himfelf up for many hours; and did the like moft *Frydayes,* and other dayes of Fafting.

He

He would by no means omit the cuftomary time of Proceffion, perfwading all both rich and poor, if they defired the prefervation of Love, and their Parifh Rights and Liberties, to accompany him in his Perambulation, and moft did fo; in which Perambulation, he would ufually exprefs more pleafant Difcourfe than at other times, and would then alwayes drop fome loving and facetious obfervations to be remembred againft the next year, efpecially by the boyes and young people; ftill inclining them and all his prefent Parifhioners, to meeknefs, and mutual kindneffes, and love; *becaufe Love thinks not evil, but covers a multitude of Infirmities.*

He was diligent to inquire who of his Parifh were fick, or any wayes diftreft, and would often vifit them unfent for; fuppofing, that the fitteft time to difcover thofe Errors to which health and profperity had blinded them; and having by pious reafons and prayers, moulded them into holy refolutions for the time to come, he would incline them to confeffion, and bewailing their fins, with purpofe to forfake them, and then to receive the Communion, both as a ftrengthning of thofe holy refolutions, and as a feal betwixt God and them of his Mercies to their Souls, in cafe that prefent ficknefle did put a period to their lives.

And

And as he was thus watchful and charitable to the sick, so he was as diligent to prevent Law-sutes, still urging his Parishioners and Neighbours, to bear with each others infirmities, and live in love, because (as St. *John* sayes) *he that lives in love, lives in God, for God is love.* And to maintain this holy fire of love constantly burning on the Altar of a pure heart, his advice was to watch and pray, and alwayes keep themselves fit to receive the Communion; and then to receive it often, for it was both a confirming and a strengthning of their graces; this was his advice: And at his entrance or departure out of any house, he would usually speak to the whole Family, and bless them by name; insomuch, that as he seem'd in his youth to be taught of God, so he seem'd in this place to teach his precepts, as *Enoch* did by walking with him, in all holiness and humility, making each day a step towards a blessed Eternity. And though in this weak and declining Age of the World, such Examples are become barren, and almost incredible, yet let his memory be blest with this true Recordation, because he that praises *Richard Hooker*, praises God, who hath given such gifts to men; and let this humble and affectionate Relation of him, become such a pattern, as may invite Posterity to imitate his vertues.

This

This was his conſtant behaviour at *Borne*, ſo he walk't with God; thus he did tread in the footſteps of primitive piety; and yet, as that great example of meekneſs and purity, even our bleſſed *Jeſus* was not free from falſe accuſations, no more was this Diſciple of his, this moſt humble, moſt innocent holy man; his was a ſlander parallel to that of chaſte *Suſannah's* by the wicked Elders, or that againſt St. *Athanaſius*, as it is recorded in his life, for that holy man had heretical enemies, and which this Age calls *Trepanning*; the particulars need not a repetition; and that it was falſe, needs no other Teſtimony than the publick puniſhment of his Accuſers, and their open confeſſion of his Innocency; 'twas ſaid that the accuſation was contrived by a diſſenting Brother, one that endur'd not Church-Ceremonies, hating him for his Books ſake, which he was not able to anſwer; and his name hath been told me, but I have not ſo much confidence in the relation, as to make my Pen fix a ſcandal on him to poſterity; I ſhall rather leave it doubtful till the great day of Revelation: But this is certain, that he lay under the great charge, and the anxiety of this accuſation, and kept it ſecret to himſelf for many months; and being a helpleſs man, had lain long under this heavy burthen, but that the protector of the innocent gave ſuch an accidental occaſion as forced him to make it known to his two deareſt friends, *Edwyn Sandys*, and
George

George Cranmer, who were so sensible of their Tutors sufferings, that they gave themselves no rest, till by their disquisitions and diligence they had found out the fraud, and brought him the welcome News, that his Accusers did confess they had wrong'd him, and beg'd his pardon: To which, the good mans reply was to this purpose, *The Lord forgive them*, and *the Lord bless you for this comfortable News :* Now I have a just occasion to say with *Solomon, Friends are born for the dayes of adversity*, and such you have prov'd to me ; and to my God I say, as did the mother of St. *John Baptist, Thus hath the Lord dealt with me, in the day wherein he looked upon me, to take away my reproach among men: And, oh my God, neither my life, nor my reputation are safe in mine own keeping, but in thine, who didst take care of me, when I yet hanged upon my mothers breast ; blessed are they, that put their trust in thee O Lord ; for when false Witnesses were risen up against me, when shame was ready to cover my face, when I was bowed down with an horrible dread, and went mourning all the day long, when my nights were restless, and my sleeps broken with a fear worse than death, when my Soul thirsted for a deliverance, as the Hart panteth after the rivers of waters, then thou Lord didst hear my complaints, pity my condition, and art now become my deliverer ; and as long as I live I will hold up my hands in this manner, and magnifie thy mercies, who didst not give me over as a prey to mine enemies.*

mies. Oh bleſſed are they that put their truſt in thee ; and no proſperity ſhall make me forget thoſe dayes of ſorrows, or to perform thoſe vows that I have made to thee in the dayes of my affliction; for with ſuch Sacrifices, thou, O God, art well pleaſed, and I will pay them.

Thus did the joy and gratitude of this good mans heart break forth; and 'tis obſervable, that as the invitation to this ſlander was his meek behaviour and Dove-like ſimplicity, for which he was remarkable; ſo his Chriſtian charity ought to be imitated : for, though the ſpirit of revenge is ſo pleaſing to Mankind, that it is never conquered but by a ſupernatural grace, being indeed ſo deeply rooted in humane Nature, that to prevent the exceſſes of it (for men would not know Moderation) Almighty God allows not any degree of it to any man, but ſayes, *Vengeance is mine.* And, though this be ſaid by God himſelf, yet this revenge is ſo pleaſing, that man is hardly perſwaded to ſubmit the menage of it to the Time, and Juſtice, and Wiſdom of his Creator, but would haſten to be his own Executioner of it. And yet nevertheleſs, if any man ever did wholly decline, and leave this pleaſing paſſion to the time and meaſure of God alone, it was this *Richard Hooker* of whom I write ; for when his Slanderers were to ſuffer, he laboured to procure their pardon; and when that was denied him, his Reply was, *That how-ever he would faſt and pray, that God would give*
                                                              them

them repentance, and patience to undergo their punishment. And his prayers were so far returned into his own bosom, that the first was granted; if we may believe a penitent behaviour, and an open confession. And 'tis observable, that after this time he would often say to Dr. *Saravia, Oh with what quietness did I enjoy my Soul after I was free from the fears of my Slander! and how much more after a conflict and victory over my desires of Revenge!*

About the Year 1600, and of his Age 46, he fell into a long and sharp sickness, occasioned by a cold taken in his passage betwixt *London* and *Gravesend*, from the malignity of which he was never recovered; for, till his death he was not free from thoughtful Dayes, and restless Nights; but a submission to his Will that makes the sick mans Bed easie by giving rest to his Soul, made his very languishment comfortable: and yet all this time he was sollicitous in his Study, and said often to Dr. *Saravia* (who saw him daily, and was the chief comfort of his life) *That he did not beg a long life of God, for any other reason, but to live to finish his three remaining Books of P O L I T Y; and then, Lord, let thy servant depart in peace,* which was his usual expression. And God heard his prayers, though he denied the Church the benefit of them, as compleated by himself; and 'tis thought he haftened his own death, by haftening to give life to his Books : But this is certain, that the nearer

he

he was to his death, the more he grew in *Humility*, in *Holy Thoughts* and *Resolutions.*

About a month before his death, this good man, that never knew, or at least never consider'd the pleasures of the Palate, became first to lose his appetite, then to have an averseness to all food; insomuch, that he seem'd to live some intermitted weeks by the smell of meat only, and yet still studied and writ. And now his guardian Angel seem'd to foretell him, that the day of his dissolution drew near, for which his vigorous Soul appear'd to thirst. In this time of his Sickness, and not many dayes before his Death, his House was rob'd ; of which he having notice, his Question was, *Are my Books and written Papers safe ?* And being answered, *That they were* ; his Reply was, *then it matters not, for no other loss can trouble me.*

About one day before his Death, Dr. *Saravia,* who knew the very secrets of his Soul, (for they were supposed to be Confessors to each other) came to him, and after a Conference of the Benefit, the Necessity, and Safety of the Churches Absolution, it was resolved the Doctor should give him both that and the Sacrament the day following. To which end, the Doctor came, and after a short retirement and privacy, they return'd to the company, and then the Doctor gave him, and some of those friends which were with him, the blessed Sacrament of the body and blood of our Jesus.

Which

Which being performed, the Doctor thought he saw a reverend gaity and joy in his face; but it lasted not long, for his bodily Infirmities did return suddenly, and became more visible, in so much that the Doctor apprehended Death ready to seize him; yet, after some amendment, left him at Night, with a promise to return early the day following, which he did, and then found him in better appearance, deep in Contemplation, and not inclinable to Discourse; which gave the Doctor occasion to require his present Thoughts: to which he replied, *That he was meditating the number and nature of Angels, and their blessed obedience and order, without which, peace could not be in Heaven; and oh that it might be so on Earth.* After which words he said, *I have lived to see this world is made up of perturbations, and I have been long preparing to leave it, and gathering comfort for the dreadful hour of making my account with God, which I now apprehend to be near; and though I have by his grace lov'd him in my youth, and fear'd him in mine age, and labour'd to have a conscience void of offence to him, and to all men; yet, if thou, O Lord, be extreme to mark what I have done amiss, who can abide it? and therefore, where I have failed, Lord shew mercy to me, for I plead not my righteousness, but, the forgiveness of my unrighteousness, for his merits who dyed to purchase pardon for penitent sinners; and since I owe thee a death, Lord let it not be terrible, and then take thine own time, I*

G   *submit*

submit to it; let not mine, O Lord, but let thy Will be done; with which expression he fell into a dangerous slumber, dangerous as to his recovery; yet recover he did, but it was to speak only these few words, *Good Doctor, God hath heard my daily petitions, for I am at peace with all men, and he is at peace with me; and from that blessed assurance I feel that inward joy, which this world can neither give nor take from me.* More he would have spoken, but his spirits failed him; and, after a short conflict betwixt Nature and Death, a quiet Sigh put a period to his last breath, and so he fell asleep.

And here I draw his Curtain, till with the most glorious company of the *Patriarchs* and *Apostles,* the most Noble Army of *Martyrs* and *Confessors,* this most learned, most humble, holy man, shall also awake to receive an eternal Tranquillity, and with it a greater degree of Glory than common Christians shall be made partakers of.

In the mean time, bless O Lord! Lord bless his Brethren, the Clergy of this Nation, *with effectual endeavours to attain, if not to his great learning, yet to his* remarkable meekness, *his* godly simplicity, *and his* Christian moderation; *for, these bring peace at the last : And, Lord ! let his most excellent Writings be blest with what he design'd, when he undertook them :* which was, Glory to Thee O God on High, Peace in thy Church, and, Good Will to Mankind. *Amen, Amen.*   This

This following Epitaph was long since presented to the World, in memory of Mr. *Hooker*,
by Sir *William Cooper*, who also built him a
fair Monument in *Borne Church*, and acknow-
ledges him to have been his Spiritual Father.

Though nothing can be spoke worthy his fame,
   Or the remembrance of that precious name,
Judicious Hooker; *though this cost be spent*
On him, that hath a lasting Monument
In his own Books, yet ought we to express,
If not his Worth, yet our Respectfulness.
Church-Ceremonies he maintain'd, then why
Without all Ceremony should he dye?
Was it because his Life and Death should be
Both equal patterns of Humility?
Or that perhaps this only glorious one
Was above all to ask, why had he none?
Yet he that lay so long obscurely low,
Doth now preferr'd to greater Honours go.
Ambitious men, learn hence to be more wise,
Humility is the true way to rise:
And God in me this Lesson did inspire,
To bid this humble man, Friend sit up higher.

A N

A N

APPENDIX

To the LIFE of

Mr. *RICH. HOOKER.*

Nd now having by a long and laborious search satisfied my self, and I hope my Reader, by imparting to him the true Relation of Mr. *Hookers* Life: I am desirous also to acquaint him with some observations that relate to it, and which could not properly fall to be spoken till after his death, of which my Reader may expect a brief and true account in the following **Appendix.**

And first it is not to be doubted, but that he dyed in the Forty-seventh, if not in the Forty-sixth year of his Age ; which I mention, because many have believed him to be more aged; but I have so examined it, as to be confident I mistake not ; and for the year of his death, Mr. *Cambden,* who in his Annals of Queen *Elizabeth* 1599. mentions him with a high commendation of his life and learning, declares him to dye in the year 1599. and yet in that Inscription of his Monument set up at the charge of Sir *William Cooper*

Cooper in *Borne Church,* where Mr. *Hooker* was buried, his death is said to be in *Anno* 1603. but doubtless both mistaken ; for I have it attested under the hand of *William Somner* the Archbishops Register for the Province of *Canterbury,* that *Richard Hookers* Will bears date *Octob.* 26. in *Anno* 1600. and that it was prov'd the third of *December* following * .

* Since I first writ this Appendix to the Life of Mr. *Hooker,* Mr. *Fulman* of *Corpus Christi Colledge,* hath shewed me a good Authority for the very day and hour of Mr. *Hookers* death, in one of his Books of *Politie,* which was *Archbishop Lauds.* In which Book, beside many considerable Marginal Notes of some passages of his time , under the *Bishops* own hand, there is also written in the Title page of that Book (which now is Mr. *Fulmans*) this Attestation :

Richardus Hooker vir summis Doctrinæ dotibus ornatus de Ecclesia præcipuè Anglicana optimè meritus, obiit Novemb. 2. *circiter horam secundam post meridianam.* Anno 1600.

And that at his death he left four Daughters, *Alice, Cicily, Jane* and *Margaret,* that he gave to each of them an hundred pound; that he left *Jone* his Wife his sole Executrix, and that by his Inventory, his Estate (a great part of it being in Books) came to 1092 *l.* 9 *s.* 2 *d.* which was much more than he thought himself worth ; and, which was not got by his care, much less by the good huswifery of his Wife, but saved by his trusty servant *Thomas Lane,* that was wiser than his Master in getting money for him, and more frugal than his Mistress in keeping of it ; of which Will I shall say no more, but that his dear friend *Thomas*, the father of *George Cranmer*, of whom I have spoken, and shall have occasion to say more, was one of the witnesses to it.

One of his elder Daughters was married to one *Chalinor*, sometime a School-master in *Chichester*, and both dead long since. *Margaret* his youngest Daughter was married unto *Ezekiel Chark*, Batchelor in Divinity, and Rector of St. *Nicholas* in *Harble down* near *Canterbury*, who dyed about 16 years past, and had a son *Ezekiel*, now living, and in Sacred Orders, being at this time Rector of *Waldron* in *Suffex*; she left also a Daughter, with both whom I have spoken not many months past, and find her to be a Widow in a condition that wants not, but far from abounding; and these two attested unto me, that *Richard Hooker* their Grandfather had a Sister, by name *Elizabeth Harvey*, that liv'd to the Age of 121 Years, and dyed in the month of *September*, 1663.

For his other two Daughters I can learn little certainty, but have heard they both dyed before they were marriageable; and for his Wife, she was so unlike *Jeptha*'s Daughter, that she staid not a comely time to bewail her Widdow-hood; nor liv'd long enough to repent her second Marriage, for which doubtless she would have found cause, if there had been but four months betwixt Mr. *Hookers* and her death: But she is dead, and let her other infirmities be buried with her.   Thus

Thus much briefly for his Age, the Year of his Death, his Eſtate, his Wife, and his Children. I am next to ſpeak of his Books, concerning which, I ſhall have a neceſſity of being longer, or ſhall neither do right to my ſelf, or my Reader, which is chiefly intended in this Appendix.

I have declared in his Life, that he propoſed eight Books, and that his firſt four were printed *Anno* 1594. and his fifth Book firſt printed, and alone, *Anno* 1597. and that he liv'd to finiſh the remaining three of the propoſed eight, but whether we have the laſt three as finiſh't by himſelf, is a juſt and material Queſtion; concerning which I do declare, that I have been told almoſt 40 Years paſt, by one that very well knew Mr. *Hooker,* and the affairs of his Family, that about a month after the death of Mr. *Hooker,* Biſhop *Whitgift,* then Archbiſhop of *Canterbury,* ſent one of his Chaplains to enquire of Mrs. *Hooker,* for the three remaining Books of Polity, writ by her Husband, of which ſhe would not, or could not give any account; and that about three months after, the Biſhop procured her to be ſent for to *London,* and then by his procurement ſhe was to be examined, by ſome of Her Majeſties Council, concerning the diſpoſal of thoſe Books, but by way of preparation for the next dayes examination, the Biſhop invited her to *Lambeth,* and, after ſome friendly queſtions, ſhe confeſſed to him, *That one*

Mr.

Mr. Charke, *and another Minifter that dwelt near* Canterbury, *came to her, and defired that they might go into her Husbands Study, and look upon fome of his Writings ; and that there they two burnt and tore many of them, affuring her, that they were Writings not fit to be feen, and that fhe knew nothing more concerning them.* Her lodging was then in *King-ftreet* in *Weftminfter,* where fhe was found next morning dead in her Bed, and her new Husband fufpected and queftioned for it, but declared innocent of her death.

And I declare alfo, that Dr. *John Spencer* (mentioned in the life of Mr. *Hooker*) who was of Mr. *Hookers* Colledge, and of his time there, and betwixt whom there was fo friendly a friendfhip, that they continually advifed together in all their Studies, and particularly in what concern'd thefe Books of Polity: This Dr. *Spencer,* the three perfect Books being loft, had delivered into his hands (I think by Bifhop *Whitgift*) the imperfect Books, or firft rough draughts of them, to be made as perfect as they might be, by him, who both knew Mr. *Hookers* hand writing, and was beft acquainted with his intentions. And a fair Teftimony of this may appear by an Epiftle firft and ufually printed before Mr. *Hookers* five Books (but omitted, I know not why, in the laft impreffion of the eight printed together in *Anno* 1662. in which the Publifhers feem to impofe the three doubtful, as the undoubted Books of Mr. *Hooker*)

with

with thefe two Letters *J. S.* at the end of the
faid Epiftle, which was meant for this *John
Spencer,* in which Epiftle the Reader may find
thefe words, which may give fome Authority
to what I have here written.

*And though Mr.*Hooker *haftened his own death
by haftening to give life to his Books, yet he held out
with his eyes to behold thefe* Benjamins, *thefe fons
of his right hand, though to him they prov'd* Benonies, *fons of pain and forrow. But fome evil difpofed minds, whether of malice, or covetoufnefs, or
wicked blind zeal, it is uncertain, as foon as they
were born, and their father dead, fmother'd them,
and, by conveying the perfect Copies, left unto us
nothing but the old imperfect mangled draughts
difmembred into pieces ; no favour, no grace, not
the fhadow of themfelves remaining in them ; had
the father lived to behold them thus defaced, he
might rightly have named them* Benonies, *the fons
of forrow ; but being the learned will not fuffer
them to dye and be buried, it is intended the world
fhall fee them as they are ; the learned will find in
them fome fhadows and refemblances of their fathers face. God grant, that as they were with their
Brethren dedicated to the Church for meffengers of
peace ; fo, in the ftrength of that little breath of
life that remaineth in them, they may profper in
their work, and by fatisfying the doubts of fuch as
are willing to learn, they may help to give an end
to the calamities of thefe our Civil Wars.*

J. S.

And

And next the Reader may note, that this Epiſtle of Dr. *Spencers*, was writ and firſt printed within four years after the death of Mr. *Hooker*, in which time all diligent ſearch had been made for the perfect Copies ; and, then granted not recoverable, and therefore endeavoured to be compleated out of Mr. *Hookers* rough draughts, as is expreſt by the ſaid Dr. *Spencer*, ſince whoſe death it is now 50 Years.

And I do profeſs by the faith of a Chriſtian, that Dr. *Spencers* Wife (who was my Aunt and Siſter to *George Cranmer*, of whom I have ſpoken) told me forty Years ſince, in theſe, or in words to this purpoſe, *That her Husband had made up, or finiſh't Mr.* Hookers *laſt three Books ; and that upon her Husbands Death-bed , or in his laſt Sickneſs, he gave them into her hand, with a charge they ſhould not be ſeen by any man, but be by her delivered into the hands of the then Archbiſhop of* Canterbury, *which was* Dr. Abbot , *or unto Dr.* King *then Biſhop of* London, *and that ſhe did as he injoin'd her.*

I do conceive, that from Dr. *Spencers*, and no other Copy, there have been divers Tranſcripts, and were to be found in ſeveral places, as namely, Sir *Thomas Bodlies* Library, in that of Dr. *Andrews*, late Biſhop of *Winton* , in the late Lord *Conwayes*, in the Archbiſhop of *Canterburies*, and in the Biſhop of *Armaghs*, and in many others, and moſt of theſe pretended to be the Authors own hand, but much diſagreeing, being indeed

indeed 'altered and diminisht, as men have thought fittest to make Mr. *Hookers* judgement suit with their fancies, or give authority to their corrupt designs; and for proof of a part of this, take these following Testimonies.

Dr. *Barnard*, sometime Chaplain to Dr. *Usher*, late Lord Archbishop of *Armagh*, hath declar'd in a late Book called *Clavi Trebales*, printed by *Richard Hodgkinson*, *Anno* 1661. that in his search and examination of the said Bishops Manuscripts, he found the three written Books which were supposed the 6, 7, and 8, of Mr. *Hookers* Books of Ecclesiastical Polity; and that in the said three Books (now printed as Mr. *Hookers*) there are so many omissions, that they amount to many Paragraphs, and which cause many incoherencies; the omissions are by him set down at large in the said printed Book, to which I refer the Reader for the whole; but think fit in this place to insert this following short part of them.

First, as there could be in Natural Bodies no Motion of any thing, unless there were some first which moved all things, and continued unmoveable; even so in Politick Societies, there must be some unpunishable, or else no man shall suffer punishment; for sith punishments proceed alwayes from Superiors, to whom the administration of justice belongeth, which administration must have necessarily a fountain that deriveth it to all others, and recei-

receiveth not from any, because otherwise the course of justice should go infinitely in a Circle, every Superior having his Superior without end, which cannot be; therefore, a Well-spring, it followeth, there is, a Supreme head of Justice whereunto all are subject, but it self in subjection to none. Which kind of preheminency if some ought to have in a Kingdom, who but the King shall have it? Kings therefore, or no man can have lawful power to judge.

If private men offend, there is the Magistrate over them which judgeth; if Magistrates, they have their Prince; if Princes, there is Heaven, a Tribunal, before which they shall appear; on Earth they are not accomptable to any. Here, sayes the Doctor, it breaks off abruptly.

And I have these words also attested under the hand of Mr. *Fabian Philips*, a man of Note for his useful Books. *I will make Oath, if I shall be required, that Dr.* Sanderson, *the late Bishop of* Lincoln, *did a little before his death, affirm to me, he had seen a Manuscript, affirmed to him to be the hand-writing of Mr.* Richard Hooker, *in which there was no mention made of the King or Supreme Governours being accomptable to the People; this I will make Oath that that good man attested to me.*

Fabian Philips.

So

So that there appears to be both Omiſſions and Additions in the ſaid laſt three printed Books; and this may probably be one reaſon why Dr. *Sanderſon*, the ſaid learned Biſhop (whoſe Writings are ſo highly and juſtly valued) gave a ſtrict charge near the time of his Death, or in his laſt Will, *That nothing of his that was not already printed, ſhould be printed after his Death.*

It is well known how high a value our learned King *James* put upon the Books writ by Mr. *Hooker*, as alſo that our late King *Charles* (the Martyr for the Church) valued them the ſecond of all Books, teſtified by his commending them to the reading of his Son *Charles*, that now is our gracious King; and you may ſuppoſe that this *Charles* the Firſt, was not a ſtranger to the pretended three Books, becauſe in a Diſcourſe with the Lord *Say*, when the ſaid Lord required the King to grant the truth of his Argument, becauſe it was the judgement of Mr. *Hooker* (quoting him in one of the three written Books) the King replied, *They were not allowed to be Mr.* Hookers *Books*; but, however *he would allow them to be Mr.* Hookers, *and conſent to what his Lordſhip propoſed to prove out of thoſe doubtful Books, if he would but conſent to the Judgement of Mr.* Hooker *in the other five that were the undoubted Books of Mr.* Hooker.

In

In this relation concerning thefe three doubt-ful Books of Mr. *Hookers*, my purpofe was to enquire, then fet down what I obferv'd and know, which I have done, not as an engaged perfon, but indifferently; and now leave my Reader to give fentence, for their legitimation, as to himfelf, but fo, as to leave others the fame liberty of believing, or disbelieving them to be Mr. *Hookers*; and 'tis obfervable, that as Mr. *Hooker* advis'd with Dr. *Spencer*, in the defign and manage of thefe Books, fo alfo, and chiefly with his dear Pupils *George Cranmer* (whofe Sifter was the Wife of Dr. *Spencer*) of which this following Letter may be a Teftimony, and doth alfo give Authority to fome things men-tioned both in this Appendix, and in the Life of Mr. *Hooker*, and is therefore added.

George

GEORGE CRANMER'S
LETTER unto
Mr. *Richard Hooker*.
February 1598.

Hat Posterity is likely to judge of these matters concerning Church-Discipline, we may the better conjecture, if we call to mind what our own Age, within few years, upon better Experience, hath already judged concerning the same. It may be remembred, that at first the greatest part of the Learned in the Land, were either eagerly affected, or favourably inclined that way. The Books then written for the most part, favoured of the Disciplinary stile; it sounded every where in Pulpits, and in common phrase of mens speech: the contrary part began to fear they had taken a wrong course, many which impugned the Discipline, yet so impugned it, not as not being the better Form of Government, but as not being so convenient for our State, in regard of dangerous Innovations thereby like to grow; * one man alone there was, to speak of (whom let no suspition of flattery deprive of his deserved commendation) who in the defiance of the one part, and courage of the

* *John Whitgift* the Archbishop.

other,

other, ſtood in the gap, and gave others reſpite to prepare themſelves to the defence, which by the ſudden eagerneſs and violence of their adverſaries, had otherwiſe been prevented, wherein God hath made good unto him his own Impreſs, *Vincit qui patitur* ; for what contumelious indignities he hath at their hands ſuſtained, the World is witneſs ; and what reward of Honour above his Adverſaries God hath beſtowed upon him, themſelves (though nothing glad thereof) muſt needs confeſs. Now of late years the heat of men towards the Diſcipline is greatly decayed. their judgements begin to ſway on the other ſide : the Learned have weighed it, and found it light ; wiſe men conceive ſome fear, leſt it prove not only not the beſt kind of Government, but the very bane and deſtruction of all Government. The cauſe of this change in mens Opinions, may be drawn from the general nature of Error, diſguiſed and cloathed with the name of Truth ; which did mightily and violently poſſeſs men at firſt, but afterwards, the weakneſs thereof being by time diſcovered, it loſt that reputation, which before it had gained ; as by the outſide of an houſe the paſſers by, are oftentimes deceived, till they ſee the conveniency of the Rooms within : ſo by the very name of *Diſcipline* and *Reformation*, men were drawn at firſt to caſt a fancy towards it, but, now they have not contented themſelves only to paſs by and behold afar off the Fore-front of this reformed

formed houfe; they have entered in, even at
the fpecial requeft of Mafter-workmen and
chief builders thereof: thy have perufed the
Roomes, the Lights, the Conveniencies, and
they finde them not anfwerable to that report
which was made of them, nor to that opinion
which upon report they had conceived: So as
now, the Difcipline which at firft triumphed
over all, being unmasked, beginneth to droop
and hang down her head.

This caufe of change in opinion concerning
the Difcipline, is proper to the Learned, or to
fuch as by them have been inftructed; another caufe there is more open, and more apparent to the view of all, namely, the courfe of
Practice, which the Reformers have had with
us from the beginning; the firft degree was
onely fome fmall difference about the *Cap* and
Surplice, but not fuch as either bred divifion
in the Church, or tended to the ruine of the
Government eftablifhed. This was peaceable:
the next degree more ftirring. *Admonitions*
were directed to the Parliament in perempto-
ry fort againft our whole Form of Regiment;
in defence of them, Volumes were publifhed
in Englifh, and in Latin; yet, this was no more
than writing. Devices were fet on foot to e-
rect the Practice of the Difcipline without Authority: yet, herein fome regard of Modefty,
fome moderation was ufed; Behold, at length
it brake forth into open outrage, firft in wri-

H   ting

ting by *Martin*, in whose kind of dealing these
things may be observed; first, that whereas
T. C. and others his great Masters had always
before set out the Discipline as a Queen, and
as the Daughter of God; He contrarywise, to
make her more acceptable to the people,
brought her forth as a Vice upon the Stage.
2. This conceit of his was grounded (as may
be supposed) upon this rare policy, that seing
the Discipline was by writing refuted, in Parliament rejected, in secret corners hunted out
and decryed, it was imagined that by open
rayling (which to the Vulgar is commonly
most plausible) the State Ecclesiastical might
have been drawn into such contempt and hatred, as the overthrow thereof should have
been most grateful to all men, and in a manner
desired by all the Common people. 3. It may
be noted (and this I know my self to be true)
how some of them, although they could not
for shame approve so lewd an Action: yet,
were content to lay hold on it to the advancement of their cause, by acknowledging therein the secret Judgments of God against the Bishops: and hoping that some good might be
wrought thereby for his Church; as, indeed
there was, though not according to their con-
struction. For, 4. contrary to their expectation, that railing Spirit did not only not further,
but extremely disgrace and prejudice their
Cause, when it was once perceived from how
low

low degrees of contradiction, at first, to what
outrage of Contumely and Slander they were
at length proceeded; and were also likely to
proceed further.

A further degree of outrage was also in Fact;
Certain * Prophets did arise, who deeming it
not possible that God should suffer that to be
undone, which they did so fiercely desire to
have done, Namely, that his holy Saints, the
favourers and Fathers of the Discipline, should
be enlarged, and delivered from persecution;
and seeing no means of Deliverance Ordinary, were fain to persuade themselves that
God must needs raise some extraordinary
means; and being persuaded of none so well
as of themselves, they forthwith must needs be
the instruments of this great work. Here-
upon they framed unto themselves an assured
hope that upon their Preaching out of a Pease
Cart, all the multitude would have presently joyned unto them; and, in amazement
of mind have asked them, *Viri fratres*, *quid
agimus?* whereunto it is likely they would
have returned an answer far unlike to that of
St. Peter, *Such and such are men unworthy to
govern, pluck them down; Such and such are
the dear Children of God, let them be advanced.*

Of two of these men it is meet to speak with
all Commiseration: yet so, that others by
their example may receive instruction, and

* Hacket
and Cop-
pinger.

F 2   with-

withall some light may appear, what stirring affections the Discipline is like to inspire, if it light upon apt and prepared minds.

Now if any man doubt of what Society they were? or, if the Reformers disclaim them, pretending, that by them they were condemned; let these points be considered. 1. *Whose associates were they before they entered into this frantick Passion? whose Sermons did they frequent? whom did they admire?* 2. *Even when they were entering into it, whose advice did they require? and when they were in, whose approbation? whom advertised they of their purpose? whose assistance by Prayer did they request?* But we deal injuriously with them to lay this to their charge; for they reproved and condemned it. How? did they disclose it to the Magistrate, that it might be suppressed? or were they not rather content to stand aloof of, and see the end of it, as being loath to quench that Spirit, No doubt these mad practitioners were of their society, with whom before, and in the practise of their madness they had most affinity. Hereof, read Dr. *Bancrofts* Book.

A third inducement may be to dislike of the Discipline, if we consider not only how far the Reformers themselves have proceeded, but what others upon their Foundations have built. Here come the *Brownists* in the first rank: their lineal descendants: who have seised upon a number of strange opinions: whereof of, although their Anceſtors, the Reformers, were never actually poſſeſſed, yet by right and intereſt from them derived, the *Browniſts* and *Barrowiſts* have taken poſſeſſion of them; for, if the poſitions of the Reformers be true, I cannot ſee how the main and general Concluſions of *Browniſm* ſhould be falſe; for, upon theſe two points, as I conceive, they ſtand.

1. That becauſe we have no Church, they are to ſever themſelves from us. 2. That without Civil Authority they are to erect a Church of their own. And if the former of theſe be true, the latter, I ſuppoſe will follow; for if above all things, men be to regard their Salvation; and, if out of the Church, there be no Salvation; it followeth, that if we have no Church, we have no means of Salvation; and therefore Separation from us, in that reſpect, is both lawfull and neceſſary; as alſo that men ſo ſeparated from the falſe and counterfeit Church, are to aſſociate themſelves unto ſome Church; not to ours; to the Popiſh much leſs; therefore to one of their own making. Now the grownd of all theſe Inferences being this, (*That in our Church there is no means of Salvation*) is out of the Reformers Principles moſt clearly to be proved. For, whereſoever any matter of Faith unto Salvation neceſſary is denyed, there can be no means of Salvation; But in the Church of *England*, the Diſcipline (by them accounted a matter of

H 3　　　　Faith,

Faith,) and, neceffary to Salvation, **is not
onely** denyed, but impugned, and the Profeffors
thereof oppreffed. *Ergo.*

Again, (but this reafon perhaps is weak) E-
very true Church of Chrift acknowledgeth the
whole Gofpel of Chrift: **The** Difcipline, in
their opin on, is a part of the Gofpel, and yet by
our Church refifted. *Ergo.*

Again, the Difcipline is effentially united to
the Church : by which term *Effentially*, they
muft mean either an effential part, or an effential property. Both which wayes it muft needs
be, that where that effential Difcipline is not,
neither is there any Church. If therefore between them and the *Brownifts*, there fhould be
appointed a Solemn difputation, whereof with
us they have been oftentimes fo earneft Chal-
lengers : it doth not yet appear what other anfwer they could poffibly frame to thefe and the
like arguments, wherewith they may be pref-
fed, but fairly to deny the Conclufion (for all
the Premiffes are their own) or rather ingeni-
oufly to reverfe their own Principles before
laid, whereon fo foul abfurdities have been fo
firmly built. What further proofs you can
bring out of their high words, magnifying the
Difcipline, I leave to your better rememorance:
but above all points, I am defirous this one
fhould be ftrongly inforced againft them, becaufe it wringeth them moft of all, and is of all
others (for ought I fee) the moft unanfwe-
rable

rable; you may notwithftanding fay, that you would be heartily glad thefe their pofitions might be falved as the Brownifts might not appear to have iffued out of their Loynes: but untill that be done, they muft give us le.ve to think that *they have caft the Seed whereout thefe tares are grown.*

Another fort of men there are, which have been content to run on with the Reformers for a time and to make them poor inftruments of their own defigns: Thefe are a fort of *Godlefs Politicks*, who perceiving the Plot of *Difcipline* to confift of thefe two parts, the overthrow of Epifcopal, and erections of Presbyterial Authority, and that this latter can take no place till the former be removed, are content to joyn with them in the Deftructive part of Difcipline, bearing them in hand, that in the other alfo they fhall find them as ready. But when time fhall come, it may be they would be as loath to be yoaked with that kind of Regiment, as now they are willing to be releafed from this; Thefe mens ends in all their actions, is Diftraction, their pretence and colour, Reformation. Thofe things which under this colour they have effected to their own good, are, 1. By maintaining a contrary faction, they have kept the Clergy alwayes in Aw; and thereby, made them more pliable and willing to buy their peace. 2. By maintaining an Opinion of Equality among Minifters, they have made way

F 4   to

to their own purpofes for devouring Cathedral
Churches, and Bifhops livings. 3. By exclai-
ming againft abufes in the Church, they
have carried their own corrupt dealings in
the Civil State more covertly ; for fuch is the
Nature of the multitude, that they are not able
to apprehend many things at once: fo as being poffeffed with a diflike or liking of any one
thing, many other in the mean time, may efcape
them without being perceived. 4. They have
fought to difgrace the Clergy, in entertaining
a conceit in mens minds, and confirming it by
continual practife, *That men of Learning, and
fpecially of the Clergy, which are imployed in the
chiefeft kind of Learning are not to be admitted, or
fparingly admitted to matters of State*; contrary
to the practice of all well-governed Commonwealths, and of our own till thefe late
years.

A third fort of men there are, though not
defcended from the Reformers, yet in part raifed and greatly Strengthned by them ; namely, the *curfed crew of Atheifts*. This alfo is one
of thofe points, which I am defirous you fhould
handle moft effectually, and ftrain your felf
therein to all points of motion and affection ;
as, in that of the *Brownifts*, to all ftrength and
finews of Reafon. This is a fort moft damna-
ble, and yet by the general fufpition of the
world at this day moft common. The caufes
of it, which are in the parties themfelves, although

though you handle in the beginning of the fifth
Book,)yet here again they may be touched;
but the occasions of help and furtherance, which
by the Reformers have been yielded unto
them, are, as I conceive, two; namely, *Sence-*
lefs Preaching, and *difgracing of the Miniftry*;
for how fhould not men dare to impugn that,
which neither by force of Reafon, nor by Authority of Perfons is maintained; But in the
parties themfelves thefe two caufes I conceive
of Atheifm, 1. more aboundance of Wit then
Judgment, and of Witty than Judicious Learning; whereby, they are more inclined to contradict any thing, than willing to be informed
of the Truth. They are not therefore, men
of found Learning for the moft part, but Smat-
terers; neither is their kind of Difpute fo much
by force of Argument, as by Scoffing; which
humour of fcoffing, and turning matters moft
ferious into merriment, is now become fo common, as we are not to marvail what the Prophet means by the *Seat of Scorners*, nor what
the Apoftles by foretelling of *Scorners to come*;
for our own age hath verified their fpeech unto
us; which alfo may be an Argument againft
thefe Scoffers and Atheifts themfelves, feeing it
hath been fo many ages ago foretold, that fuch
men the later dayes of the world fhould afford:
which, could not be done by any other Spirit,
fave that whereunto *things future and prefent*
are alike. And even for the main queftion of
the

the Resurrection, whereat they stick so mightily! was it not plainly foretold, that men should in the latter times say, *Where is the Promise of his Coming?* Against the Creation, the Ark, and divers other points, exceptions are said to be taken; the ground whereof is superfluity of Wit, without ground of Learning and Judgment. A second cause of Atheism is *Sensuality*, which maketh men desirous to remove all stops and impediments of their wicked life; among which, because Religion is the chiefest, so as neither in this life without shame they can persist therein, nor (if that be true) without Torment in the life to come: they therefore whet their wits to annihilate the joys of Heaven, wherein they see (if any such be) they can have no part, and likewise the pains of Hell, wherein their portion must needs be very great. They labour therefore, not that they may not deserve those pains, but that deserving them, there may be no such pains to seize upon them; But, what conceit can be imagined more base, than that man should strive to perswade himself even against the secret Instinct (no doubt) of his own Mind, that his Soul is as the Soul of a Beast, mortal and corruptible with the Body? Against which barbarous Opinion, their own Atheism is a very strong Argument. For were not the Soul a Nature separable from the Body, how could it enter into discourse of things meerly Spiritual, and nothing at all pertaining to to the Body? Surely the Soul were not able to conceive any thing of Heaven, no not so much as to dispute against Heaven and against God, if there were not in it somewhat Heavenly and derived from God.

The last which have received strength and encouragement from the Reformers are *Papists*; against whom although they are most bitter Enemies, yet unwittingly they have given them great advantage. For, what can any Enemy rather desire than the Breach and Dissention of those which are Confederates against him? Wherein they are to remember, that if our Communion with Papists in some few Ceremonies do so much strengthen them as is pretended, how much more doth this Division and Rent among our selves, especially seeing it is maintained to be, not in light matters onely, but even in matter of Faith and Salvation? Which over-reaching Speech of theirs, because it is so open an advantage for the *Barrowist* and the *Papist*, we are to wish and hope for, that they will acknowledge it to have been spoken rather in heat of Affection, than with soundness of Judgment; and that though their exceeding love to that Creature of *Discipline* which themselves have bred, nourished, and maintained, their mouth in commendation of her did so often overflow.

From hence you may proceed (but the means of connexion I leave to your self) to another
dis-

difcourfe, which I think very meet to be handled either here or elfewhere at large; the parts whereof may be thefe. 1. That in this caufe between them and us, men are to fever the proper and effential points and controverfy, from thofe which are accidental. The moft effential and proper are thefe two: overthrow of Epifcopal, and erection of Presbyterial Authority. But in thefe two points whofoever joyneth with them is accounted of their number; whofoever in all other points agreeth with them, yet thinketh the Authority of Bifhops not unlawful, and of Elders not neceffary, may juftly be fevered from their retinue. Thofe things therefore, which either in the Perfons, or in the Laws and Orders themfelves are faulty, may be complained on, acknowledged and amended; yet they no whit the nearer their main purpofe; for what if all errours by them fuppofed in our Liturgy were amended, even according to their own hearts defire? if *Non-refidence*, *Pluralities*, and the like, were utterly taken away? are their *Lay-Elders* therefore prefently Authorized? or their Soveraign Ecclefiaftical Jurifdiction eftablifhed?

But even in their complaining againft the outward and accidental matters in Church-government, they are many wayes faulty: 1. In their end which they propofe to themfelves. For in Declaming againft Abufes, their meaning is not to have them redreffed, but by difgracing

gracing the prefent State, to make way for their own Difcipline. As therefore in *Venice*, if any Senatour fhould difcoufe againft the Power of their Senate, as being either *too Soveraign,* or *too weak* in Government, with purpofe to draw their Authority to a Moderation, it might well be fuffered; but not fo, if it fhould appear he fpake with purpofe to induce another State by depraving the prefent: So, in all Caufes belonging either to Church or Commonwealth, we are to have regard what mind the Complaining part doth bear, whether of Amendment or Innovation; and, accordingly either to fuffer or fupprefs it. Their Objection therefore is frivolous, *Why may not men fpeak againft Abufes ?* Yes; but with defire to *cure the part affected, not to deftroy the whole.* 2. A fecond fault is in their Manner of Complaining, not only becaufe it is for the moft part in bitter and reproachful Terms, but alfo it is to the Common people, who are Judges incompetent and infufficient, both to determine any thing amifs, and for want of Skill and Authority to amend it. Which alfo difcovereth their Intent and Purpofe to be rather Deftructive than Corrective. 3. Thirdly, thofe very exceptions which they take are frivolous and impertinent: Some things indeed they accufe as impious, which if they may appear to be fuch, God forbid they fhould be maintained.

Againft the reft it is only alledged, that they

are

are Idle Ceremonies without ufe, and that better and more profitable might be devifed.
Wherein they are doubly deceived; for neither
is it a fufficient Plea to fay, This muft give
place, becaufe a Better may be devifed; becaufe in our Judgments of Better and Worfe,
we oftentimes conceive amifs, when we compare thofe things which are in Devife, with
thofe which are in Practice; *for the Imperfecti-
ons of the one are hid, till by Time and Trial they
be difcovered:* The others are already manifeft
and open to all. But laft of all (which is a
Point in my Opinion of great regard, and which
I am defirous to have enlarg'd) they do not fee
that for the moft part when they ftrike at the
State Ecclefiaftical, they fecretly wound the Civil State: for Perfonal faults, *What can be faid
againft the Church, which may not alfo agree to the
Commonwealth?* In both States Men have alwayes been, and will be alwayes, Men; fometimes blinded with Errour, moft commonly
perverted by Paffions: many Unworthy have
been and are advanced in both, many Worthy
not regarded. And as for Abufes which they
pretend to be in the Laws themfelves, when
they inveigh againft *Non-refidence*, do they
take it a matter lawful or expedient in the Civil State for a man to have a great and gainful
Office in the North, himfelf continually remaining in the South? *He that hath an Office, let him
attend his Office.* When they condemn *Plura-
lity*

lity of Livings Spirtual to the pit of Hell, what think they of the Infinite of Temporal Promotions? By the great Philosopher, *Pol. lib. 2. c. 9.* it is forbidden as a thing moſt dangerous to Commonwealths, that by the ſame man many great Offices ſhould be exerciſed. When they deride our Ceremonies as vain and frivolous, were it hard to apply their Exceptions even to thoſe Civil Ceremonies, which at the Coronation, in Parliament, and all Courts of Juſtice, are uſed; Were it hard to argue even againſt Circumciſion, the Ordinance of God, as being a cruel Ceremony? againſt the Paſſeover, as being ridiculous? ſhould be girt, a Staff in their hand, to eat a Lamb.

To conclude; you may exhort the Clergy, (or what if you direct your Concluſion not to the Clergy in general, but only to the Learned in or of both Univerſities?) you may exhort them to a due Conſideration of all things, and to a right Eſteem and Valuing of each thing in that degree wherein it ought to ſtand. For it oftentimes falleth out, that what Men have either deviſed themſelves, or greatly delighted in, the Price and the Excellency thereof they do admire above deſert. The chiefeſt Labour of a Chriſtian ſhould be to know; of a Miniſter, to preach Chriſt crucified: in regard whereof, not onely Worldly things, but things otherwiſe precious, even the Diſcipline it ſelf is vile and baſe: Where-

Whereas now by the heat of Contention, and violence of Affection; the Zeal of men towards the one hath greatly decayed their Love to the other. Hereunto therefore they are to be exhorted, to *Preach Chriſt crucified*, the *Mortification* of the *Fleſh*, the Renewing of the *Spirit*; not thoſe things which in time of Strife ſeem precious, but (Paſſions being allayed) are vain and childiſh.

F I N I S.

The LIFE

OF

Mr. *GEORGE HERBERT.*

Wifdom of Salom. 4. 10.

He pleafed God , and was beloved of him : fo that whereas he lived among finners, he tranflated him.

LONDON,

Printed by *Tho: Newcomb,* for *Richard Marriott,* fold by moft Bookfellers. M,DC.LXX.

IMPRIMATUR,

April 21.
1670.

Sam: Parker *Reverendiſſimo in Chriſto Patri ac Domino, Domino* Gilberto *Archi-ep:* Cantuar: *à Sac: Domeſt.*

To his very Worthy and much Honoured FRIEND, Mr. Izaack Walton, upon his Excellent Life of Mr. George Herbert.

I.

HEav'ns youngeſt Son, its *Benjamin,*
  Divinity's next Brother, *Sacred Poeſie,*
No longer ſhall a Virgin reckoned be,
  (What ere with others tis) by me,
  A Female Muſe, as were the Nine:
  But (full of Vigor Maſculine)
An Eſſence Male, with Angels his Companions
                                  [ſhine.
With Angels firſt the heavenly youth was bred,
And, when a Child, inſtructed them to ſing,
  The praiſes of th' Immortal King,
  Who *Lucifer* in Triumph led :
For, as in Chains the Monſter ſank to Hell,
And tumbling headlong down the precipice fell,
By him firſt taught, *How art thou fallen thou*
                      [*morning ſtar:* they ſaid   * *Rapha-*
Too fondly then, we have fancy'd him a Maid: *el Urbin*
We, the vain Brethren of the rhyming trade ; the fa-
A femal Angel leſs would *Urbins* skill upbraid. mous
                A 2   II. Thus painter.

II.

Thus 'twas in Heav'n: This, *Poefy's* Sex and Age;
And, when he thence t'our lower World came
[down,
    He chofe a Form more like his own,
And *Ieffe's* youngeft Son infpir'd with holy rage.
The fprightiy Shepherd felt unufual Fire,
    And up he took his tuneful Lyre;
He took it up, and ftruck't, and his own foft
[touches did admire.
    Thou, Poefie, on him didft beftow:
Thy choiceft gift, a honor fhew'd before to none;
And, to prepare his way to th'Hebrew Throne,
    Gav'ft him thy Empire, and Dominion;
    The happy Land of Verfe, where flow
Rivers of milk, and Woods of Laurel grow;
    Wherewith, thou, didft adorn his brow,
And mad'ft his firft, more flourifhing, and trium-
[phant Crown.
Affift me thy great Prophets praife to fing,
David, the Poets, and blefs'd *Ifraels* King;
And, with the dancing Echo, let the mountains
[ring!
Then, on the wings of fome aufpicious wind,
Let his great name from earth, be rais'd on high,
And in the ftarry volume of the Sky
    A lafting Record find:
    Be with his mighty *Pfaltery* joyn'd;
Which, taken long fince up in to the Aire,
And call'd the *Harp,* makes a bright Conftella-
[tion there.
        III. Wor-

III.

Worthy it was to be tranflated hence,
And, there, in view of all, exalted hang :
To which fo oft the Princely Prophet fang,
    And mvſtick Oracles did difpence.
Though, had it ſtill remain'd below,
    More wonders of it we had feen,
How great the mighty *Herberts* skill had been ;
Herbert, who could fo much without it do ;
Herbert, who did its Chords diſtinctly know ;
More perfectly, than any Child of Verfe below.
    O ! Had we known him half fo well !
But then, my friend, there had been left for you
Nothing fo fair, and worthy praife to do ;
Who, fo exactly all his Story tell,
    That, though he did not want his Bayes,
    Nor all the Monuments vertue can raife,
Your hand, he did, to Eternize his Praife.
    Herbert, and *Donne,* again are joyn'd,
    Now here below, as they're above ;
Thefe friends, are in their old embraces twin'd ;
And, fince by you the Enterview's defign'd,
    Too weak, to part them, death does prove ;
For, in this book they meet again : as, in one
        [Heav'n they love.

Benſted,
Apr. 3.
1670.
        Sam: Woodforde.

The LIFE

OF

Mr. *GEORGE HERBERT.*

THE

Introduction.

IN *a late retreat from the buſineſs of this World, and thoſe many little cares with which I have too often incumbred my ſelf, I fell into a Contemplation of ſome of thoſe Hiſtorical paſſages that are recorded in* Sacred Story ; *and, more particularly, of what had paſt betwixt our* Bleſſed Saviour, *and that wonder of Women, and Sinners, and* Mourners, Saint Mary Magdalen. *I call her* Saint, *becauſe I did not then, nor do now conſider her, as when ſhe was poſſeſt with ſeven Devils ; not as when her wanton Eyes, and diſsheveld Hair, were deſigned and manag'd, to charm and inſnare amorous Beholders : But, I did then, and do now conſider her, as after ſhe had expreſt a viſible and ſacred ſorrow for her ſenſualities ; as, after thoſe Eyes had*

wept

wept such a flood of penitential tears as did wash, and that hair had wip't, and she most passionately kist the feet of hers, and our blessed Jesus. And, I do now consider, that because she lov'd much, not only much was forgiven her : but that, beside that blessed blessing of having her sins pardoned, she also had from him a testimony, that her alablaster box of precious oyntment poured on his head and feet, and that Spikenard, and those Spices that were by her dedicated to embalm and preserve his sacred body from putrefaction, should so far preserve her own memory, that these demonstrations of her sanctified love, and of her officious, and generous gratitude should be recorded and mentioned wheresoever his Gospel should be read ; intending thereby, that as his, so her name should also live to succeeding generations, even till time shall be no more.

Upon occasion of which fair example, I did lately look back, and not without some content (at least to my self) that I have endeavour'd to deserve the love, and preserve the memory of my two deceased friends, Dr. Donne, and Sir Henry Wotton, by declaring the various employments and accidents of their Lives : And, though Mr. George Herbert (whose Life I now intend to write) were to me a stranger as to his person : yet, since he was, and was worthy, to be their friend ; and, very many of his have been mine, I judge it may not be unacceptable to those that knew any of

A 4   them

them in their lives, or do now know their Wri-
tings, to see this Conjunction of them after their
deaths; without which many things that concern'd
them, and some things that concern'd the Age in
which they liv'd, would be less perfect, and lost to
posterity.

For these Reasons I have undertaken it, and
if I have prevented any abler person, I beg pardon of him, and my Reader.

T H E

The Life.

Eorge *Herbert* was born the Third day of *April*, in the Year of our Redemption 1593. The place of his Birth was near to the Town of *Montgomery*, and in that *Caſtle* that did then bear the name of that Town and County; that *Caſtle* was then a place of ſtate and ſtrength, and had been ſucceſſively happy in the Family of the *Herberts,* who had long poſſeſt it: and, with it, a plentiful Eſtate, and hearts as liberal to their poor Neighbours. A Family, that hath been bleſt with men of remarkable wiſdom, and with a willingneſs to ſerve their Countrey, and indeed, to do good to all Mankind; for which, they were eminent: But alas! this Family did in the late Rebellion ſuffer extremely in their Eſtates; and the Heirs of that *Caſtle*, ſaw it laid level with that earth that was too good to bury thoſe Wretches that were the cauſe of it.

The Father of our *George*, was *Richard Herbert* the Son of *Edward Herbert* Knight, the Son of *Richard Herbert* Knight, the Son of the famous Sir *Richard Herbert* of *Colebrook* in the County

County of *Monmouth* Banneret, who was the youngeſt Brother of that memorable *William Herbert* Earl of *Pembroke*, that liv'd in the Reign of our King *Edward* the fourth.

His Mother was *Magdalen Newport*, the youngeſt Daughter of Sir *Richard*, and Siſter to Sir *Francis Newport* of *High Arkall* in the County of *Salop* Knight, and Grand-father of *Francis* Lord *Newport*, now Comptroller of His Majeſties Houſhold. A Family, that for their Loyalty, have ſuffered much in their Eſtates, and ſeen the ruine of that excellent Structure, where their Anceſtors have long liv'd, and been memorable for their Hoſpitality.

This Mother of *George Herbert* (of whoſe perſon, and wiſdom, and vertue, I intend to give a true account in a ſeaſonable place) was the happy Mother of ſeven Sons, and three Daughters, which ſhe would often ſay, was *Jobs* number; and as often bleſs God, that they were neither defective in their ſhapes, or in their reaſon; and, often reprove them that did not praiſe God for ſo great a bleſſing. I ſhall give the Reader a ſhort accompt of their names, and not ſay much of their Fortunes.

Edward the eldeſt was firſt made Knight of the *Bath*, at that glorious time of our late Prince *Henries* being inſtall'd Knight of the Garter; and after many years uſeful travel, and the attainment of many Languages, he was by King *James* ſent Ambaſſador Reſident to the then

He was made xt of the Bathe at yⁱ coronation of K. James

then French King, *Lewis* the Thirteenth. There, he continued about two Years; but, he could not subject himself to a compliance with the humors of the Duke *de Luines*, who was then the great and powerful Favourite at Court: so that upon a complaint to our King, he was call'd back into *England* in some displeasure; but at his return he gave such an honourable account of his employment, and so justified his Comportment to the Duke, and all the Court, that he was suddenly sent back upon the same Embassie, from which he return'd in the beginning of the Reign of our good King *Charles* the first, who made him first Baron of *Castle-Island*; and not long after of *Cherberie* in the County of *Salop*: *He was a man of great learning and reason, as appears by his printed Book* de veritate; *and, by his History of the Reign of King* Henry *the Eight, and by several other Tracts.*

The second and third Brothers were *Richard* and *William*, who ventur'd their lives to purchase Honour in the Wars of the *Low Countries*, and dyed Officers in that employment. *Charles* was the fourth, and dyed Fellow of *New-Colledge* in *Oxford.* *Henry* was the sixth, who became a menial servant to the Crown in the dayes of King *James*, and hath continued to be so for fifty years: during all which time he hath been Master of the Revels; a place, that requires a diligent wisdome, with which God hath blest him. The seventh Son was *Thomas*, who being

being made Captain of a Ship in that Fleet with which Sir *Robert Mansell* was sent againſt *Algiers*, did there ſhew a fortunate and true Engliſh valor. Of the three Siſters, I need not ſay more, then that they were all married to perſons of worth, and plentiful fortunes; and, liv'd to be examples of *vertue*, and to do good in their generations.

I now come to give my intended account of *George*, who was the fifth of thoſe ſeven Brothers.

George Herbert ſpent much of his Childhood in a ſweet content under the eye and care of his prudent mother, and the tuition of a Chaplain or Tutor to him, and two of his Brothers in her own Family (for ſhe was then a Widow) where he continued, till about the age of twelve years; and being at that time well inſtructed in the Rules of Grammar, he was not long after commended to the care of Dr. *Neale*, who was then Dean of *Weſtminſter*; and by him to the care of Mr. *Ireland*, who was then chief Maſter of that School; where the beauties of his pretty behaviour and wit, ſhin'd and became ſo eminent and lovely in this his innocent age, that he ſeem'd to be marked out for piety, and to become the care of Heaven, and of a particular Angel to guard and guide him. And thus, he continued in that School, till he came to be perfect in the learned Languages, and eſpecially in the Greek Tongue, in which he after prov'd an excellent Critick.   About

About the age of Fifteen, he, being then a Kings Scholar, was elected out of that School for *Trinity Colledge* in *Cambridge*, to which place he was tranfplanted about the year 1608. And his prudent mother well knowing, that he might eafily lofe, or leffen that virtue and innocence which her advice and example had planted in his mind; did therefore procure the generous and liberal Dr. *Nevil,* who was then Dean of *Canterbury,* and Mafter of that Colledge, to take him into his particular care, and provide him a Tutor; which he did moft gladly undertake, for he knew the excellencies of his Mother, and how to value fuch a friendfhip.

This was the method of his Education, till he was fetled in *Cambridge,* where we will leave him in his Study, till I have paid my promis'd account of his excellent mother, and I will endeavour to make it fhort.

I have told her birth, her Marriage, and the Number of her Children, and, have given fome fhort account of them: I fhall next tell the Reader, that her husband dyed when our *George* was about the Age of four years: and that fhe continued twelve years a Widow: that fhe then maried hapily to a Noble Gentleman, the brother and Heir of the Lord *Danvers* Earl of *Danby,* who did highly value both her perfon and moft excellent endowments of her mind.

In

In this time of her Widowhood, she being desirous to give *Edward* her eldest son, such advantages of Learning, and other education as might suit his birth and fortune: and thereby make him the more fit for the service of his Country: did at his being of a fit age, remove from *Montgomery Castle* with him, and some of her yonger sons to *Oxford*; and, having entred *Edward* into *Queens Colledge*, and provided him a fit *Tutor*, she commended him to his Care; yet, she continued there with him, and still kept him in a moderate awe of herself: and so much under her own eye, as to see and converse with him dayly; but she managed this power over him without any such rigid sourness, as might make her company a torment to her Child, but, with such a sweetness and complyance with the recreations and pleasure of youth, as did incline him willingly to spend much of his time in the company of his dear and careful mother: which was to her great content; for, she would often say, *That as our bodies take a nourishment sutable to the meat on which we feed: so, our souls do as insensibly take in vice by the example or Conversation with wicked Company:* and, would therefore, as often say, *That ignorance of Vice was the best preservation of Vertue:* and, that *the very knowledge of wickedness was as tinder to inflame and kindle sin, and to keep it burning:* For these reasons, she indeared him to her own Company: and,

conti-

continued with him in *Oxford* four years: in
which time, her *great* and *harmless wit* , her
chearful gravity , and her *oblieging behaviour*,
gain'd her an acquaintance and friendship with
most of any eminent worth or learning, that
were at that time in or near that University: and
particularly, with Mr. *John Donne*, who then
came accidentally to that place, in this time of
her being there: it was that *John Done* who
was after *Doctor Donne* , and Dean of *Saint
Pauls London:* and he at his leaving *Oxford*,
writ and left there a Character of the Beauties of her body, and minde; of the first, he
fayes,

No Spring *nor* Summer-Beauty, *has such grace*

As I have seen in an Autumnal *face,*

Of the latter he fayes,

In all her words to every hearer fit

You may at Revels, *or at* Council *fit.*

The rest of her Character, may be read in
his printed Poems, in that Elegy which bears
the name of the *Autumnal Beauty.* For both
he and she were then past the meridian of mans
life.

This

This Amity begun at this time, and place, was not *Amity* that polluted their Souls; but, an *Amity* made up of a chain of sutable inclinations and vertues; an *Amity*, like that of St. *Chrysostoms* to his dear and vertuous *Olimpias*; whom, in his Letters, he calls his *Saint*: Or, an *Amity* indeed more like that of St. *Hierom* to his *Paula*; whose affection to her was such, that he turn'd Poet in his old Age, and then made her *Epitaph*; wishing, all his Body were turn'd into Tongues, that he might declare her just praises to posterity. And this *Amity* betwixt her and Mr. *Donne,* was begun in a happy time for him, he being then about the Fortieth year of his Age (which was some years before he entred into Sacred Orders:) A time, when his necessities needed a daily supply for the support of his Wife, seven Children, and a Family: And in this time she prov'd one of his most bountiful Benefactors; and he, as grateful an acknowledger of it. You may take one testimony of what I have said of them, from this following *Letter,* and *Sonnet.*

MADAM,

MADAM,

*Y*OUR *Favours to me are every where; I use
them, and have them. I enjoy them at*
London, *and leave them there; and yet find them
at* Micham : *Such Riddles as these become things
unexpressible; and, such is your goodness. I was
almost sorry to find your Servant here this day, because I was loth to have any witness of my not
coming home last Night, and indeed of my coming
this Morning : But, my not coming was excusable,
because earnest business detain'd me ; and my
coming this day, is by the example of your St.* Mary Magdalen, *who rose early upon* Sunday, *to seek
that which she lov'd most, and so did I. And, from
her and my self, I return such thanks as are due to
one to whom we owe all the good opinion, that they
whom we need most, have of us——by this Messenger, and on this good day, I commit the inclosed*
Holy Hymns *and* Sonnets (*which for the matter, not the workmanship, have yet escap'd the fire*)
*to your judgment, and to your protection too, if you
think them worthy of it ; and I have appointed
this inclosed* Sonnet *to usher them to your happy
hand.*

Your unworthiest Servant ,

unless your accepting him,

have mended him.

Jo. Donne.

B   To

To the Lady Magdalen Herbert, of St. Mary Magdalen.

HEr of your name, whose fair inheritance
　　Bethina was, and jointure Magdalo:
An active faith so highly did advance,
　　That she once knew, more than the Church did
The Resurrection; so much good there is (know
　　Deliver'd of her, that some Fathers be
Loth to believe one Woman could do this;
　　But, think these Magdalens were two or three.
Increase their number, Lady, and their fame:
　　To their Devotion, add your Innocence;
Take so much of th' example, as of the name;
　　The latter half; and in some recompence
That they did harbour Christ himself, a Guest.
　　Harbour these Hymns, to his dear name addrest.

J. D.

These *Hymns* are now lost to us; but, doubtless they were such, as they two now sing in *Heaven*.

There might be more demonstrations of the Friendship, and the many sacred Indearments betwixt these two excellent persons (for I have
many

many of their Letters in my hand) and much more might be said of her great prudence and piety; but my design was not to write hers, but the life of her Son; and therefore I shall only tell my Reader, that about that very day twenty years, that this Letter was dated, and sent her, I saw and heard this Mr. *John Donne* (who was then Dean of St. *Pauls*) weep, and preach her Funeral Sermon, in the Parish-Church of *Chelsey* near *London*, where she now rests in her quiet Grave, and where we must now leave her, and return to her Son *George*, whom we left in his Study in *Cambridge*.

And in *Cambridge* we may find our *George Herberts* behaviour to be such, that we may conclude, he consecrated the first fruits of his early age to vertue, and a serious study of learning. And that he did so, this following Letter and Sonnet which were in the first year of his going to *Cambridge* sent his dear Mother for a New-years gift, may appear to be some testimony.

—— But I fear the heat of my late Ague *hath dryed up those springs, by which Scholars say, the Muses use to take up their habitations. However, I need not their help, to reprove the vanity of those many Love-poems, that are daily writ and consecrated to* Venus; *nor to bewail that so few are writ, that look towards* God *and* Heaven. *For my own part, my meaning* (dear Mother) *is in*

B 2 *these*

these Sonnets, to declare my resolution to be , that my poor Abilities in Poetry, *shall be all, and ever consecrated to Gods glory. And——*

M Y *God , where is that ancient heat towards*
[*thee,*
Wherewith whole showls of Martyrs *once did*
[*burn,*
Besides their other flames.   Doth Poetry
Wear Venus *Livery? only serve her turn ?*
Why are not Sonnets *made of thee ? and layes*
Upon thine Altar burnt? Cannot thy love
Heighten a spirit to sound out thy praise
As well as any she ? Cannot thy Dove
Out-strip their Cupid *easily in flight ?*
Or, since thy wayes are deep, and still the same,
Will not a verse run smooth that bears thy name!
Why doth that fire. which by thy power and might
Each breast does feel, no braver fuel choose
Than that, which one day, Worms, *may chance*
[*refuse.*

Sure Lord, there is enough in thee to dry
Oceans of Ink ; *for, as the Deluge did*
Cover the Earth, so doth thy Majesty :
Each Cloud distills thy praise, and doth forbid
Poets *to turn it to another use.*
Roses and Lillies *speak thee ; and to make*
A pair of Cheeks of them, is thy abuse.
Why should I Womens *eyes for Chrystal take ?*
Such poor invention burns in their low mind
Whose

Whofe fire is wild, and doth not upward go
To praife and on thee Lord, fome Ink *beftow.*
Open the bones, and you fhall nothing find
In the beft face *but* filth, *when Lord, in thee*
The beauty *lies, in the* difcovery.

G. H.

This was his refolution at the fending this Letter to his dear Mother; about which time, he was in the Seventeenth year of his Age; and, as he grew older, fo he grew in learning, and more and more in favour both with God and man: infomuch, that in this morning of that fhort day of his life, he feem'd to be mark'd out for vertue, and to become the care of Heaven; for God ftill kept his foul in fo holy a frame, that he may, and ought to be a pattern of vertue to all pofterity; and efpecially, to his Brethren of the Clergy, of which the Reader may expect a more exact account in what will follow.

I need not declare that he was a ftrict Student, becaufe, that he was fo, there will be many teftimonies in the future part of his life. I fhall therefore only tell, that he was made *Minor Fellow* in the year 1609. *Batchelor of Art* in the year 1611. *Major Fellow* of the *Colledge, March* 15. 1615. And, that in that year, he was alfo made *Mafter of Arts,* he being then in the 22d year of his Age; during all which time,
B 3   all,

all, or the greatest diversion from his Study,
was the practice of Musick, in which he became a great Master; and of which, he would
say, *That it did relieve his drooping spirits, com-*
pose his distracted thoughts, and raised his weary
Soul so far above Earth, that it gave him an ear-
nest of the joyes of Heaven, before he possest them.
And it may be noted, that from his first entrance into the Colledge, the generous Dr.
Nevil was a cherisher of his Studies, and such a
lover of his person, his behaviour, and the excellent endowments of his mind, that he took
him often into his own company, by which he
confirm'd his native gentileness; and, if during
this time he exprest any Error, it was, that he
kept himself too much retir'd, and at too great
a distance with all his inferiours; and his cloaths
seem'd to prove, that he put too great a value
on his parts and parentage.

This may be some account of his disposition,
and of the employment of his time, till he was
Master of Arts, which was *Anno* 1615. and in
the year 1619. he was chosen Orator for the
University. His two precedent Orators, were
Sir *Robert Nanton,* and Sir *Francis Nethersoll:*
The first was not long after made Secretary of
State; and, Sir *Francis,* not long after his be-
ing Orator, was made Secretary to the Lady
Elizabeth Queen of *Bohemia.* In this place of
Orator, our *George Herbert* continued eight
years; and manag'd it with as becoming, and
grave

grave a gaity, as any had ever before, or fince his time. For, *He had acquir'd great Learning, and was bleft with a high fancy, a civil and fharp wit, and with a natural elegance, both in his behaviour, his tongue, and his pen.* Of all which, there might be very many particular evidences, but I will limit my felf to the mention of but three.

And the firft notable occafion of fhewing his fitnefs for this employment of *Orator*, was manifefted in a Letter to King *James*, who had fent the Univerfity his Book, called *Bafilicon Doron*; and their Orator was to acknowledge this great honour, and return their gratitude to His Majefty for fuch a condefcention; at the clofe of which Letter, he writ,

Quid Vaticanam Bodleianamque objicis hofpes!
Unicus eft nobis Bibliotheca Liber.

This Letter was writ in fuch excellent Latin, was fo full of Conceits, and all the expreffions fo futed to the *genius* of the King, that he inquired the Orators name, and then ask'd *William* Earl of *Pembroke,* if he knew him? whofe anfwer was, *That he knew him very well; and, that he was his Kinfman, but he lov'd him more for his learning and vertue, than for that he was of his name and family.* At which anfwer, the King fmil'd, and asked the Earl leave, *that he might love him too; for, he took him to be the Jewel of that Univerfity.*

B 4   The

The next occasion that he had to shew his great Abilities, was, with them, to shew also his great affection to that Church in which he received his *Baptism*; and, of which he profest himself a member, and the occasion was this: There was one *Andrew Melvin*, a Gentleman of *Scotland*, who was in his own Countrey possest with an aversness, if not a hatred of *Church-government by Bishops*; and, he seem'd to have a like aversness to our manner of *Publick Worship*, and of *Church-prayers* and *Ceremonies*. This Gentleman had travail'd *France*, and resided so long in *Geneva*, as to have his opinions the more confirm'd in him by the practice of that place; from which he return'd into *England* some short time before, or immediately after Mr. *Herbert* was made *Orator*. This Mr. *Melvin* was a man of learning, and was the Master of a great wit, a wit full of *knots* and *clenches*: a wit sharp and satyrical; exceeded, I think, by none of that Nation, but their *Bucanen*. At Mr. *Melvins* return hither, he writ and scattered in Latin, many pieces of his wit against our *Altars*, our *Prayers*, and our *Publick Worship* of God; in which, Mr. *Herbert* took himself to be so much concern'd, that as fast as *Melvin* writ and scatter'd them, Mr. *Herbert* writ and scatter'd answers, and reflections of the same sharpness, upon him and them; I think, to the satisfaction of all un-ingaged persons. But, this Mr. *Melvin*, was not only so busie against

against the *Church*, but at last so bold with the *King* and *State*, that he rayl'd, and writ himself into the *Tower*; at which time, the Lady *Arabella* was an innocent prisoner there; and, he pleas'd himself much in sending the next day after his Commitment, these two Verses to the good Lady; which, I will under-write, because they may give the Reader a taste of his others, which were like these.

Causa tibi mecum est communis, Carceris, Ars-Bella; tibi causa est, Araque sacra mihi.

I shall not trouble my Reader with an account of his enlargement from that Prison, or his Death; but tell him, Mr. *Herberts* Verses were thought so worthy to be preserv'd, that Dr. *Duport* the learned Dean of *Peterborough*, hath lately collected, and caus'd them to be printed, as an honourable memorial of his friend Mr. *George Herbert*, and the Cause he undertook.

And, in order to my third, and last observation of his great Abilities, it will be needful to declare, that about this time King *James* came very often to hunt at *New-market* and *Royston*; and was almost as often invited to *Cambridge*, where his entertainment was suted to his pleasant humor *, and where Mr. *George Herbert* was to welcome him with *Gratulations*, and the *Applauses* of an *Orator*; which he alwayes performed

* *Albumizer.*
Ignoramus.

form'd so well, that he still grew more into the
Kings favour; insomuch, that he had a particular appointment to attend His Majesty at *Royston*, where after a Discourse with him, His Majesty declar'd to his Kinsman, the Earl of *Pembroke, That he found the Orators learning and wisdom, much above his age or wit.* The year following, the King appointed to end His progress
at *Cambridge,* and to stay there certain dayes;
at which time, he was attended by the great
Secretary of Nature, and all Learning, Sir
Francis Bacon (Lord *Virulam*) and by the ever
memorable and learned Dr. *Andrews* Bishop of
Winchester, both which did at that time begin a
desir'd friendship with our *Orator*. Upon whom
the first put such a value on his judgement, that
he usually desir'd his approbation, before he
would expose any of his Books to be printed;
and thought him so worthy of his friendship,
that having translated many of the Prophet
Davids Psalms into English Verse, he made
George Herbert his Patron of them, by a publick dedication of them to him, as the best
Judge of *Divine Poetry*. And, for the learned
Bishop, it is observable, that at that time, there
fell to be a modest debate about *Predestination,*
and *Sanctity of life*; of both which, the *Orator*
did not long after send the Bishop some safe and
useful *Aphorisms*, in a long Letter written in
Greek; which, was so remarkable for the language, and matter, that after the reading of it,
                                              the

the Bishop put it into his bosom, and did often
shew it to Scholars, both of this, and forreign
Nations; but did alwayes return it back to the
place where he first lodg'd it, and continu'd it
so near his heart, till the last day of his
life.

To these, I might add the long and intire
friendship betwixt him and Sir *Henry Wotton*,
and Dr. *Donne*, but I have promis'd to contract
my self, and shall therefore only add one testimony to what is also mentioned in the Life of
Dr. *Donne*; namely, that a little before his
death, he caused many *Seals* to be made, and in
them to be ingraven the figure of *Christ crucified* on an *Anchor*, which is the emblem of hope,
and of which Dr. *Donne* would often say, *Crux
mihi Anchora*. These Seals, he sent to most of
those friends on which he put a value; and, at
Mr. *Herberts* death, these Verses were found
wrap't up with that Seal which was by the
Doctor given to him.

When my dear Friend, could write no more,
He gave this Seal, *and, so gave ore.*

When winds and waves rise highest, I am sure,
This Anchor *keeps my* faith, *that, me secure.*

At this time of being *Orator*, he had learnt
to understand the *Italian*, *Spanish*, and *French*
Tongues very perfectly; hoping, that as his
Pre de-

Predeceffor, fo he might in time attain the place
of a *Secretary of State*, being then high in the
Kings favour ; and , not meanly valued and
lov'd by the moft eminent and moft powerful
of the Court Nobility: This, and the love of
a Court-converfation mixt with a laudable ambition to be fomething more then he then was ,
drew him often from *Cambridge* to attend the
King, who then gave him a *Sine Cure* , which
fell into His Majefties difpofal, I think, by the
death of the Bifhop of St. *Afaph*. It was the
fame, that Queen *Elizabeth* had formerly given
to her Favourite Sir *Philip Sidney* ; and valued
to be worth an hundred and twenty pound *per*
Annum.   With this, and his Annuity, and the
advantage of his Colledge, and of his Orator-
fhip, he enjoy'd his gentile humour for Cloaths,
and Court-like company, and feldom look'd
towards *Cambridge*, unlefs the King were there,
and then he never fail'd ; but, at other times,
left the manage of his Orators place , to his
learned friend Mr. *Herbert Thorndike*, who is now
Prebend of *Weftminfter*.

I may not omit to tell, that he had often defign'd to leave the Univerfity, and decline all
Study, which he judg'd did impair his health ;
for he had a body apt to a *Confumption*, and to
Fevers, and other infirmities which he judg'd
were increas'd by his Studies ; for he would
often fay, *He had a Wit, like a Pen-knife in a*
narrow fheath, too fharp for his Body : But his Mother

ther would by no means allow him to leave the University, or to travel; to which, though he inclin'd very much, yet he would by no means satisfie his own desires at so dear a rate , as to prove an undutiful Son to so affectionate a Mother; but, did alwayes submit to her wisdom : And, what I have now said, may partly appear in a Copy of Verses in his printed Poems; 'tis one of those that bears the title of *Affliction:* And it appears to be a pious reflection on Gods providence, and some passages of his life, and in which he sayes,

WHereas my birth and spirit rather took
  The way that takes the Town:
Thou did'st betray me to a lingring Book,
  And wrap me in a Gown.
I was intangled in a World of strife,
Before I had the power to change my life.

Yet for I threatned oft the Siege to raise,
  Not simpring all mine age:
Thou often didst with Academick praise,
  Melt, and dissolve my rage;
I took the sweetned Pill, till I came where
I could not go away, nor persevere.

Yet, least perchance, I should too happy be
  In my unhappiness;
Turning my purge to food, thou throw'st me
  Into more sicknesses.

        Thus

Thus doth thy power, Cross-byas me, not making
Thine own gifts good; yet, me from my wayes ta-
　　　　　　　　　　　　　　　　[*king.*

Now I am here, what thou wilt do with me
　　　None of my Books will shew :
I read, and sigh, and wish I were a Tree,
　　　For then sure I should grow
To fruit or shade; at least, some Bird would trust
Her Houshold with me, and I would be just.

Yet, though thou troublest me, I must be meek;
　　　In weaknefs must be stout :
Well, I will change my service, and go seek
　　　Some other Master out :
Ah my dear God! though I am clean forgot,
Let me not love thee, if I love thee not.

　　　　　　　　　　　G. H.

In this time of Mr. *Herberts* attendance and expectation of some good occasion to remove him from *Cambridge*, to Court; God, in whom there is an unseen Chain of Causes, did in a short time put an end to the lives of two of his most oblieging and most powerful friends, *Lodowick* Duke of *Richmond*, and *James* Marquess of *Hamilton*; and not long after him, King *James* dyed, and with them, all Mr. *Herbert*'s Court-hopes: So that he presently betook

took himself to a Retreat from *London*, to a
Friend in *Kent*, where he liv'd very privately,
and was such a lover of solitariness, as was judg'd
to impair his health.   In this time of Retirement, he had many Conflicts with himself,
Whether he should return to the painted pleasures of a Court-life, or betake himself to a
study of Divinity, and enter into Sacred Orders?
(to which his dear Mother had often perfuaded
him) These were such Conflicts, as they only
can know, that have endur'd them ; for, ambitious Desires, and the outward Glory of this
World, are not easily laid aside; but, at last,
God inclin'd him to put on a resolution to serve
at his Altar.

He did at his return to *London*, acquaint a
Court friend with his resolution to enter into
Sacred Orders, who persuaded him to alter it, as
too mean an employment, and too much below
his birth, and the excellent abilities and endowments of his mind.   To whom he replied, *It
hath been formerly judg'd, that the Domestick
Servants of the King of Heaven, should be of
the noblest Families on Earth : and, though the
Iniquity of the late Times have made Clergy-men
meanly valued, and the sacred name of Priest contemptible; yet, I will labour to make it honourable, by consecrating all my learning, and all my poor
abilities, to advance the glory of that God that
gave them; knowing, that I can never do too
much for him, that hath done so much for me, as to*
make

make me a Christian.   *And I will labour to be like my Saviour, by making Humility lovely in the eyes of all men, and by following the merciful and meek example of my dear Jesus.*

This was then his resolution, and the God of Constancy, who intended him for a great example of vertue, continued him in it ; for within that year he was made Deacon, but the day when, or by whom, I cannot learn; but that he was about that time made Deacon, is most certain ; for I find by the Records of *Lincoln,* that he was made Prebend of *Layton Ecclesia,* in the Dioces of *Lincoln, July* 15. 1626. and that this Prebend was given him, by *John,* then *Lord Bishop of that See.* And now, he had a fit occasion to shew that Piety and Bounty that was deriv'd from his generous Mother, and his other memorable Anceftors, and the occasion was this.

This *Layton Ecclesia ,* is a Village near to *Spalden* in the County of *Huntington,* and the greatest part of the Parish was fallen down, and that of it which stood, was so decayed, so little, and so useless, that the Parishioners could not meet to perform their Duty to God in publick prayer and praises ; and thus it had been for almost 20 years, in which time there had been some faint endeavours for a publick Collection, to enable the Parishioners to rebuild it ; but, with no success, till Mr. *Herbert* undertook it ; and he, by his own, and the contribution of many

ny of his Kindred, and other noble Friends, undertook the Re-edification of it; and, made it
so much his whole business, that he became restless, till he saw it finisht as it now stands; being, for the workmanship, a costly *Mosaick*: for
the form, an *exact Cross*; and, for the decen-
cy and beauty, I am assur'd it is the most remarkable Parish-Church, that this Nation af-
fords. He liv'd to see it so Wainscoated, as
to be exceeded by none; and, by his order, the
Reading Pew, and Pulpit, were a little distant
from each other, and both of an equal height;
for, he would often say, *They should neither have
a precedency or priority of the other: but, that*
Prayer *and* Preaching *being equally useful, might
agree like Brethren, and have an equal honour and
estimation.*

Before I proceed farther, I must look back to
the time of Mr. *Herberts* being made Prebend,
and tell the Reader, that not long after, his
Mother being inform'd of his intentions to Re-
build that Church; and, apprehending the
great trouble and charge that he was like to
draw upon himself, his Relations, and Friends,
before it could be finisht; sent for him from
London to *Chelsey* (where he then dwelt) and
at his coming, said--*George, I sent for you, to persuade you to commit Simony, by giving your Patron as good a gift as he has given to you; namely, that you give him back his Prebend; for,*
George, *it is not for your weak body, and empty*
C *purse,*

purse, to undertake to build Churches. To which, he defir'd he might have a Dayes time to confider, and then make her an Anfwer: And at his return to her at the next Day, when he had firft defired her blessing, and fhe given it him, his next requeft was, *That fhe would at the Age of Thirty three Years, allow him to become an undutiful Son ; for, he had made a kind of Vow to God, that if he were able, he would Re-build that Church:* And then, fhew'd her fuch reafons for his refolution, that fhe prefently fubfcribed to be one of his Benefactors, and undertook to follicit *William* Earl of *Pembroke*, to be another, who fubfcribed for 50 *l.* and not long after, by a witty, and perfuafive Letter from Mr. *Herbert*, made it 50 *l.* more. And in this nomination of fome of his Benefactors, *James* Duke of *Lenox*, and his brother Sir *Henry Herbert*, ought to be remembred ; and the bounty of Mr. *Nicholas Farrer*, and Mr. *John Woodnot* ; the one, a Gentleman in the Neighbourhood of *Layton*, and the other, a Goldfmith in *Fofterlane, London*, ought not to be forgotten ; for the memory of fuch men ought to out-live their lives. Of Mr. *Farrer*, I fhall hereafter give an account in a more feafonable place ; but before I proceed farther, I will give this fhort account of Mr. *John Woodnot.*

He was a man, that had confider'd, over-grown Eftates do often require more care and watchfulnefs to prefeive, than get them ; and,

that

that there be many Difcontents, that Riches cure not; and did therefore fet limits to himfelf as to the defire of wealth: And having attain'd fo much as to be able to fhew fome mercy to the Poor, and preferve a competence for himfelf, he dedicated the remaining part of his life to the fervice of God; and being ufeful for his Friends, he prov'd to be fo to Mr. Herbert; for, befide his own bounty, he collected and return'd moft of the money that was paid for the Re-building of that Church; he kept all the account of the charges, and would often go down to ftate them, and fee all the Workmen paid. When I have faid, that this good man was a ufeful Friend to Mr. Herberts Father, to his Mother, and continued to be fo to him, till he clos'd his eyes on his Death-bed; I will forbear to fay more, till I have the next fair occafion to mention the holy friendfhip that was betwixt him, and Mr. Herbert.

About the year 1 6 2 9. and the 34th of his Age, Mr. Herbert was feiz'd with a fharp Quotidian Ague, and thought to remove it by the change of Air; to which end, he went to Woodford in Effex, but thither more chiefly, to enjoy the company of his beloved Brother Sir Henry Herbert, and other Friends. In his Houfe he remain'd about Twelve Months, and there became his own Phyfitian, and cur'd himfelf of his Ague, by forbearing Drink, and eating no Meat, no not Mutton, nor a Hen, or Pidgeon,

C 2   unlefs

unlefs they were falted ; and by fuch a conftant
Dyet, he remov'd his Ague, but with inconve-
niencies that were worfe ; for he brought upon himfelf a difpofition to Rheums, and other
weakneffes, and a fuppofed Confumption. And
it is to be Noted, that in the fharpeft of his
extream Fits, he would often fay, *Lord abate my*
great affliction, and increafe my patience ; but,
Lord I repine not, I am dumb, Lord, before thee,
becaufe thou doeft it.   By which, and a fanctified fubmiffion to the Will of God, he fhewed
he was inclinable to bear the fweet yoke of
Chriftian Difcipline, both then, and in the latter
part of his life ; of which, there will be many
true Teftimonies.

And now his care was to recover from his
Confumption by a change, from *Woodford* into
fuch an air as was moft proper to that end. And
his remove was from *Woodford* to *Dantfey* in
Wiltfhire , a noble Houfe which ftands in a
choice Air, the owner of it then was, the Lord
Danvers Earl of *Danby,* who lov'd Mr. *Her-*
bert mu h, and allow'd him fuch an apartment
in that Houfe, as might beft fute Mr. *Herberts*
accomodation and liking.   And, in this place,
by a fpare Dyet, declining all perplexing Studies, moderate exercife, and a chearful converfation ; his health was apparently improv'd to
a good degree, of ftrength and chearfulnefs :
And then, he declar'd his refolution to marry,
and to enter into the Sacred Orders of Prieft-
hood:

hood: Thefe had long been the defires of h's Mother, and his other Relations; but, fhe liv'd not to fee either: for, fhe dyed in the year 1627. And, though he was difobedient to her about *Layton* Church, yet, in conformity to her will, he kept his Fellowfhip in *Cambridge*, and his Orators place, till after her death; and then, declin'd both: And, the laft, the more willingly, that he might be fucceeded by his friend *Robert Creighton*, who now is Dr. *Creighton*, and the worthy Dean of *Wells*.

I fhall now proceed to his Marriage, in order to which, it will be convenient, that I firft give the Reader a fhort view of h's perfon, and then, an account of his Wife, and of fome circum-ftances concerning both.——*He was for his perfon of a ftature inclining towards Tallnefs; his body was very ftrait, and fo far from being cumbred with too much flefh that he was lean to an extre-mity. His afpect was chearful, and his fpeech and motion did both declare him a Gentleman; and were all fo meek and obliging, that both then, and at his death, he was faid to dye without an Enemy.*

Thefe, and his other vifible vertues, begot him fo much love from a Gentleman of a No-ble fortune, and a near Kinfman to his friend the Earl of *Danby*; namely, from Mr. *Charles Dan-vers* of *Bainton*, in the County of *Wilts* Efq; That Mr. *Danvers* having known him long, and familiarly, did fo much affect him, that he often,

and

and publickly declar'd a desire that Mr. *Herbert* would marry any of his Nine Daughters (for he had so many) but rather, his Daughter *Jane*, than any other, because *Jane* was his beloved Daughter : And he had often said the same to Mr. *Herbert* himself ; and, that if he could like her for a Wife, and she him for a Husband, *Jane* should have a *double blessing* : And Mr. *Danvers* had so often said the like to *Jane*, and so much commended Mr. *Herbert* to her, that *Jane* became so much a Platonick, as to fall in love with Mr. *Herbert* unseen.

This was a fair preparation for a Marriage ; but alas, her father dyed before Mr. *Herberts* retirement to *Dantsey* ; yet some friends to both parties, procur'd their meeting ; at which time, a mutual affection entered into both their hearts ; and as a Conqueror, enters into a surprized City, so Love having got that possession govern'd, and made there such Laws and Resolutions, as neither party was able to resist ; insomuch, that she chang'd her name into *Herbert*, the third day after this first Interview.

This haste, might in others be thought a Love-phrensie, or worse, but it was not ; for they wooed so like Princes, as to have select Proxies ; such, as were friends to both parties ; such, as well understood Mr. *Herberts*, and her temper of mind ; and, their Estates so well, before this Interview, that, the suddenness was justifiable, by the strictest Rules of prudence:

dence:

dence : And, the more, becaufe it prov'd fo happy to both parties ; for, the eternal lover of Mankind, made them happy in each others mutual affections, and compliance ; fo happy, that there never was any oppofition betwixt them, unlefs it were a Conteft which fhould moft incline to a compliance with the others defires. And, though this begot, and continued in them, fuch a mutual love and joy, and content, as was no way defective ; yet, this mutual content and love, and joy, did receive a daily augmentation, by fuch daily obligingnefs to each other, as ftill added fuch new affluences to the former fulnefs of thefe divine Souls, as was only improvable in Heaven, where they now enjoy it.

About three months after his Marriage, Dr. *Curle*, who was then Rector of *Bemerton* in *Wiltfhire*, was made Bifhop of *Bath* and *Wells*, (and not long after Tranflated to *Winchefter*) and by that means the prefentation of a Clerk to *Bemerton*, did not fall to the Earl of *Pembroke* (who was the undoubted Patron of it) but to the King, by reafon of Dr. *Curles* advancement : But *Philip*, then Earl of *Pembroke* (for *William* was lately dead) requefted the King to beftow it upon his Kinfman *George Herbert* ; and the King faid, *Moft willingly to Mr.* Herbert, *if it were worth his acceptance :* And the Earl as willingly and fuddenly fent it him, without feeking ; but though Mr. *Herbert* had formerly put on a re-

C 4   folution

solution for the Clergy : yet, the apprehension
of the laſt great Account that he was to make
for the Cure of ſo many Souls, made him faſt
and pray, and conſider, for not leſs than a
month; in which time, he had ſome reſolutions
to decline both the Prieſthood, and that living.
And in this time of conſidering, *He endur'd* (as
he would often ſay) *ſuch ſpiritual Conflicts, as
none can think, but only thoſe that have endur'd them.*

In the midſt of theſe Conflicts, his old and
dear friend Mr. *John Woodnot,* took a journey
to ſalute him at *Bainton* (where he then was
with his Wives Friends and Relations) and was
joyful to be an Eye-witneſs of his Health, and
happy Marriage. And after they had rejoyc'd
together ſome few dayes, they two took a
Journey to *Wilton,* the famous Seat of the
Earls of *Pembroke*; at which time, the King,
the Earl, and the whole Court were there, or
at *Salisbury,* which is near to it. At which time
Mr. *Herbert* preſented his Thanks to the Earl,
for his preſentation to *Bemerton,* but had not
yet reſolv'd to accept of it, and told him the
reaſon why; but that Night, the Earl acquainted Dr. *Laud,* the Archbiſhop of *Canterbury,*
with his Kinſmans irreſolution. And the Biſhop
did the next day ſo convince Mr. *Herbert, That
the refuſal of it was a ſin*; that a Taylor was
ſent for to come ſpeedily from *Salisbury* to *Wilton,* to take meaſure, and make him Canonical
Cloaths,

Cloaths, againſt next day , which the Taylor
did; and Mr. *Herbert* being ſo habited, went
with his preſentation to the learned Dr. *Dave-*
nant, who was then Biſhop of *Salisbury,* and he
gave him Inſtitution immediately (for Mr. *Her-*
bert had been made Deacon ſome years before)
and he was alſo the ſame day (which was *April*
26. 1630. inducted into the good and more
pleaſant, than healthful Parſonage of *Bemerton,*
which is a Mile from *Salisbury.*

I have now brought him to his Parſonage of
Bemerton, *and to the Thirty ſixth Year of his*
Age, and muſt now ſtop, and beſpeak the Reader
to prepare for an almoſt incredible ſtory , of the
great ſanctity of the ſhort remainder of his holy
life ; a life ſo full of Charity, Humility, *and all*
Chriſtian *vertues, that it deſerves the eloquence*
of St. Chryſoſtom *to commend and declare it.*
A life, that if it were related by a Pen *like his,*
there would then be no need for this Age to look
back into times paſt for the examples of primitive
piety ; for they might be all found in the life of
George Herbert. *But now, alas, who is fit to un-*
dertake it, I confeſs I am not, and am not pleas'd
with my ſelf that muſt ; and profeſs my ſelf
amaz'd, when I conſider how few of the Clergy
liv'd like him then ; and, how many live ſo un-
like him now: But it becomes not me to cenſure,
my deſign is rather to aſſure the Reader , that I
have uſed very great diligence to inform my
ſelf , that I might inform him of the truth of
                                    what

what follows, and I will do that with sincerity.

When at his Induction he was shut into *Bemerton* Church, being left there alone to Toll the Bell, as the Law requires him; he staid so much longer than an ordinary time, before he return'd to his Friends that staid expecting him at the Church-door; that his Friend, Mr. *Woodnot*, looked in at the Church-window, and saw him lie prostrate on the ground before the Altar: at which time and place (as he after told Mr. *Woodnot*) he set some Rules to himself, for the future manage of his life; and then and there made a vow, to labour to keep them.

And the same night that he had his Induction, he said to Mr. *Woodnot, I now look back upon my aspiring thoughts, and think my self more happy than if I had attain'd what I so ambitiously thirsted for: And, I can now behold the Court with an impartial Eye, and see plainly, that it is made up of Fraud, and Titles, and Flattery, and many other such empty, imaginary painted Pleasures. Pleasures, that are so empty, as not to satisfie when they are enjoy'd; but, in God and his service, is a fulness of all joy and pleasure, and no satiety: And I will now use all my endeavours to bring my Relations and Dependants to a love and reliance on him, who never fails those that trust him. But above all, I will be sure to live well, because the vertuous life of a Clergy-man, is the most power-*

ful

ful eloquence to perswade all that see it, to reverence and love, and at least to desire to live like him. And this I will do, *because I know we live in an Age that hath more need of good examples, than precepts.* And I beseech that God, *who hath honour'd me so much as to call me to serve at his Altar : that, as by his special grace he hath put into my heart these good desires, and resolutions : so, he will by his assisting grace enable me to bring the same to good effect ; and, that my humble and charitable life, may so win upon others, as to bring glory to my Jesus, whom I have this day taken to be my Master and Governour ; and am so proud of his service, that I will always observe, and obey, and do his Will, and always call him Jesus my Master : and I will always contemn my birth, or any title or dignity that can be conferr'd upon me, when I shall compare them with any title of being a Priest, and serving at the Altar of Jesus my Master.*

And that he did so, may appear in many parts of his Book of *Sacred Poems* ; especially, in that which he calls *the Odour.* In which he seems to rejoyce in his thoughts of that word Jesus, and to say the adding these words *my Master* to it, and the often repetition of them, seem'd to perfume his mind, and leave an oriental fragrancy in his very breath. And for his unforc'd choice to serve at Gods Altar, he seems in another place (*the Pearl*, Matth. 13.) to rejoyce and say--- *He knew the wayes of Learning :*
knew,

knew, what nature does willingly ; and what, when 'tis forc'd by fire : knew the wayes of honour, and when glory inclines the Soul to noble expressions ; knew the Court ; knew the wayes of pleasure , of love, of wit, of musick, and upon what terms he declined all these for the service of his Master Je-sus ; and concludes, saying,

That, through these Labyrinths, not my groveling
(*Wit :*
But, thy Silk-twift, let down from Heaven to me ;
Did, both conduct, and teach me, how by it,
To climb to thee.

The third day after he was made Rector of *Bemerton,* and had chang'd his sword and silk Cloaths into a Canonical Coat ; he return'd so habited with his friend Mr. *Woodnot* to *Bainton :* And, immediately after he had seen and saluted his Wife, he said to her——*You are now a Mini-sters Wife, and must now so far forget your fathers house, as not to claim a precedence of any of your Parishioners ; for you are to know, that a Priests Wife can challenge no precedence or place, but that which she purchases by her obliging humility ; and, I am sure, places so purchased, do best become them.* And, let me tell you, *That I am so good a Herald, as to assure you that this is truth.* And she was so meek a Wife, *as to assure him it was no vexing News to her, and that he should see her observe it with a chearful willingness.* And indeed her

unforc'd

unforc'd humility, that humility that was in her
so original, as to be born with her, made her so
happy as to do so ; and her doing so, begot her
an unfeigned love, and a serviceable respect
from all that converst with her; and this love
followed her in all places, as inseparably, as sha-
dows follow substances in Sun-shine.

It was not many dayes before he return'd
back to *Bemerton*, to view the Church, and repair the Chancel ; and indeed, to re-build three
parts of his house which was fall'n down by
reason of his Predecessors living at a better Parsonage house ; namely, at *Minal*, 16 or 20 miles
from this place. At which time of Mr. *Herberts* coming alone to *Bemerton*, there came to
him a poor old Woman, with an intent to acquaint him with her necessitous condition, and
with some troubles of her mind; but after she
had spoke some few words to him, she was surpriz'd with a fear and shortness of breath, so
that her spirits and speech fail'd her; which he
perceiving, did so compassionate her, that he
took her by the hand, and said, *Speak good Mother, be not afraid to speak to me; for, I am a
man that will hear you with patience; and will relieve your necessities too, if I be able: and this I
will do willingly, and therefore, Mother, be not
afraid to acquaint me with what you desire.* After
which comfortable speech, he again took her
by the hand, made her sit down by him, and un-
derstanding she was of his Parish, he told her, *He
                                                        would*

*would be acquainted with her, and take her into
his care:* And having with patience heard and
underſtood her wants (and it is ſome relief to
be but hear'd with patience) he comforted her
by his meek behaviour and counſel; but becauſe that coſt him nothing, he reliev'd her with
money too, and ſo ſent her home with a chearful heart, praiſing God, and praying for him.
Thus worthy, and (like *Davids* bleſſed man)
thus lowly, was Mr. George Herbert *in his own
eyes.*

At his return that Night to his Wife at
Bainton, he gave her an account of the paſſages
'twixt him and the poor Woman, with which
ſhe was ſo affected, that ſhe went next day to
Salisbury, and there bought a pair of Blankets,
and ſent them as a Token of her love to the
poor Woman, and with them a Meſſage, *That
ſhe would ſee and be acquainted with her, when
her houſe was built at* Bemerton.

There be many ſuch paſſages both of him
and his Wife, of which, ſome few will be related; but I ſhall firſt tell, that he haſted to get
the Pariſh-Church repair'd; then, to beautifie
the Chappel (which ſtands near his houſe)
and that at his own great charge. He then proceeded to re-build the Parſonage-houſe, which
he did alſo very compleatly, and at his own
charge; and having done this good work, he
caus'd theſe Verſes to be writ upon, or ingraven
in the Mantle of the Chimney in his Hall.

T O

TO MY
SUCCESSOR.

If thou chance for to find
A new House to thy mind,
And built without thy Cost:
 Be good to the Poor,
 As God gives thee store,
And then, my Labour's not lost.

We will now by the Readers favour suppose him fixt at *Bemerton*, and grant him to have seen the Church repair'd, and the Chappel belonging to it very decently adorn'd, at his own great charge (which is a real Truth) and having no fixt him there, I shall proceed to give an account of the rest of his behaviour to his Parishioners, and those many others that knew him.

Doubtless Mr. *Herbert* had consider'd and given Rules to himself for his Christian carriage both to God and man before he enter'd into *Holy Orders*. And 'tis not unlike, but that he renewed those resolutions at his prostration before the *Holy Altar*, at his Induction into the Church of *Bemerton*; but as yet he was but a

Deacon,

Deacon, and therefore long'd for the next *Ember-week*, that he might be ordain'd *Priest*, and made capable of administring both the Sacraments. At which time, the Reverend Doctor *Humphrey Hinchman*, now Lord Bishop of *London* (who does not mention him, but with some veneration for the life and excellent learning of Mr. *George Herbert*) tells me, *He laid his hand on Mr.*Herberts *Head, and (alas !) within less than three Years, lent his Shoulder to carry his dear Friend to his Grave.*

And, that Mr. *Herbert* might the better preserve those holy Rules which such a *Priest* as he intended to be, ought to observe; and, that time might not insensibly blot them out of his memory, but the next year shew him his variations from this years resolutions; he therefore, did set down his Rules in that order, as the World now sees them printed in a little Book, call'd, *The Countrey Parson*, in which some of his Rules are:

The Parsons Knowledge.
The Parson on Sundayes.
The Parson Praying.
The Parson Preaching.
The Parsons Charity.
The Parson comforting the Sick.
The Parson Arguing.
The Parson Condescending.
The Parson in his Journey.

The

The Parson in his Mirth.
The Parson with his Church-wardens.
The Parsons Blessing the People.

And his behavior toward God and man, may be said to be a practical Comment on these, and the other holy Rules set down in that useful Book. A Book, so full of plain, prudent and useful Rules, that, that *Countrey Parson*, that can spare 12 *d.* and yet wants, is scarce excusable; because it will both direct him what he is to do, and convince him for not having done it.

At the Death of Mr. *Herbert*, this Book fell into the hands of his friend Mr. *Woodnot*; and he commended it into the trusty hands of Mr. *Bar. Oly.* who publish't it with a most conscientious, and excellent Preface; from which I have had some of those Truths, that are related in this life of Mr. *Herbert*.

The Text for his first Sermon, was taken out of *Solomons Proverbs*, and the words were, *Keep thy heart with all diligence.* In which first Sermon, he gave his Parishioners many necessary, holy, safe Rules, for the discharge of a good Conscience, both to God and man. And, deliver'd his Sermon after a most florid manner, both with great learning and eloquence. And at the close of his Sermon, told them, *That should not be his constant way of Preaching, and that he would not fill their heads with unnecessary*

D   *Notions;*

Notions : but. that for their fakes, his language and his expreffions fhould be more plain and practical in his future Sermons. And he then made it his humble requeft, *That they wou d be conftant to the Afternoons Service, and Catechifing.* And fhewed them convincing reafons why he defir'd it ; and his obliging examp'e and perfwafions, brought them to a willing conformity to his defires.

The Texts for all his Sermons, were conftantly taken out of the Gofpel for the day ; and he did as conftantly declare why the Church did appoint that portion of Scripture to be that day read : And in what manner the *Collect* for every Sunday does refer to the *Gofpel,* or to the *Epiftle* then read to them ; and, that they might pray with underftanding, he did ufually take occafion to explain, not onl, the *Collect* for every particular day, but the reafons of all the other *Collects* and *Refponfes* in our Service ; and, made it appear to them, that, *the whole Service of the Church,* was a reafonable, and therefore an acceptable Sacrifice to God ; as namely, that we begin with *Confeffion of our felves to be vile, miferable finners* ; and that we begin fo, becaufe till we have confeffed our felves to be fuch, we are not capable of that mercy which we acknowledge we need, and pray for ; but having in the prayer of our Lord, begg'd pardon for thofe fins which we have conteft : And hoping, that as the *Prieft*
hath

hath declar'd our Abfolution, fo by our publick Confeffion, and real Repentance, we have obtain'd that pardon: Then, we dare proceed to beg of the Lord; *to open our lips, that our mouths may fhew forth his praife*; for, till then, we are neither able, nor worthy to praife him : But this being fuppos'd, we are then fit to fay, *Glory be to the Father, and to the Son, and to the Holy Ghoft*; and fit to proceed to a further fervice of our God, in the *Collects*, and *Pfalms*, and *Lauds* that follow in the Service.

And, as to thefe *Pfalms* and *Lauds*, he proceeded to inform them, why they were fo often, and fome of them daily repeated in our *Churchfervice* : namely, the *Pfalms* every Month, becaufe they be an *Hiftorical* and thankful repetition of mercies paft ; and, fuch a compofition of prayers and praifes, as ought to be repeated often, and publickly ; for, *with fuch Sacrifices, God is honour'd, and well-pleafed.* This, for the *Pfalms*.

And for the *Hymns* and *Lauds*, appointed to be daily repeated or fung after the firft and fecond Leffons were read to the Congregation, he proceeded to inform them, that it was moft reafonable, after they have heard the will and goodnefs of God declar'd or preach't by the *Prieft* in his reading the two Chapters, that it was then a feafonable Duty to rife up and exprefs their gratitude to Almighty God for thofe his mercies to them, and to all Mankind, and say with the *blessed Virgin*, *That their Souls do magnifie the Lord, and that their spirits do also rejoyce in God their Saviour :* And that it was their Duty also to rejoyce with *Simeon* in his Song, and say with him, *That their eyes have also seen their salvation;* for they have seen that salvation which was but prophesied till his time; and he then broke out in expressions of joy to see it : but they live to see it daily, in the History of it, and therefore ought daily to rejoyce, and daily to offer up their Sacrifices of praise to their God, for that and all his mercies. A service, which is now the constant employment of that *blessed Virgin*, and *Simeon*, and all those blessed Saints that are possest of Heaven; and where they are at this time interchangeably, and constantly singing, *Holy, Holy, Holy Lord God, Glory be to God on High , and on Earth peace.* And he taught them, that to do this, was an acceptable service to God, because the Prophet *David* sayes in his Psalms, *He that praiseth the Lord, honoureth him.*

He made them to understand, how happy they be that are freed from the incumbrances of that Law which our Fore-fathers groan'd under: namely; from the *Legal Sacrifices*; and from the many *Ceremonies of the Levitical Law:* freed from *Circumcision*, and from the strict observation of the *Jewish Sabbath*, and the like : And he made them know, that having receiv'd so many, and so great blessings, by being born

since

since the dayes of our Saviour, it muſt be an acceptable Sacrifice to Almighty God, for them to acknowledge thoſe bleſſings, and ſtand up and worſhip, and ſay as *Zacharias* did, *Bleſſed be the Lord God of* Iſrael, *for he hath* (in our dayes) *viſited and redeemed his people ; and* (he hath in our dayes) *remembred, and ſhewed that mercy which by the mouth of the Prophets, he promiſed to our Fore-fathers :* and this he hath done, *according to his holy Covenant made with them:* And we live to ſee and enjoy the benefit of it, in his *Birth,* in his *Life,* his *Paſſion,* his *Reſurrection* and *Aſcenſion* into Heaven, where he now ſits ſenſible of all our temptations and infirmities ; and where he is at this preſent time making interceſſion for us, to his, and our Father, and therefore they ought daily to expreſs their publick gratulations, and ſay daily with *Zacharias, Bleſſed be that Lord God of* Iſrael *that hath thus viſited, and thus redeemed his people.* -- Theſe were ſome of the reaſons by which Mr. *Herbert* inſtructed his Congregation for the uſe of the *Pſalms,* and the *Hymns* appointed to be daily ſung or ſaid in the Church-ſervice.

He inform'd them, when the *Prieſt* did pray only for the Congregation, and not for himſelf ; and when they did only pray for him, as namely, after the repetition of the *Creed,* before he proceeds to pray the Lords prayer, or any of the appointed Collects, the Prieſt is directed to kneel down, and pray for them, saying—*The Lord be with you* --And then they pray for him, saying-- *And with thy spirit.* and he assur'd them, that when there is such mutual love , and such joint prayers offer'd for each other , then the holy Angels look down from Heaven, and are ready to carry such charitable desires to God Almighty, and he as ready to receive them; and that a Christian Congregation calling thus upon God, with one heart, and one voyce, and in one reverend and humble posture look as beautifully as *Jerusalem,* that is at peace with it self.

He instructed them, why the prayer of our Lord was pray'd often in every full service of the Church; namely, at the conclusion of the several parts of that Service; and pray'd then, not only because it was compos'd and commanded by our Jesus that made it, but as a perfect pattern for our less perfect Forms of prayer, and therefore fittest to sum up and conclude all our imperfect Petitions.

He instructed them, that as by the second Commandment we are requir'd not to bow down, or worship an Idol, or false god; so, by the contrary Rule, we are to bow down and kneel, or stand up and worship the true God: And he instructed them, why the Church requir'd the Congregation to stand up, at the repetition of the Creeds; namely, because they did thereby declare both their obedience to the
Church,

Church, and an assent to that faith into which they had been baptiz'd.   And he taught them, that in that sho ter Creed, or Doxology so often repeated daily; they also stood up to testifie their belief to be, that, *the God that they trusted in was one God, and three persons the Father, the Son, and the Holy Ghost; to whom, the Priest gave glory:* And because there had been Hereticks that had denied some of these three persons to be God, therefore the Congregation stood up and honour'd him, by confessing and saying, *It was so in the beginning, is now so, and shall ever be so World without end.* And a l gave their assent to this belief, by saying *Amen.*

He instructed them, what benefit they had, by the Churches appointing the celebration of Holy-dayes, and the excellent use of them; namely, that they were set apart for particular Commemorations of particular mercies received from Almighty God; and (as Reverend Mr. *Hooker* sayes) to be the *Land marks* to distinguish times; for by them we are taught to take notice how the years pass by us; and, that we ought not to let them pass without a Celebration of praise for those mercies which they give us occasion to remember; and therefore the year is appointed to begin the 25*th* day of *March*; a day, in which we commemorate the *Angels* appearing to the *B.Virgin*,with the joyful tydings that *she should conceive and bear a Son, that should be the redeemer of Mankind*; and, she did so Forty weeks after this joyful salutation; namely, at our *Christmas*, a day in which we commemorate his Birth, with joy and praise; and that eight dayes after this happy Birth, we celebrate his *Circumcision*; namely, in that which we call *New-years day*. And that upon that we call *Twelfth-day*, we commemorate the manifestation of the unsearchable riches of Jesus to the *Gentiles*: And that day we also celebrate the memory of his goodness in sending a *Star* to guide the *three wise men* from the *East* to *Bethlem*, that they might there *worship*, and present him with their oblations of *Gold, Frankincense*, and *Myrrhe*. And he (Mr. *Herbert*) instructed them, that *Jesus* was Forty dayes after his Birth, presented by his blessed mother in the *Temple*; namely, on that day which we call, *the Purification of the blessed Virgin, Saint Mary*. And he instructed them, that by the *Lent-fast*, we imitate and commemorate our Saviours humiliation in fasting Forty dayes; and, that we ought to endeavour to be like him in purity, And, that on *Good-friday* we commemorate and condole his *Crucifixion*. And, at *Easter*, commemorate his *glorious Resurrection*. And he taught them, that after Jesus had manifested himself to his Disciples, to be that *Christ* that was crucified, dead and buried; that then by his appearing and conversing with them for the space of Forty dayes after his *Resurrection*, he then, and not till then, ascended into

Heaven,

Heaven, in the fight of his Difciples, namely, on that day which we call the *Afcenfion,* or *Holy Thurfday.* And that we then celebrate the performance of the promife which he made to his Difciples, at or before his Afcenfion; namely, *that though he left them, yet he would fend them the Holy Ghoft to be their Comforter;* and he did fo on that day which the Church calls *Whitfunday*——Thus the Church keeps an Hiftorical and circular Commemoration of times, as they pafs by us; of fuch times, as ought to incline us to occafional praifes, for the particular bleffings which we do, or might receive at thofe holy times.

He made them know, why the Church hath appointed *Ember-weeks*; and, to know the reafon why the *Commandements,* and the *Epiftles* and *Gofpels* were to be read at the *Altar,* or *Communion Table:* why the Prieft was to pray the *Litany* kneeling; and, why to pray fome *Collects* ftanding; and he gave them many other obfervations, fit for his plain Congregation, but not fit for me now to mention; for I muft fet limits to my Pen, and not make that a Treatife, which I intended to be a much fhorter account than I have made it; but I have done, when I have told the Reader, that he was conftant in *Catechifing* every *Sunday* in the Afternoon, and that his Catechifing was after his fecond leffon, and in the Pulpit, and that he never exceeded his half hour, and was always fo happy as to have a full Congregation.   But

But to this I muſt add, That if he were at any time too zealous in his Sermons, it was, in reproving the indecencies of the peoples behaviour, in the time of Divine Service; and of thoſe Miniſters that hudled up the Church-prayers, without a viſible reverence and affection; namely, ſuch as ſeem'd to ſay the Lords prayer, or a Collect in a breath; but for himſelf, his cuſtom was, to ſtop betwixt every Collect, and give the peop'e time to conſider what they had pray'd, and to force their deſires affectionate'y to God, before he engag'd them into new Petitions.

And by this account of his diligence, to make his Pariſhioners underſtand what, and why they pray'd, and prais'd, and ador'd their Creator. I hope I ſhall the more eaſily obtain the Readers belief to the following account of Mr. *Herberts* own practice; which was, to appear conſtantly with his Wife, and three Neeces (the daughters of a deceaſed Siſter) and his whole Family, twice a day at the Church-prayers, in the Chappel which does almoſt join to his Parſonage-houſe. And for the time of his appearing, it was ſtrictly at the Canonical hours of Ten and Four; and then, and there, he lifted up pure and charitable hands to God in the midſt of the Congregation. And he would joy to have ſpent that time in that place, where the honour of his Maſter Jeſus dwelleth; and there, by that inward devotion which he teſtifi-

ed

ed conſtantly by an humble behaviour, and viſible adoration, he, like _David_, brought not
only _his own Houſhold thus to ſerve the Lord_;
but brought moſt of his Pariſhioners, and many
Gentlemen in the Neighbourhood, conſtantly
to make a part of his Congregation twice a
day; and ſome of the meaner ſort of his Pa-
riſh, did ſo love and reverence Mr. _Herbert_, that
they would let their Plow reſt when Mr. _Her-
berts Saints-Bell_ rung to Prayers, that they
might alſo offer their devotions to God with
him, and would then return back to their Plow.
And his moſt holy life was ſuch, that it begot
ſuch reverence to God, and to him, that they
thought themſelves the happier, when they carried Mr. _Herberts_ bleſſing back with them to
their labour. Thus powerful was his reaſon,
and example, to perſwade others to a practical
piety.

And his conſtant publick Prayers did never
make him to neglect his own private devotions, nor thoſe prayers that he thought himſelf
bound to perform with his Family; which alwayes were a Set-form, and not long; and he
did alwayes conclude them with that Collect
which the Church hath appointed for the day
or week.——_Thus he made every dayes ſanctity a
ſtep towards that Kingdom where Impurity cannot
enter._

His chiefeſt recreation was Muſick, in which
heavenly Art he was a moſt excellent Maſter,
and

and, compos'd many *divine Hymns* and *Anthems*, which he set and sung to his *Lute* or *Viol*; and, though he was a lover of retirednefs, yet his love to *Mufick* was fuch, that he went ufually twice every week on certain appointed dayes, to the *Cathedral Church* in *Salisbury*; and at his return would fay, *That his time fpent in Prayer, and Cathedral Mufick, elevated his Soul, and was his Heaven upon Earth:* But before his return thence to *Bemerton*, he would ufually fing and play his part, at an appointed private Mulick meeting; and, to juftifie this practice, he would often fay, *Religion does not banifh mirth, but only moderates, and fets rules to it.*

And, as his defire to enjoy *his Heaven upon Earth*, drew him twice every week to *Salisbury*, fo, his walks thither, were the occafion of many happy accidents to others, of which, I will mention fome few.

In one of his walks to *Salisbury*, he overtook a Gentleman that is ftill living in that City, and in their walk together, Mr. *Herbert* took a fair occafion to talk with him, and humbly begg'd to be excus'd, if he ask'd him fome account of his faith; and faid, *I do this, the rather, becaufe though you are not of my Parifh, yet I receive Tythe from you by the hand of your Tenant; and, Sir, I am the bolder*

to

to do it, because I know there be some Sermon-hearers, that be like those Fishes, that alwayes live in salt water, and yet are alwayes fresh.

After which expression, Mr. *Herbert* asked him some needful Questions, and having received his answer, gave him such Rules for the tryal of his sincerity, and for a practical piety, and in so loving and meek a manner, that the Gentleman did so fall in love with him, and his discourse, that he would often contrive to meet him in his walk to *Salisbury*, or to attend him back to *Bemerton*; and still mentions the name of Mr. *George Herbert* with veneration, and still praises God that he knew him.

In another of his *Salisbury* walks, he met with a Neighbour Minister, and after some friendly Discourse betwixt them, and some Condolement for the wickedness of the Times, and Contempt of the Clergy, Mr. *Herbert* took occcasion to say,

One Cure for these Distempers, would be for the Clergy themselves to keep the Ember-Weeks *strictly, and begg of their Parishioners to joyn with him in* Fasting *and* Prayers, *for a more Religious Clergy.*

And

And another Cure would be, *for them to re-store the great and neglected duty of* Catechi-*sing, on which the salvation of so many of the poor and ignorant Lay-people does depend; but prin-cipally, that the Clergy themselves would be sure to live unblameably; and that the dignified Cler-gy especially, which preach Temperance, would avoid Surfeting, and take all occasions to express a visible humility, and charity in their lives; for this would force a love and an imitation, and an unfeigned reverence from all that knew them:* (And for proof of this, we need no other Te-stimony, than the life and death of Dr. *Lake,* late Lord Bishop of *Bath* and *Wells*) *This,* (said Mr. *Herbert*) *would be a Cure for the wickedness and growing Atheism of our Age. And,* my dear Brother, *till this be done by us, and done in ear-nest, let no man expect a reformation of the man-ners of the* Laity: *for 'tis not learning, but this, this only, that must do it; and till then, the fault must lie at our doors.*

In another walk to *Salisbury,* he saw a poor man, with a poorer horse, that was fall'n under his Load; they were both in distress, and need-ed present help; which Mr. *Herbert* perceiv-ing, put off his Canonical Coat, and help'd the poor man to unload, and after to load his horse: The poor man blest him for it; and he blest the poor man, and was so like the *good Samaritan,* that he gave him money to refresh both himself and his horse; and told him, *That*
if

if he lov'd himself, he should be merciful to his Beast. Thus he left the poor man, and at his coming to his musical friends at *Salisbury,* they began to wonder that Mr. *George Herbert,* which us'd to be so trim and clean, came into that company so soyl'd and discompos'd; but he told them the occasion: And when one of the company told him, *He had disparag'd himself by so dirty an employment;* his answer was, *That the thought of what he had done, would prove Musick to him at Midnight; and the omission of it, would have upbraided and made discord in his Conscience, whensoever he should pass by that place; for if I be bound to pray for all that be in distress, I am sure I am bound so far as it is in my power to practise what I pray for. And though I do not wish for the like occasion every day yet let me tell you, I would not willingly pass one day of my life, without comforting a sad soul, or shewing mercy; and I praise God for this occasion:* And now let's tune our Instruments.

Thus, as our blessed Saviour after his Resurrection, did take occasion to interpret the Scripture to *Cleopas,* and that other Disciple which he met with and accompanied too in their journey to *Emmaus;* so Mr. *Herbert,* in his path toward Heaven, did daily take any fair occasion to instruct the ignorant, or comfort any that were in affliction; and did alwayes confirm his precepts, by shewing mercy.

And

And he was most happy in his Wifes un-forc'd compliance with his acts of Charity, whom he made his *Almoner*, and paid constant-ly into her hand, *a tenth penny* of what money he receiv'd for Tythe, and gave her a power to dispose that to the poor of his Parish, and with it a power to dispose a tenth part of the Corn that came yearly into his Barn; which trust she did most faithfully perform, and would often offer to him *an account of her stewardship*, and as often beg an inlargement of his bounty, for she rejoyc'd in the employment; and this was usually laid out by her in *Blankets* and *Shooes*, for some such poor people, as she knew to stand in most need of them.   This, as to her Chari-ty———And for his own, he set no limits to it; nor did ever turn his face from any that he saw in want, but would relieve them, especially his poor Neighbours, to the meanest of whose Houses, he would go and inform himself of their wants, and relieve them chearfully if they were in distress; and would alwayes praise God, as much for being willing, as for being able to do it.   And, when he was advis'd by a friend to be more frugal, because he might have Children, his answer was, *He would not see the danger of want so far off*; *but, being the Scri-pture does so commend Charity, as to tell us, that Charity is the top of Christian vertues, the co-vering of sins, the fulfilling of the Law, the life of Faith. And, that Charity hath a promise of*
the

the bleſſings of this life, and of a reward in that life which is to come; being theſe, and more excellent things are in Scripture ſpoken of thee O Charity; and being all my Tythes, and Church-dues, are a Deodate from thee O my God; make me, O my God, ſo far to truſt thy promiſe, as to return them back to thee: and, by thy grace, I will do ſo, in diſtributing them to any of thy poor members that are in diſtreſs, or do but bear the image of Jeſus my Maſter. Sir (ſaid he to his friend) my Wife hath a competent maintenance ſecur'd her after my death, and therefore as this is my prayer, ſo this my reſolution ſhall by Gods grace be unalterable.

This may be ſome account of the excellencies of the active part of his life, and thus he continued, till a Conſumption ſo weakned him, as to confine him to his Houſe, or to the Chappel, which does almoſt join to it; in which, he continued to read Prayers conſtantly twice every day, though he were very weak; in one of which times of his reading, his Wife obſerv'd him to read in pain, and told him ſo, and that it waſted his ſpirits, weakned him, and he confeſs'd it, but ſaid, *His life could not be better ſpent, than in the ſervice of his Maſter Jeſus, who had done and ſuffered ſo much for him:* But, he ſaid, *I will not be wilful, for* Mr. Boſtock *ſhall be appointed to read* Prayers *for me to morrow, and I will now be only a hearer of them, till this mortal ſhall put on immortality.* And Mr. Boſtock

E　　　　did

did the next day undertake and continue th's
happy employment, till Mr. *Herberts* death.---
This Mr. *Bostock* was a learned and vertuous
man, an old friend of Mr. *Herberts,* and then
his Curate to the Church of *Fulston,* which is
a mile from *Bemerton,* to which Church, *Be-*
merton is but a *Chappel of ease.*--- And, this Mr.
Bostock did also constantly supply the *Church-*
service for Mr. *Herbert* in that Chappel, when
the Musick-meeting at *Salisbury,* caus'd his absence from it.

About one month before his death, h's friend
Mr. *Farrer* (for an account of whom I am by
promise indebted to the Reader, and intend to
make him sudden payment) sent Mr. *Edmund*
Duncon (who is now Rector of *Fryer Barnet* in
the County of *Middlesex*) from his House of
Gidden Hal', w! i h is near to *Huntington,* to see
Mr. *Herbert,* and to assure him, he wanted not
his daily prayers for his recovery ; and Mr. *Dun-*
con was to return back to *Gidden,* with an account of Mr. *Herberts* condition. Mr. *Dun-*
con found him at that time lying on his Bed, or
on a Pallet ; but at his seeing Mr. *Duncon,* he
rais'd himself vigorously, saluted him, and with
some earnestness inquir'd the health of his brother *Farrer,* of which Mr. *Duncon* satisfied
him ; and after a conference of Mr. *Farrers*
holy life, and the manner of his constant serving
God, he said to Mr. *Duncon*---*Sir, I see by your*
habit that you are a Priest, and I desire you to pray
with

with me; which being granted, Mr. *Duncon*
ask'd him, *what Prayers?* to which, Mr. *Her-*
berts anſwer was, *O Sir, the Prayers of my Mo-*
ther, the Church of England, *no other Prayers are*
equal to them; but, *at this time, I beg of you to*
pray only the Litany. *for I am weak and faint*, and
Mr. *Duncon* did ſo. After which, and ſome
other diſcourſe of Mr. *Farrer*, M·s. *Herbert*
provided Mr. *Duncon* a plain Supper, and a clean
Lodging, and he betook himſelf to reſt--*This*
Mr. *Duncon tells me*; and, that at his firſt view
of Mr. *Herbert*, he ſaw ʋ ajeſty and humility ſo
reconcil'd in his looks and behaviour, as begot
in him an awful reverence for his perſon, and
ſayes, his diſcourſe was ſo pious, and his motion ſo gentile and meek, that after almoſt forty
years, they remain ſtill freſh in his memory.

The next morning, Mr. *Duncon* left him, and
betook himſelf to a Journey to *Bath*, but with
a promiſe to return back to him within five
dayes, and he did ſo; but before I ſh ll ſay any
thing of what diſcourſe then fell betwixt them
two, I will pay my promis'd account of Mr.
Farrer.

Mr. *Nicholas Farrer* (who got the reputation of being call'd Saint *Nicholas*, at the age of
ſix years) was born in *London*, and doubtleſs
had good education in his youth; but certainly, was at a fit age made Fellow of *Clare-Hall*
in *Cambridge*, where he continued to be eminent

E 2 for

for his temperance and learning. .About the
26th year of h s Age, he betook himſelf to
Travel, in which ﬁe added to his Latin and
Greek, a peﬁect knowledg: of all the Languages ſpoken in the Weſte.n parts of our Chriſtian world and underſtood well the principles
of their Religion, and their manner, and the
reaſons of their worſhip. In this his Travel,
he met with many perſwaſions to come into a
communion with that Church which calls it
ſelf *Catholick*, but he return'd from his Travels
as he went, eminent for his obedience to his
Mother, *the Church of England*. In his abſence
from *England* Mr. *Farrers* father (who was a
Merchant) allow'd him a liberal m intenance;
and, not long after his return into *England*, he
had by the death of his father, or an elder brother, an Eſtate left him, that enabled him to
buy Land to the value of 500 *l.* a year, the
greateſt part of which Land was at *Little Gidden*, four or ſix miles from *Huntington*, and a-
bout 18 from *Cambridge*, which place he choſe
for the privacy of it, and the Hall, which had
the Pariſh-Church, or Chappel belonging, and
adjoining near to it; for Mr. *Farrer* having
ſeen the manners and vanities of the World,
and found them to be, as Mr. *Herbert* ſayes, *A
nothing between two Diſhes*; he did ſo contemn
the World, that he reſolv'd to ſpend the remainder of his life in mortifications, and in devotion, and charity, and to be alwayes prepar'd
for

for Death. —— And his Life was spent thus.

He, and his Family, which were like a little Colledge, and about Thirty in number, did most of them keep *Lent,* and all *Ember-weeks* strictly, both in fasting, and using all those prayers that the Church hath appointed to be then used ; and he and they, did the like on *Fridayes,* and on the *Vigils,* or Eves appointed to be fasted before the Saints dayes ; and, this frugality and abstinence, turn'd to the relief of the Poor ; but, this was but a part of his charity, none but God and he knew the rest.

This Family, which I have said to be in number about Thirty, ere a part of them his Kindred, and the rest chosen to be of a temper fit to be moulded into a devout life ; and all of them were for their dispositions serviceable and quiet, and humble, and free from scandal. Having thus fitted himself for his Family, he did about the year 1630. betake himself to a constant and methodical service of God, and it was in this manner.——He did himself use to read the Com non prayers (for he was a Deacon) every day, at the appointed hours of ten and four, in the Church which was very near his House, and which he had both repair'd and adorn'd ; for it was fall'n into a great ruine, by reason of a depopulation of the Village before Mr. *Farrer* bought the Mannor. And he did also constantly read the *Mattins* every morning

E 3 at

at the hour of six, either in the Church, or in
an Oratory, which was within his own House:
And many of the Family did there continue
with him after the Prayers were ended , and
there they spent some hours in singing Hymns,
or Anthems, sometimes in the Church, and
often to an Organ in the Oratory. And, they
sometimes betook themselves to meditate, or
to pray privately, or to read a part of the New
Testament, or to continue their praying or
reading the Psalms; and in case the Psalms
were not all read in the day, then Mr. *Farrer*,
and others of the Congregation, did at Night,
at the ring of a Watch-bell, repair to the
Church or Oratory, and there betake themselves to prayers, and lauding God, and reading
the Psalms that had not been read in the day;
and when these, or any part of the Congregation grew weary, or faint, the Watch-bell was
rung, sometimes before, and sometimes after
Midnight; and then a part of the Family rose,
and maintain'd the Watch, sometimes by praying, or singing Lauds to God, or reading the
Psalms; and when after some hours they also
grew weary or faint, then they rung the Watch-
bell, and were reliev'd by some of the former,
or by a new part of the Society, which continued their devotions (as hath been mentioned)
until morning.---And it is to be noted, that in
this continued serving of God, the Psalter, or
whole Book of Psalms, was in every four and
twenty

twenty hours, fung or read over, from the firft to the laft verfe, and this done as conftantly, as the Sun runs his Circle every day about the World, and then begins it again the fame inftant that it ended.

Thus did Mr. *Farrer* and his happy Family, ferve God day and night. Thus did they alwayes behave themfelves, as in his prefence. And they did alwayes eat and d.ink by the ftricteft rules of Temperance; eat and drink fo, as to be ready to rife at Midnight, or at the call of a Watch-bell, and perform their devotions to God.---And 'tis fit to tell the Reader, that many of the Clergy that were more inclin'd to practical piety, and devotion, then to doubtful and needlefs Difputations , did often come to *Gidden Hall*, and make themfelves a part of that happy Society, and ftay a week or more, and join with Mr. *Farrer*, and the Family in thefe Devotions, and affift and eafe him or them in their Watch by Night ; and thefe various Devotions, had never lefs than two of the domeftick Family in the Night; and the Watch was alwayes kept in the Church or Oratory unlefs in extreme cold Winter-nights, and then it was maintain'd in a Parlor which had a fire in it, and the Parlor was fitted for that purpofe; and this courfe of piety, and great liberality to his poor Neighbours, Mr. *Farrer* maintain'd till his death, which was in the year 1639.

E 4   Mr.

Mr. *Farrers*, and Mr. *Herberts* devout lives, were both so noted, that the general report of their sanctity, gave them occasion to renew that slight acquaintance which was begun at their being Contemporaries in *Cambridge*, and, this new holy friendship was maintain'd without any interview, but only by loving and endearing Letters. And, one testimony of their friendship, and pious designs, may appear by Mr. *Farrers* commending the considerations of *John Valdesso* (a Book which he had met with in his Travels, and Translated out of *Spanish* into *English*) to be examin'd and censur'd by Mr. *Herbert*; which Book, Mr. *Herbert* did read, and return back with many marginal Notes, as they be now printed with that excellent Book; and with them, Mr. *Herberts* affectionate Letter to Mr. *Farrer*.

This *John Valdesso* was a *Spaniard*, and was for his Learning and Vertue, much valued and lov'd by the great Emperour *Charles the fifth*, whom *Valdsso* had followed as a *Cavalier* all the time of his long and dangerous Wars; and when *Valdesso* grew old, and weary of the World he took his fair opportunity to declare to the Emperour, that his resolution was to decline His Majesties Service, and betake himself to a quiet an contemplative life, *because there ought to be a vacancy of time, betwixt fighting and dying.*---The Emperor had himself, for the same, or other reasons, put on the same resolutions;

tions; but God and himself did then only know them; and he did for those, or other reasons, desire *Valdesso* to consider well of what he had said, but keep his purpose within his own breast, till they two had another like opportunity of a friendly Discourse, which *Valdesso* promis'd.

In the mean time, the Emperour aproints privately a day for him and *Valdesso* to receive the Sacrament publickly, and appointed an eloquent and devout Fryer, to preach a Sermon of contempt of the World, and of the happiness and benefit of a quiet and contemplative life, which the Fryer did most affectionately. After which Sermon, the Emperour declar'd openly, *That the Preacher had begot in him a resolution to lay down his Dignities, to forsake the World, and betake himself to a Monastical life.* And, he pretended, he had perswaded *John Valdesso* to do the like; but this is most certain, that after the Emperour had called his son *Philip* out of *England*, and resign'd to him all his Kingdoms, that then the Emperour, and *John Valdesso*, did perform their resolutions.

This account of *John Valdesso*, I receiv'd from a Friend, that had it from the mouth of Mr. *Farrer:* And, the Reader may note, that in this retirement, *John Valdesso* writ his 110 considerations, and many other Treatises of worth, which want a second Mr. *Farrer* to procure, and Translate them.

After

After this account of Mr. *Farrer*, and *John Valdesso*, I proceed to my account of Mr. *Herbert*, and Mr. *Duncon*, who, according to his promise, return'd the fifth day, and found Mr. *Herbert* much weaker than he left him, and therefore their Discourse could not be long; but at Mr. *Duncons* parting with him, Mr. *Herbert* spoke to this purpose--- *Sir, I pray give my brother* Farrer *an account of my decaying condition, and tell him, I beg him to continue his prayers for me, and let him know, that I have consider'd, That God only is what he would be; and, that I am by his grace become now so like him, as to be pleas'd with what pleaseth him, and do not repine at my want of health; and tell him, my heart is fixed on that place where true joy is only to be found; and, that I long to be there, and will wait my appointed change with hope and patience.*—And having said this, he did with such a humility as seem'd to exalt him, bow down to Mr. *Duncon*, and with a thoughtful and contented look, say to him, *Sir, I pray deliver this little Book to my dear brother* Farrer, *and tell him, he shall find in it a picture of the many spiritual Conflicts that have past betwixt God and my Soul, before I could subject mine to the will of* Jesus *my Master, in whose service I have now found perfect freedom; desire him to read it, and then if he can think it may turn to the advantage of any dejected poor Soul, let it be made publick; if not, let him burn it, for I and it, are less than the least of Gods*

mer-

mercies.---Thus meanly did this humble man think of this excellent Book, which now bears the name of *The TEMPLE: Or, Sacred Poems, and Private Ejaculations*; of which, Mr. *Farrer* would say, *There was the picture of a Divine Soul in every page; and, that the whole Book, was such a harmony of holy passions, as would enrich the World with pleasure and piety.* And, it appears to have done so, for there have been Ten thousand of them sold since the first Impression.

And this ought to be noted, that when Mr. *Farrer* sent this Book to *Cambridge* to be Licensed for the Press, the *Vice-Chancellor* would by no means allow the two so much noted Verses

Religion stands a Tip-toe in our Land,
Ready to pass to the American *Strand.*

to be printed; and, Mr. *Farrer*, would by no means allow the Book to be printed, and want them: But after some time, and some arguments for, and against their being made publick, the *Vice-Chancellor* said, *I knew Mr.* Herbert *well, and know that he had many heavenly Speculations, and was a Divine Poet; but, I hope the World will not take him to be an inspired Prophet, and therefore I License the whole Book:* So that it came to be printed, without the diminution or addition of a syllable, since it was deliver'd ver'd into the hands of Mr. *Duncon*, save only, that Mr. *Farrer* hath added that excellent Preface that is printed before it.

At the time of Mr. *Duncons* leaving Mr. *Herbert*, which was about three Weeks before his death, his old and dear friend Mr. *Woodnot*, came from *London* to *Bemerton*, and never left him, till he had seen him draw his last breath, and clos'd his Eyes on his Death-bed. In this time of his decay, he was often visited and pray'd for by all the Clergy that liv'd near to him, especially by the Bishop and Prebends of the Cathedral Church in *Salisbury*; but by none more devoutly, than his Wife, his three Neeces (then a part of his Family) and Mr. *Woodnot*, who were the sad Witnesses of his daily decay, to whom he would often speak to this purpose.-- *I now look back upon the pleasures of my life past, and see the content I have taken in beauty, in wit, in musick, and pleasant Conversation, ~~but they~~ are now all past by me, as a shadow that returns not, and are all become dead to me, or I to them; that as my father and generation hath done before me, so I shall now suddenly (with* Job) *make my Bed also in the dark ; and, I praise God, I am prepar'd for it ; and, that I am not to learn patience, now I stand in such need of it ; and, that I have practised Mortification, and endeavour'd to dye daily, that I might not dye eternally ; and, my hope is, that I shall shortly leave this valley of tears, and be free from all fevers* and

and pain : and which will be a more happy condition, I shall be free from sin, and all the temptations and anxieties that attend it ; and this being past, I shall dwell in the new Jerusalem *, dwell there with men made perfect ; dwell, where these eyes shall see my Master and Saviour* Jesus *; and, with him, see my dear mother, and relations, and friends ; but I must dye, or not come to that happy place : And, this is my content, that I am going daily towards it ; and, that every day that I have liv'd, hath taken a part of my appointed time from me ; and, that I shall live the less time, for having liv'd this, and the day past.* ---These, and the like expressions, which he utter'd often, may be said to be his enjoyment of Heaven, before he enjoy'd it. The *Sunday* before his death, he rose Suddenly from his Bed or Couch, call'd for one of his Instruments, took it into hand, and said--*My God, my God,* .

> *My Musick shall find thee ,*
>   *And every string*
> *shall have his attribute to sing.*

And having tun'd it, he play'd and sung:

> *The Sundayes of mans life ,*
> *Thredded together on times string ,*
> *Make Bracelets, to adorn the Wife*
> *Of the eternal glorious King :*
> *On Sundayes, Heavens dore stands ope ;*
> *Blessings are plentiful and rife,*
>   *More plentiful than hope.*

Thus he sung on earth such Hymns and Anthems, as the Angels and he, and Mr. *Farrer,* now sing in Heaven.   Thus

Thus he continued meditating and praying, and rejoycing, till the day of his death, and on that day said to Mr. *Woodnot, My dear Friend, I am sorry I have nothing to present to my merciful God but sin and misery; but the first is pardon'd, and a few hours will put a period to the latter.* Upon which expression, Mr. *Woodnot* took occasion to remember him of the Re-edifying *Layton* Church, and his many Acts of mercy; to which he made answer, saying, *They be good works, if they be sprinkled with the blood of Christ, and not otherwise.* After this Discourse, he became more restless, and his Soul seem'd to be weary of her earthly Tabernacle; and this uneasiness became so visible, that his Wife, his three Neeces, and Mr. *Woodnot,* stood constantly about his Bed, beholding him with sorrow, and an unwillingness to lose the sight of him whom they could not hope to see much longer. As they stood thus beholding him, his Wife observ'd him to breath faintly, and with much trouble; and, observ'd him to fall into a sudden Agony; which so surpriz'd her, that she fell into a sudden passion, and requir'd of him to know *how he did?* to which his answer was, *That he had past a Conflict with his last Enemy, and had overcome him, by the merits of his Master Jesus.* After which answer, he look'd up, and saw his Wife and Neeces weeping to an extremity, and charg'd them, *If they lov'd him, to withdraw into the next Room, and there pray every one alone*
for

for him, for nothing but their lamentations could make his death uncomfortable. To which request, their sighs and tears would not suffer them to make any reply, but they yielded him a sad obedience, leaving only with him Mr. *Woodnot*, and Mr. *Bostock.* Immediately after they had left him, he said to Mr. *Bostock, Pray Sir open that door, then look into that Cabinet, in which you may easily find my last Will, and give it into my hand;* which being done, he deliver'd it into the hand of Mr. *Woodnot,* and said, *My old Friend, I here deliver you my last Will, in which you will find that I have made you my sole Executor for the good of my Wife and Neeces, and I desire you to shew kindness to them, as they shall need it; I do not desire you to be just, for I know you will be so for your own sake; but I charge you, by the Religion of our friendship, to be careful of them.* And having obtain'd Mr. *Woodnots* promise to be so, he said, *I am now ready to dye;* after which words he said, *Lord, grant me mercy, for the merits of my Jesus, and now, Lord, receive my Soul.* And with those words breath'd forth his Divine Soul, without any apparent disturbance, Mr. *Woodnot,* and Mr. *Bostock,* attending his last breath, and closing his eyes.

Thus he liv'd, and thus he dy'd like a Saint, unspotted of the World, full of Almf-deeds, full of Humility, and all the examples of vertuous life; which I cannot conclude better, than with this borrowed observation:

—— *All*

———————— *All must to the cold Graves :*
But, the religious actions of the just,
Smell sweet in death, and blossom in the dust.

Mr. *George Herberts* have done so to this, and will doubtless do so to succeeding Generations.

F I N I S.

THere is a Debt juſtly due to the memory of Mr. Herberts vertuous Wife, a part of which I will endeavour to pay by a very ſhort account of the remainder of her life, which ſhall follow.

She continued his diſconſolate Widow five years, bemoaning her ſelf, and complaining, That ſhe had loſt the delight of her eyes; but more, that ſhe had loſt the ſpiritual guide for her poor ſoul; and would often ſay, O that I had like holy Mary, the Mother of Jeſus, treaſur'd up all his ſayings in my heart; but ſince I have not been able to do that, I will labour to live like him, that where he now is, I may be alſo. And ſhe would often ſay (as the Prophet David for his ſon Abſolon) O that I had dyed for him. Thus ſhe continued mourning, till time and converſation had ſo moderated her ſorrows, that ſhe became the happy Wife of Sir Robert Cook of Higham in the County of Glouceſter Knight: And, though he put a high value on the excellent accompliſhments of her mind and body; and was ſo like Mr. Herbert, as not to govern like a Maſter, but as an affectionate Husband; yet, ſhe would even to him often take occaſion to mention the name of Mr. George Herbert, and ſay, That name muſt live in her memory. till ſhe put off mortality. By Sir Robert, ſhe had only one Child, a Daughter, whoſe parts and plentiful eſtate make her happy in this world, and her well uſing

F

of

of them, gives a fair testimony, that she will be so in that which is to come.

Mrs. Herbert *was the Wife of Sir* Robert *eight years, and liv'd his Widow nine; all which time, she took a pleasure in mentioning, and commending the excellencies of Mr.* George Herbert. *She dyed in the year* 1663. *and lies buried at* Higham, *Mr.* Herbert *in his own Church, under the Altar, and cover'd with a Grave-stone without any inscription.*

This Lady Cook, *had preserv'd many of Mr.* Herberts *private Writings, which she intended to make publick; but they, and* Higham *house, were burnt together, by the late Rebels; and by them was also burnt or destroyed a choice Library, which Mr.* Herbert *had fastned with Chains, in a fit room in* Mountgomery *Castle, being by him dedicated to the succeeding* Herberts, *that should become the owners of it. He dyed without an Enemy, if* Andrew Melvin *dyed before him?*

F I N I S.

LETTERS

WRITTEN BY

Mr. *GEORGE HERBERT*,

At his being in

Cambridge :

With others to his Mother, the Lady
MAGDALEN HERBERT:

WRITTEN BY

John Donne,

AFTERWARDS
Dean of St. *PAULS*.

LONDON,

Printed by *Tho: Newcomb*, for *Richard Marriott*,
Sold by moſt Bookſellers. M.DC.LXX.

Mr. *GEORGE HER-BERT* to *N. F.* the Translatour of *Valdeſſo.*

MY dear and deſerving Brother, your Val-
deſſo *I now return with many thanks,
and ſome notes, in which perhaps you will diſcover ſome care, which I forbear not in the midſt
of my griefs ; Firſt for your ſake ; becauſe, I
would do nothing negligently that you commit unto me ; Secondly for the Authors ſake, whom I
conceive to have been a true ſervant of God ;
and to ſuch, and all that is theirs, I owe diligence ; Thirdly for the Churches ſake, to whom
by Printing it, I would have you conſecrate it. You
owe the Church a debt, and God hath put this into your hands (as he ſent the Fiſh with money to
St. Peter) to diſcharge it : happily alſo with this
(as his thoughts are fruitful) intending the honour of his ſervant the Author, who being obſcu-
red in his own Countrey, he would have to flouriſh
in this land of light, and region of the Goſpel,
among his choſen. It is true, there are ſome
things which I like not in him, as my frag-
ments will expreſs, when you read them ; nevertheleſs I wiſh you by all means to publiſh*

it,

it, for these three eminent things observable there-in: First, *that God in the midst of* Popery *should open the eyes of one to understand and express so clearly, and excellently the intent of the Gospel in the acceptation of Chrifts righteousness :* (*as he sheweth through all his* Considerations,) *a thing strangely buried, and darkned by the Adverfaries, and their great stumbling block.* Secondly, *the great honour and reverence, which he everywhere bears towards our dear Master and Lord ; concluding every Consideration almost with his holy Name, and setting his merit forth so pioufly ; for which I do so love him, that were there nothing else, I would Print it, that with it the honour of my Lord might be publifhed.* Thirdly, *the many pious rules of ordering our life, about Mortification, and obfervation of Gods Kingdom within us, and the working thereof ; of which he was a very diligent obferver.* These three things are very eminent in the Author, and overweigh the Defects (as I conceive) towards the publifhing thereof.*

From his Parfonage
of *Bemerton,* near
Salisbury, Sept.

To Sir *J. D.*

SIR,

THough I had the beſt wit in the World,
yet it would eaſily tyre me, to find out
variety of thanks for the diverſity of your favours, if I ſought to do ſo ; but, I profeſs it not :
And therefore let it be ſufficient for me, that the
ſame heart, which you have won long ſince, is ſtill
true to you, and hath nothing elſe to anſwer
your infinite kindneſſes, but a conſtancy of obedience; only hereafter I will take heed how I
propoſe my deſires unto you, ſince I find you ſo
willing to yield to my requeſts ; for, ſince your
favours come a Horſe-back, there is reaſon, that
my deſires ſhould go a-foot : neither do I make
any queſtion, but that you have performed your
kindneſs to the full, and that the Horſe is every way fit for me, and I will ſtrive to imitate
the compleatneſs of your love, with being in ſome
proportion, and after my manner,

Your moſt obedient Servant,

George Herbert.

　　　　　　For

For my dear fick Sifter.

Moft dear Sifter,

THink not my filence forgetfulnefs; or, that
my love is as dumb as my papers, though
bufineffes may ftop my hand, yet my heart, a much
better member, is alwayes with you : and which is
more, with our good and gracious God, inceffantly
begging fome eafe of your pains, with that earneftnefs, that becomes your griefs, and my love. God
who knows and fees this Writing, knows alfo that
my folliciting him has been much, and my tears
many for you ; judge me then by thofe waters, and
not by my ink, and then you fhall juftly value

Your moft truly,

moft heartily,

*Decem.*6. 16 20.   affectionate Brother,

Trin: Coll.

and Servant,

George Herbert.

S I R,

SIR,

I Dare no longer be *silent*, *leaft while I think I am modeft*, *I wrong both my felf*, *and alfo the confidence my Friends have in me*; *wherefore I will open my cafe unto you*, *which I think deferves the reading at the leaft*; *and it is this*, *I want Books extremely*; *You know Sir*, *how I am now fetting foot into Divinity*, *to lay the platform of my future life*, *and fhall I then be fain alwayes to borrow Books*, *and build on anothers foundation?* *What Tradef-man is there who will fet up without his Tools?* *Pardon my boldnefs Sir*, *it is a moft ferious Cafe*, *nor can I write coldly in that*, *wherein confifteth the making good of my former education*, *of obeying that Spirit which hath guided me hitherto*, *and of atchieving my (I dare fay) holy ends. This alfo is aggravated*, *in that I apprehend what my Friends would have been forward to fay*, *if I had taken ill courfes*, Follow your Book, and you fhall want nothing : *You know Sir*, *it is their ordinary fpeech*, *and now let them make it good*; *for*, *fince*, *I hope*, *I have not deceived their expectation*, *let not them deceive mine:* *But perhaps they will fay*, *you are fickly*, *you muft not ftudy too hard*; *it is true (God knows) I am weak*, *yet not fo*, *but that every day*, *I may ftep one ftep towards my journies end:*

and

and I love my friends so well, as that if all
things proved not well, I had rather the fault
should lie on me, than on them ; but they will
object again. What becomes of your Annuity?
Sir, if there be any truth in me, I find it
little enough to keep me in health. You know
I was sick last Vacation, neither am I yet recovered, so that I am fain ever and anon, to
buy somewhat tending towards my health; for
infirmities are both painful and costly. Now
this Lent I am forbid utterly to eat any Fish,
so that I am fain to dyet in my Chamber at
mine own cost; for in our publick Halls, you
know, is nothing but Fish and Whit-meats.
Out of Lent also, twice a Week, on Fridayes
and Saturdayes, I must do so, which yet sometimes I fast. Sometimes also I ride to New-
market, and there lie a day or two for fresh
Air; all which tend to avoiding of costlier matters, if I should fall absolutely sick: I protest
and vow, I even study Thrift, and yet I am
scarce able with much ado to make one half
years allowance, shake hands with the other:
And yet if a Book of four or five Shillings
come in my way, I buy it, though I fast for
it; yea, sometimes of Ten Shillings : But, a-
las Sir, what is that to those infinite Volumes
of Divinity, which yet every day swell, and
grow bigger. Noble Sir, pardon my boldness, and consider but these three things. First,
the Bulk of Divinity. Secondly, the time
when

*when I desire this (which is now, when I must
lay the foundation of my whole life.) Thirdly,
what I desire, and to what end, not vain pleasures, nor to a vain end. If then, Sir,
there be any course, either by engaging my
future Annuity, or any other way, I desire
you, Sir, to be my Mediator to them in my behalf.*

*Now I write to you, Sir, because to you I
have ever opened my heart; and have reason,
by the Patents of your perpetual favour to do
so still, for I am sure you love*

Your faithfullest Servant,

March 18. 1617.

Trin: Coll.

George Herbert:

SIR,

SIR,

THis Week hath loaded me with your Favours; I wish I could have come in person to thank you, but it is not possible; presently
after Michaelmas, I am to make an Oration to the
whole University of an hour long in Latin, and my
Lincoln journey, hath set me much behind hand :
neither can I so much as go to Bugden, and deliver your Letter, yet have I sent it thither by a
faithful Messenger this day : I beseech you all, you
and my dear Mother and Sister to pardon me, for
my Cambridge necessities are stronger to tye me
here, than yours to London : If I could possibly
have come, none should have done my message to
Sir Fr: Netherfole for me; he and I are ancient acquaintance, and I have a strong opinion of
him, that if he can do me a courtesie, he will of
himself; yet your appearing in it, affects me
strangely. I have sent you here inclosed a Letter
from our Master in my behalf, which if you can
send to Sir Francis before his departure, it will do
well, for it expresseth the Universities inclination
to me ; yet if you cannot send it with much con-
venience, it is no matter, for the Gentleman needs
no incitation to love me.

The Orators place (that you may understand
what it is) is the finest place in the University,
though not the gainfullest; yet that will be about
30 l. per an. but the commodiousness is beyond
                                              the

the *Revenue* ; *for the* Orator *writes all the* University Letters, *makes all the* Orations, *be it to* King, Prince, *or whatever comes to the* University *; to requite these pains, he takes place next the* Doctors, *is at all their* Assemblies *and* Meetings, *and sits above the* Proctors, *is* Regent *or* Non-regent *at his pleasure, and such like* Gaynesses, *which will please a young man well.*

I long to hear from Sir Francis, *I pray Sir send the Letter you receive from him to me as soon as you can, that I may work the heads to my purpose. I hope I shall get this place without all your* London *helps, of which I am very proud, not but that I joy in your favours, but that you may see, that if all fail, yet I am able to stand on mine own legs.* Noble Sir, *I thank you for your infinite favours, I fear only that I have omitted some fitting circumstance, yet you will pardon my haste, which is very great, though never so, but that I have both time and work to be*

Your extreme Servant,

George Herbert.

SIR,

SIR,

I Have received the things you sent me, safe; and now the only thing I long for, is to hear of my dear sick Sister; first, how her health fares, next, whether my peace be yet made with her concerning my unkind departure. Can I be so happy, as to hear of both these that they succeed well? Is it not too much for me? Good Sir, make it plain to her, that I loved her even in my departure, in looking to her Son, and my charge. I suppose she is not disposed to spend her eye-sight on a piece of paper, or else I had wrote to her; when I shall understand that a Letter will be seasonable, my Pen is ready. Concerning the Orators place all goes well yet, the next Friday it is tryed, and according you shall hear. I have forty businesses in my hands, your Courtesie will pardon the haste of

Jan. 19. 1619.

Trin: Coll.

　　　　　Your humblest Servant,

　　　　　　　　　　George Herbert.

SIR.

SIR,

I *Underſtand by Sir* Francis Netherſols *Letter, that he fears I have not fully reſolved of the matter, ſince this place being civil may divert me too much from Divinity, at which, not without cauſe, he thinks, I aim; but, I have wrote him back, that this dignity, hath no ſuch earthineſs in it, but it may very well be joined with Heaven; or if it had to others; yet to me it ſhould not, for ought I yet knew; and therefore I deſire him to ſend me a direct anſwer in his next Letter. I pray Sir therefore, cauſe this incloſed to be carried to his brothers houſe of his own name (as I think) at the ſign of* the Pedler *and the* Pack *on* London-bridge, *for there he aſſigns me. I cannot yet find leiſure to write to my Lord, or Sir* Benjamin Ruddyard; *but I hope I ſhall ſhortly, though for the reckoning of your favours, I ſhall never find time and paper enough, yet am I*

Your readieſt Servant,

Octob. 6. 1619.

Trin: Coll.

George Herbert.

I remember my moſt humble duty to my Mother, who cannot think me lazy, ſince I rode 200 mile to ſee a Siſter, in a way I knew not, in the midſt of much buſineſs, and all in a Fortnight, not long ſince. To

To the truly Noble Sir *J. D.*

SIR,

I *Understand by a Letter from my Brother* Henry, *that he hath bought a parcel of Books for me, and that they are coming over. Now though they have hitherto travelled upon your charge, yet if my Sister were acquainted that they are ready, I dare say she would make good her promise of taking five or six pound upon her, which she hath hitherto deferred to do, not of her self, but upon the want of those Books which were not to be got in* England ; *for that which surmounts, though your noble disposition is infinitely free, yet I had rather flie to my old ward, that if any course could be taken of doubling my Annuity now, upon condition that i should surcease from all title to it, after I enter'd into a Benefice, I should be most glad to entertain it, and both pay for the surplusage of these Books, and for ever after cease my clamorous and greedy bookish requests. It is high time now that I should be no more a burden to you, since I can never answer what I have already received; for your favours are so ancient,*

that

that they prevent my memory, and yet still grow
upon

Your humblest Servant,

George Herbert.

I remember my most humble duty to my Mother.
I have wrote to my dear sick Sister this week
already, and therefore now I hope may be ex-
cused.

I pray Sir, pardon my boldness of inclosing my
Brothers Letter in yours, for it was because
I know your Lodging, but not his.

G   To

To the worthieſt Lady, Mrs. Magdalen Herbert.

Madam,

EVery excuſe hath in it ſomewhat of accuſation ; and ſince I am innocent , and
yet muſt excuſe, how ſhall I do for that part of
accuſing.   By my troth, as deſperate and perplexed men, grow from thence bold ; ſo muſt
I take the boldneſs of accuſing you , who
would draw ſo dark a Curtain betwixt me and
your purpoſes, as that I had no glimmering ,
neither of your goings, nor the way which my
Letters might haunt.   Yet, I have given this
Licence to Travel, but I know not whether, nor
it.   It is therefore rather a Pinnace to diſcover ;
and the intire Colony of Letters , of Hundreds and Fifties, muſt follow ; whoſe employment is more honourable, than that which our
State meditates to *Virginia*, becauſe you are
worthier than all that Countrey, of which that
is a wretched inch ; for you have better treaſure, and a harmleſsneſs.   If this ſound like a
flattery, tear it out.   I am to my Letters as
rigid a Puritane, as *Cæſar* was to his Wife.   I
can as ill endure a ſuſpitious and miſinterpreta-
ble

ble word as a fault; but remember, that nothing is flattery which the Speaker believes; and of the groffest flatteries there is this good use, that they tell us what we fhould be. But, *Madam*, you are beyond inftruction, and therefore there can belong to you only praife; of which, though you be no good hearer, yet allow all my Letters leave to have in them one part of it, which is thankfulnefs towards you.

Your unworthieft Servant,

Michin,
July 11.
1607.

Except your accepting

have mended him,

John Donne.

To the worthiest Lady, Mrs. Magdalen Herbert.

Madam,

THis is my second Letter, in which though I cannot tell you what is good, yet this is the worst, that I must be a great part of it; yet to me, that is recompensed, because you must be mingled. After I knew you were gone (for I must, little less then accusingly tell you, I knew not you would go) I sent my first Letter, like a *Bevis* of *Hampton*, to seek Adventures. This day I came to Town, and to the best part of it, your House; for your memory, is a State-cloth and Presence; which I reverence, though you be away; though I need not seek that there, which I have about and within me. There, though I found my accusation, yet any thing to which your hand is, is a pardon: yet I would not burn my first Letter, because as in great destiny no small passage can be omitted or frustrated, so in my resolution of writing almost daily to you, I wou'd have no link of the Chain broke by me, both because my Letters interpret one another, and because only their number can give them weight:

If

If I had your Commiffion and Inftructions to
do you the fervice of a Legier Ambaffadour
here, I could fay fomething of the Countefs of
Devon: of the States, and fuch things.   But
fince to you, who are not only a World alone,
but the Monarchy of the World your felf, nothing can be added, efpecially by me ; I will
fuftain my felf with the honour of being

London,
July 23.
1607.

Your Servant Extraordinary,

And without place,

John Donne.

To

To the worthiest Lady, Mrs. Magdalen Herbert.

Madam,

AS we muft dye before we can have full glory and happinefs, fo before I can have this degree of it, as to fee you by a Letter, I muft almoft dye, that is, come to *London*, to plaguy *London*; a place full of danger, and vanity, and vice, though the Court be gone. And fuch it will be, till your return redeem it: Not that, the greateft vertue in the World, which is you, can be fuch a Marfhal, as to defeat, or difperfe all the vice of this place; but as higher bodies remove, or contract themfelves when better come, fo at your return we fhall have one door open to innocence. Yet *Madam*, you are not fuch an *Ireland*, as produceth neither ill, nor good; no Spiders, nor Nightingales, which is a rare degree of perfection: But you have found and practifed that experiment, That even nature, out of her detefting of emptinefs, if we will make that our work, to remove bad, will fill us with good things. To abftain from it, was therefore but the Childhood, and Minority of your Soul, which

which hath been long exercifed fince, in your manlier active part, of doing good. Of which fince I have been a witnefs and fubject, not to tell you fome times, that by your influence and example I have attained to fuch a ftep of goodnefs, as to be thankful, were both to accufe your power and judgement of impotency and infirmity.

Auguft 2d.
1607.

Your Ladifhips in all Services,

John Donne.

F I N I S.

On Mr. *George Herbert's* Book, Intituled, *The Temple* of *Sacred Poems*, sent to a Gentlewoman.

*K*Now you *Fair*, on what you look?
　Divinest Love lies in this Book:
Expecting Fire from your Eyes ,
To kindle this his Sacrifice.
When your hands untye these strings,
Think you've an Angel by the wings.
One that gladly will be nigh ,
To wait upon each morning sigh.
To flutter in the balmy Air,
Of your well perfumed Prayer
These white Plumes of his Hee'll lend you,
Which every day to Heaven will send you,
To take acquaintance of the Sphere,
And all the smooth-fac'd Kindred there.
　And though Herberts *Name do owe*
　These Devotions, Fairest ; *know*
　That while I lay them on the shrine
　Of your white Hand, they are mine.

F I N I S.